38TH PARALLEL
SEOUL
Inchon
Suwon
Osan
Ansong
Pyongtaek
Chonan
Chongju
Chochiwon
Kongju
Taepyong-ni
TAEJON
Yusong
Okchon
KUM RIVER
Nonsan
Chinsan
Kumsan
Yongdong
Muju
Kumchon
Yongdam
Sangjon-myon
Chonju
Chinan
POINT OF GENERAL'S CAPTURE
TAEGU
NAKTONG RIVER
PUSAN
General's wanderings for 35 days as fugitive
Main Roads
Railroads

GENERAL DEAN'S STORY

GENERAL DEAN'S STORY

as told to William L. Worden by

MAJOR GENERAL
WILLIAM F. DEAN

New York · 1954

THE VIKING PRESS

PUBLISHED BY THE VIKING PRESS IN MAY 1954
PUBLISHED ON THE SAME DAY IN THE DOMINION OF CANADA
BY THE MACMILLAN COMPANY OF CANADA LIMITED

Parts of this book appeared in a serial version in *The Saturday Evening Post* under the title "My Three Years as a Dead Man."

Library of Congress catalog card number: 54-7569

PRINTED IN U. S. A. BY H. WOLFF BOOK MANUFACTURING COMPANY

To the many friends

who for three long years

never gave up hope

Table of Contents

▶▶▶▶◀◀◀◀

Photographs

ABOVE AND BEYOND THE CALL OF DUTY

Mrs. William F. Dean of Berkeley, California, receives from President Truman, on January 9, 1951, the Congressional Medal of Honor awarded to her husband, Major General William F. Dean, missing in action in Korea. Brigadier General Robert Landry is at center. (*Wide World Photos*)

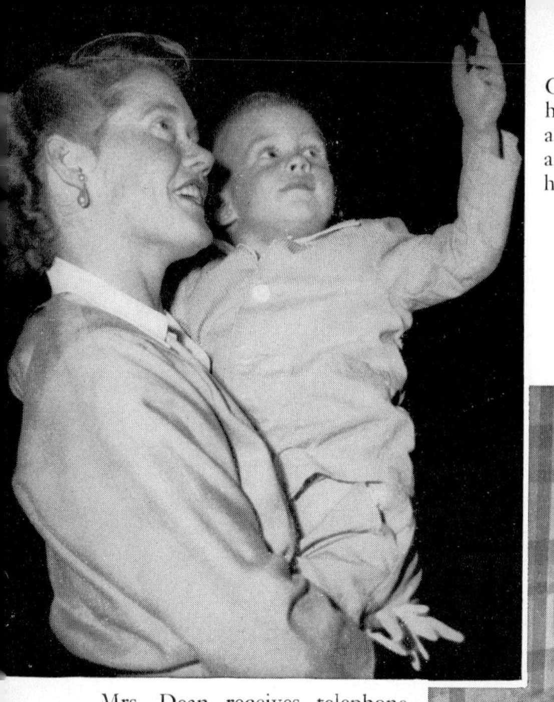

General Dean's daughter, June Williams, and his grandson, Robert Dean Williams, waiting at Travis Air Force Base, California, for the arrival of the plane bringing the General home. (*Photo by Lonnie Wilson for the* Oakland Tribune)

Mrs. Dean receives telephone congratulations at her home, December 18, 1951, after General Dean's name appeared on the list of prisoners of war held by the Reds in Korea. (*Wide World Photos*)

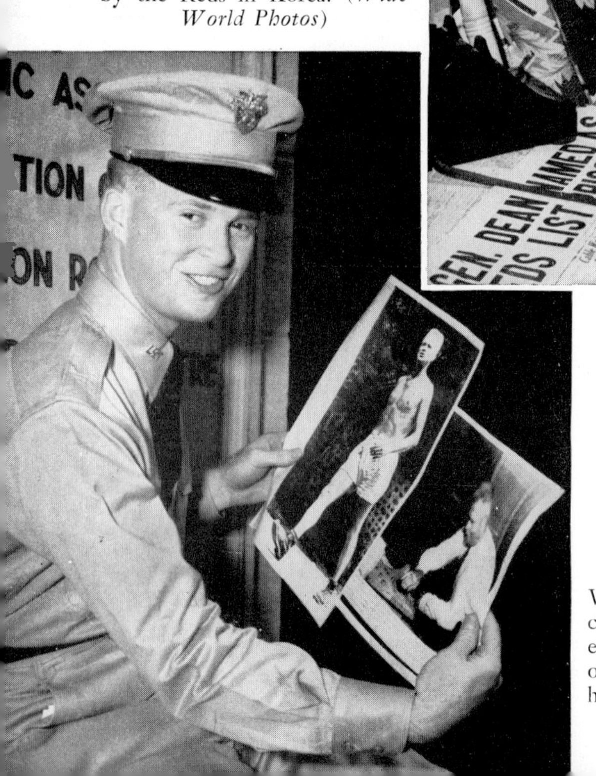

William F. Dean, Jr., then a second classman at the U.S. Military Academy, looks at some of the first pictures of his father to be made available after his release, September 4, 1953. (*Associated Press Newsphoto*)

(*Above*) General Dean embraces his mother at the airfield upon arrival, September 23, 1953. The General's wife is at the right. (*Wide World Photos*)

(*Below*) President Eisenhower welcomes General Dean during a visit to the White House, October 21, 1953. (*Wide World Photos*)

(*Above*) A lookout post on the 38th parallel. On June 24, 1950, North Korean troops invaded South Korea on a wide front. (*Wide World Photos*)

(*Below*) South Korean troops march toward the front on June 30, 1950. (*Wide World Photos*)

(*Above*) South Korean soldiers escort refugees from a burning town near the battle line, July 8, 1950. (*Wide World Photos*)

(*Below*) South Koreans applaud American soldiers as they arrive in an unidentified city shortly before moving into the front lines, July 8, 1950. (*Wide World Photos*)

(*Above*) Lieutenant General Walton H. Walker, Commanding General U.S. Eighth Army (*left*), and General Dean, Commanding General 24th Infantry Division, examine a map near the front lines, July 8, 1950. (*Wide World Photos*)

(*Below*) Three American soldiers, who worked their way back through enemy lines, are safe in Yongdong on July 27, 1950, one week after the fall of Taejon. (*Wide World Photos*)

(*Above*) Infantrymen of the 24th Division rest in a field, July 29, 1950. (*Wide World Photos*)

(*Below*) This wrecked Red tank stands on a Taejon street corner as a memorial to General Dean. After the battle he eluded the enemy for thirty-five days, until, weakened and sick, he was captured on August 25, 1950. (*Wide World Photos*)

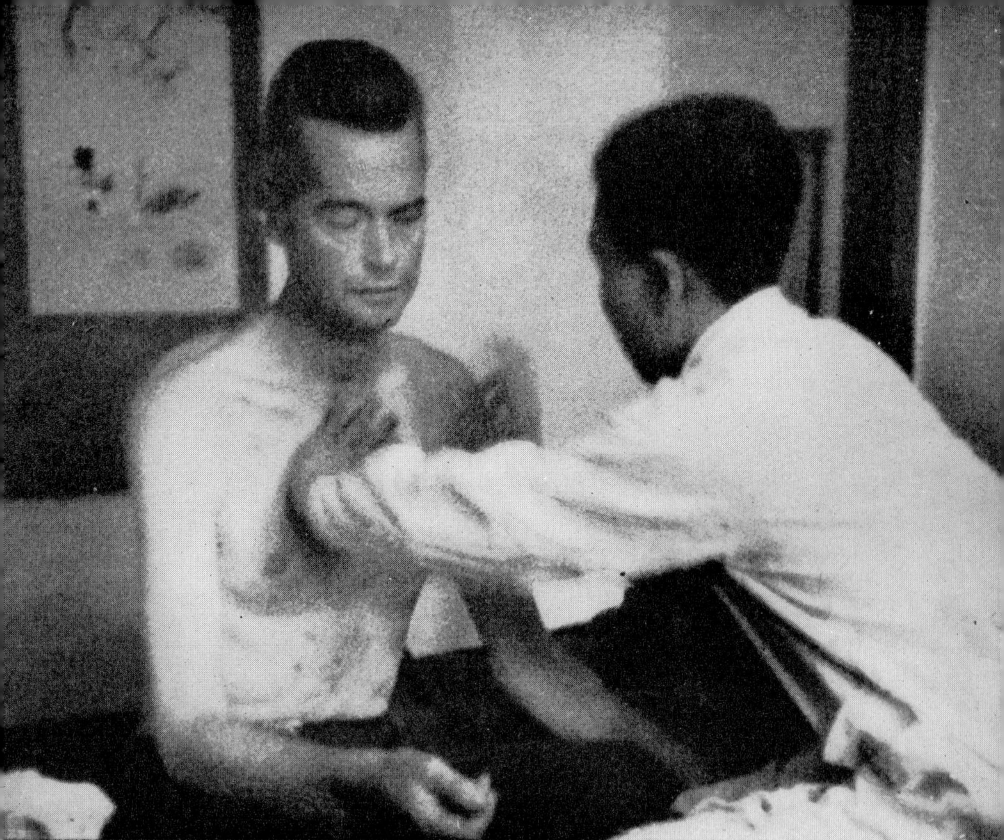

(*Eastfoto*)

These two pictures were taken by the Communists in North Korea in October 1950.

(*Eastfoto*)

The official Soviet photo agency, which distributed this picture, describes the men as American soldiers captured by North Korean forces. (*International News Photos*)

When General Dean asked his interpreter, Lee Kyu Hyun, about other American prisoners, Lee replied, "Oh, the men in your camps are very happy, very merry, very cheerful, happy. They're whistling and singing and cracking jokes all the time."

This picture of General Dean was taken on December 21, 1951, during an interview with Wilfred Burchett, correspondent of *Le Soir*. This was the General's first contact with the outside world since his capture. (*International News Photos*)

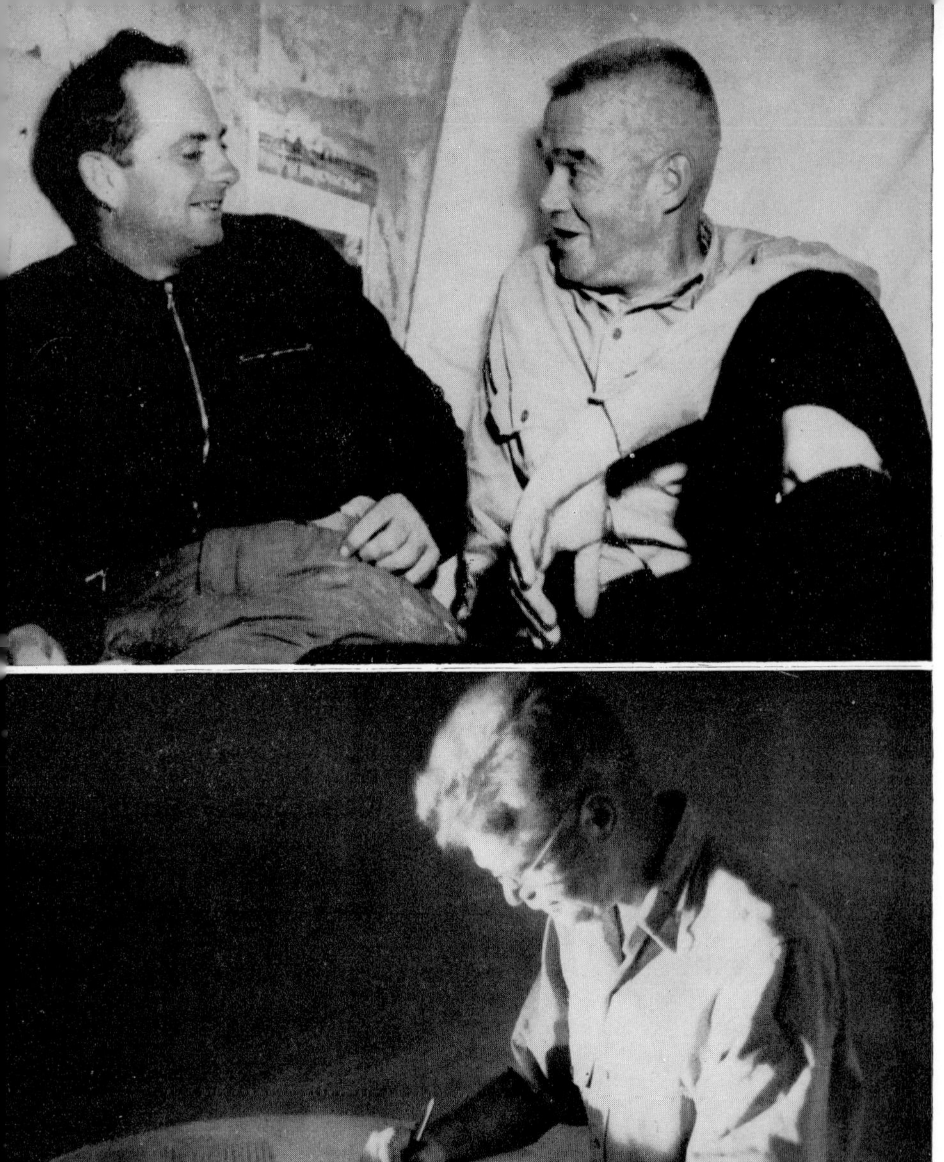

(*Above*) General Dean and Wilfred Burchett in the General's cramped quarters about ten miles from Pyongyang. (*Wide World Photos*)

(*Below*) General Dean writing letters—with difficulty. For more than a year he had been without writing materials of any kind. (*Eastfoto*)

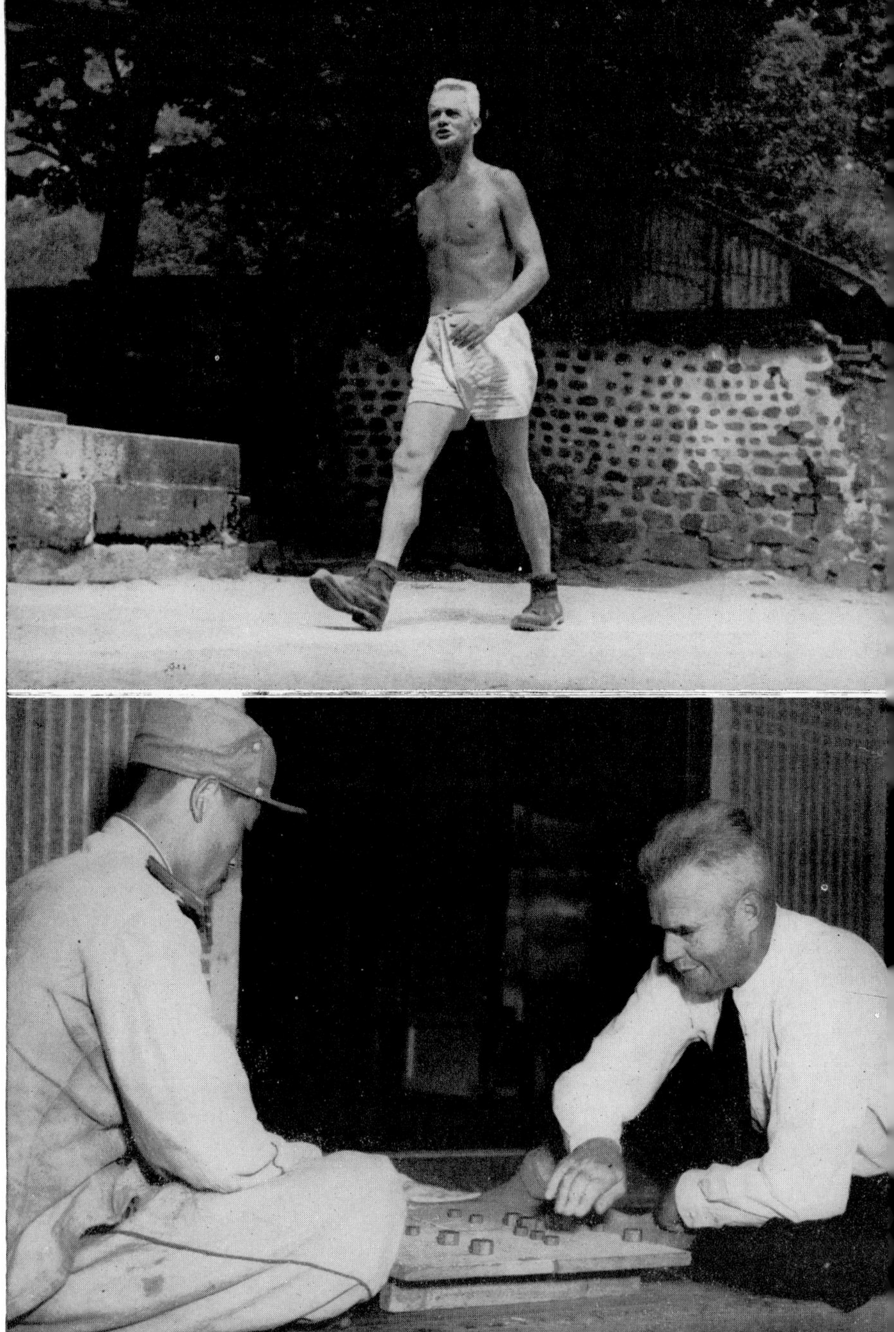

(*Above*) General Dean taking his daily walk. Because of strict orders that he was not to be seen, it was only toward the end of his captivity that he was permitted to exercise. (*Wide World Photos*)

(*Below*) General Dean passes the time immediately before his release playing chong-gun, a form of chess, with an unidentified Communist guard. (*Wide World Photos*)

General Dean arriving at Panmunjom for repatriation, September 4, 1953. (*Wide World Photos*)

General Dean speaks during an interview at Freedom Village after repatriation. (*Wide World Photos*)

General Dean is interviewed by news correspondents at Freedom Village on the first day of his release, after having been a prisoner of the Communists for three years. (*Wide World Photos*)

►►►►◄◄◄◄

Collaborator's Note

When Major General William F. Dean and I sat down to put his experiences into book form, I was equipped with a tape recorder, various maps, some reference books, and materials for writing down quickly the things he told me before I should forget them.

General Dean, on the other hand, was equipped with nothing whatever but an astonishing and almost frightening ability to recall, without props, every single thing that had happened in three years. He had forgotten nothing. For more than fifty hours he told the story of his three years day by day, hour by hour, with places, dates, the quality and quantity of meals, Korean names, temperatures, crop conditions, house plans, speeches made to him, anecdotes, military details, bits of Communist theory and practice. Seldom did he hesitate, and never did he fail to recall an important fact. A single notebook finally was produced, mainly to help with translations of Korean words—but he had possessed neither this nor any other writing materials during the first year and a half of his captivity.

It may be heresy for a writer to admit it, but the fact is, General Dean wrote this book himself by speaking it. Not only are the facts his own, without additions from me, but the language is his own. The writing consisted mainly of removing from the tape-recorder report the pauses, occasional repetitions, and sounds of rattling maps which interrupted or slowed the fascinating telling.

For two men of differing professions, I think we worked in remarkable harmony. I didn't force him to match my continual cigarette smoking; he did not insist that I arise at his customary five a.m., walk five miles a day, or run up stairways rather than use elevators.

On only one point did we have a serious disagreement. William Frishe Dean is an almost painfully honest man. I'm quite sure that he has stood off from himself in judgment, given himself the benefit of equitable doubts (but no more), and weighed his own conduct as a general, a fugitive, and a prisoner. The result is his considered and definite decision: he does *not* think General Dean is either a great commander or a true hero.

I think he is.

William L. Worden

GENERAL DEAN'S STORY

▶▶▶▶◀◀◀◀

Introductory

If the story of my Korean experiences is worth telling, the value lies in its oddity, not in anything brilliant or heroic. There were heroes in Korea, but I was not one of them. There were brilliant commanders, but I was a general captured because he took a wrong road. I am an infantry officer and presumably was fitted for my fighting job. I don't want to alibi that job, but a couple of things about it should be made clear. In the fighting I made some mistakes and I've kicked myself a thousand times for them. I lost ground I should not have lost. I lost trained officers and fine men. I'm not proud of that record, and I'm under no delusions that my weeks of command constituted any masterly campaign.

No man honestly can be ashamed of the Congressional Medal of Honor. For it and for the welcome given to me here at home in 1953, I'm humbly grateful. But I come close to shame when I think about the men who did better jobs—some who died doing them—and did not get recognition. I wouldn't have awarded myself a wooden star for what I did as a commander. Later, as fugitive and prisoner, I did things mildly out of the ordinary only at those times when I was excited and not thinking entirely straight; and the only thing I did which mattered—to my family and perhaps a few others—was to stay alive.

Other prisoners resisted torture, but I wasn't tortured.

Others hid in the hills and finally escaped, but I failed in my escape attempts. Others bluffed the Communists steadily, whereas I was lucky enough to do it only once in a while. Others starved, but I was fed and even learned to like *kimchee*. Others died for a principle, but I failed in a suicide attempt.

I can justify writing this book only because mine was an adventure—without a hero—and because I did see the face of the enemy close up, did have time to study his weaknesses and his remarkable strengths, not on the battlefield but far behind his lines. I saw communism working—with men and women of high education or none, great intelligence or little—and it was a frightening thing.

Otherwise I can guarantee only to show how a grandfather came close to hating little boys, how important standing up is when you haven't been able to stand for sixteen months—and the best way to kill a fly. I ought to know. I swatted 40,671 flies in three years and counted every carcass. There were periods when I was batting .850 and deserved to make the big leagues.

▶▶▶▶◀◀◀◀

CHAPTER I

A War Begins

As a general officer, I'm an in-between, curious sort, who never went to West Point, did not see action in World War I, and did not come up from the enlisted ranks. I was born in Carlyle, Illinois, on August 1, 1899 (almost between centuries). My dentist-father, Charles Watts Dean, was partially responsible for my interest in the Army. He took me to the 1904 St. Louis Exposition, where I saw West Point cadets and soldiers drilling—and I never quite rid myself of the interest they aroused.

Not that this interest did me any particular good for a long time. I spent my boyhood in Carlyle, much of it doing body-building exercises. I suppose I'm still something of a physical-fitness crank, in that I do daily calisthenics, try to walk at least five miles a day, and never ride an elevator if it's practicable to run up and down stairs. One of my first jobs was selling magazines to make spending money, and I developed quite a resentment against the *Saturday Evening Post* when its circulation men appointed a second agent in town during a small boom. I thought then that they had robbed me of a chance to make real profits, but I guess we're friends now. Early in 1954 the *Post* published six articles containing portions of this book.

After graduating from high school I tried for the Military

Academy at West Point and missed, which was a severe disappointment. I also tried to enlist for World War I, but my mother, Elizabeth Frishe Dean, refused her permission, so I missed on that too. (I was under-age to enter the Army without permission.)

The only military organization I could join was the Students' Army Training Corps at the University of California, where I enrolled in what now would amount to a pre-law course. The whole family moved west, and the surviving members still live in California—my mother in Berkeley; my sister, Mrs. Leonard Ver Mehr, at Antioch; and my brother David at Kenwood.

To stay in the university I earned money as a temporary stevedore on the San Francisco docks, as a trolley conductor or motorman, briefly as a restaurant dishwasher, and then as a beat-pounding patrolman on the Berkeley police force when August Vollmer, father of many modern criminology methods, was testing his ideas as chief of police.

I should have earned a bachelor of arts degree in 1921, but failed a course in legal contracts and so had to stay another year. I never did complete work for the doctor of laws degree toward which I was aiming, but I've never regretted this especially. I didn't care much for the law, and I've always been disturbed by the victories of technicalities over equity.

Besides, I just couldn't stay away from the Army. Perhaps it was my mother's German blood beginning to tell. I secured a regular commission as a second lieutenant on October 18, 1923, on the basis of my student reserve training and an examination. My first post was fairly indicative of what was to come—an assignment to troops of the 38th Infantry Regiment at Fort Douglas, Utah.

This was the period in which, contrary to the popular refrain, practically nobody loved a soldier. Enlistments were difficult, promotions for junior officers were slow to non-existent because of the "bulge" of company-grade regular officers who had stayed in the Army after World War I, and relations between military posts and adjacent cities were cool, at best, and more often on the level of ignoring each other.

But we in the Army still did have some horses, and these brought about what was to me the most important event of my three years at Fort Douglas—a young lady fell off a horse on her head. The post commandant, as a gesture toward cementing understanding between people at the fort and in Salt Lake City, had organized a Saturday riding group, and young women from the town were invited to use the Army horses. Some of the younger officers kept polo ponies, and I had a couple of my own (they could be bought for thirty dollars each, and we schooled them ourselves), but for the civilian riders we usually saddled up some of the older, presumably safer Army-owned stock. One Saturday when I had the duty of assigning the riders, I took a look at a pretty girl named Dorothy Welch and decided she had a little too much daring for most of our horses. So I put her up on old Dick, an elderly crow-bait who was the non-moving champion of our stable. I thought not even she would be able to get him past a walk, but I was wrong. Somehow she got old Dick into a gallop, and he promptly threw her in a gully.

She suffered a skull fracture and went into a coma from which she didn't recover for twelve days. I felt terribly responsible for the accident and went to her home frequently to see her. There I met one of her close friends, Mildred Dern, also of Salt Lake.

That old horse Dick was no friend of mine. After Miss Welch recovered and I had started taking Mildred riding at

Fort Douglas, he ran away with her too. But she clung to his back and ducked her head as he tried to brush her off on a stable door. Mildred married me, in spite of him; and the sale of two polo ponies helped to finance the wedding.

Immediately after we were married we were transferred to the Panama Canal Zone, for three more years of duty with troops. In both posts I coached boxing and basketball teams but never was a serious competitor myself—even though I seem to have a minor reputation as a boxer now, the result of a Communist photograph showing me shadow-boxing while in captivity.

The rest of my prewar duty was just average. I was a lieutenant for twelve years. At Fort Douglas I served with troops, then attended the Fort Benning Infantry School in 1931, serving with a tank battalion there and going on to a second course, at the Tank School. I returned to the Pacific Coast in 1932, with technical assignment to the 30th Infantry Regiment. But my actual duty was with the Civilian Conservation Corps, first as commander of Camp Hackamore, in Modoc County, California, while the corps built trails and roads, then in the CCC headquarters at Redding.

Back on more normal duty, I went to the Command and General Staff School at Fort Leavenworth, then spent two more years with troops in Oahu, T.H. After that there were more schools: the Armed Forces Industrial College in Washington; the Field Officers course at the Chemical Warfare School; the Army War College.

I was lucky to make captain in 1936, and major in 1940, when I was assigned to a series of desk jobs in Washington—first on the War Department's General Staff as a junior member, then assistant secretary of it, finally executive officer of the Requirements Division in Ground Forces headquarters.

My temporary rank went up to lieutenant colonel in 1941, to colonel in 1942. In 1943 I became head of the Requirements Division, which is concerned with new weapons, electronics, training literature, and visual aids.

I finally got what I wanted—another job with troops, this time as assistant commander of the 44th Infantry Division, just preparing to go to Europe in late 1943—but I nearly missed my second war. During a demonstration of flame-throwers to division officers, the flame-thrower leaked on the lieutenant operating it. In agony as the napalm set his clothing afire, he struggled to rid himself of the weapon but instead flipped the hose, spraying napalm. Another officer and I, both rushing toward him, caught the slash of fire; but I was the lucky one. Both the other men died. I didn't even know my leg had been burned until I started to walk off after the others had been taken away in an ambulance. Then someone noticed that my trouser leg was in tatters below the knee. I too went to the hospital, but doctors saved my leg. I was still on crutches when the division sailed, but I sailed with it.

We landed in France on Omaha Beach behind the amphibious assault forces, and for the next several months moved generally east and south across France, Germany, and Austria. When Major General Robert L. Spragins was invalided home in December 1944, I took command of the division—a fine fighting group that had been trained and indoctrinated by Major General James I. Muir and brought to peak battle efficiency by General Spragins. I've always been proud of the 44th, which did fine jobs at Sarrebourg, Sarreguemines, Mannheim, and in front of Heidelberg, where one of the most outstanding artillerymen I've ever known, then Brigadier General William A. Beiderlinden, used mass time-on-target fire and a couple of other tricks to convince a whole sector of

Germans that surrender was the only course for reasonable men—and thereby avoided having to damage the city's famous old buildings. The division went on to fight at Göppingen, Ulm, Memmingen, Kempten, Fern Pass, and Resia Pass. When the war ended we were in the Inn Valley, with our headquarters at Innsbruck—and had lost only forty-two men by capture during the entire war. That minor detail especially pleased me. I've always thought that to say *Kamerad* was one of the most degrading things that could happen to a soldier.

The 44th Division came home shortly after V-E Day and was retraining to go to the Pacific when the Japanese surrendered. I left the division command almost immediately, going to Leavenworth again, this time to organize and direct new command classes.

In October 1947 I was sent to South Korea as military governor and deputy to Lieutenant General John R. Hodge, then commanding the American occupation forces. With headquarters at Seoul, I had the duty of making the South Korean civil government work during the final period before it was turned over to the Koreans and military occupation ended. I had over-all command of such activities as police work, rice collection to make sure that the hungry population had enough to eat, operation of railroads and telegraphs. The Korean constabulary was also under my command. Most of these activities were manned by Americans in executive positions, with Koreans sitting beside them to study their methods, and also filling most of the jobs on lower levels, without American opposite numbers.

This was a transition period for the Koreans. Under the Japanese, Koreans never had been allowed to hold executive positions or even jobs involving much responsibility. For example, Koreans could be railroad firemen or station agents, but not locomotive engineers. In government, they never had held policy-making positions. The result was that no trained cadre existed, once the Japanese had been ousted. So U.S. occupation forces, in contrast to the situation in Germany and Japan, not only had to change the methods and philosophy of the previous government but also had to train Korean personnel for almost every job. The whole business was complicated further by the artificial division of the country on the 38th parallel, with disruption of the entire economy, blocking of railroads, and division of families between democratic and Communist regimes.

We also had the job of setting the new Korean government-to-be on its feet. Having had no government of their own for generations and never a free election in four thousand years of their history, the Koreans were completely lacking in machinery and training for holding an election. During the troubled months preceding the election in 1948, I traveled the American-occupied part of the peninsula many times, making speeches for our rice collection and other programs, setting up election boards, even arranging for polling places and protection of voters from coercion and Communist interference.

After the elections the newly chosen Korean officials took over their own government, on August 15, 1948. The occupation ended officially, and my civil job with it. I became commander of the 7th Infantry Division, with headquarters at Seoul still, but immediately began arranging the withdrawal of that division to stations in northern Japan. We completed that movement in January 1949; and my headquarters became the city of Sapporo, on Hokkaido island. But in May, Lieutenant General Walton Walker called me to Yokohama as chief of staff for the Eighth Army. In October, when a sudden transfer left the 24th Infantry Division without a commander, I managed to talk myself into the job, and moved once more, to Kokura, on Kyushu, the most southerly Japanese island.

Kokura is only one hundred and forty miles from Pusan, the nearest point on the Korean peninsula, and faces the Korea Strait, across which Korean and Japanese fleets, armies, and fishing boats have warred for thousands of years. If you like history, this was the strait in which a divine wind—the *kamikaze*—arose to turn back a Korean fleet trying to invade ancient Japan, thus reinforcing the Japanese in their belief that the island peoples were invincible. It also provided both a rough precedent and a name for the Japanese pilots who flew their aircraft into American ships during the last days of World War II.

At Kokura, on June 24, 1950, the officers of the 24th Division headquarters staged a costume party. I am slightly more than six feet tall, and that summer I weighed two hundred and ten pounds. The black stovepipe hat of a Korean gentleman sat foolishly high on my head, and the long robes proper to a *yang-ban* (one of the people who do not work) flopped somewhere around my knees. My wife came dressed as a well-born Korean lady, and our double costume was a considerable success.

As a troop commander, I believe in hard work for officers and men; and it was quite obvious on this evening that the officers I had been working hard for several months enjoyed seeing the division commander looking thoroughly ridiculous. At the same time, the costume was a not-so-nostalgic gesture toward the short Korean chapter in my life. It had been interesting and troubling but was definitely over. I had no real reason to expect to go to Korea again. I knew only a few words of the language. I never had found an opportunity to know Korean people outside of official circles and the major cities—and I certainly was not lonesome for the variable climate of that appendix of northeastern Asia.

So I wore the costume of a yang-ban but thought about Korea only briefly, if at all, during the long evening. It was an uneventful party, just one more officers' dance like thousands of others; and the main thing I remember was that the hard hat became highly uncomfortable before the evening ended.

The next morning, when I went to the division headquarters building after attending church, the only thing on my mind was the possibility of mail from my daughter June, then en route to Puerto Rico with her husband, Captain Robert Williams, or from my son Bill, who was taking examinations for entrance to the Military Academy at West Point. But as I headed toward the post office a duty officer hailed me. North Koreans, he said, had just crossed the 38th parallel, breaking the uneasy peace of the border between communism and the newest of the U. S.-sponsored free governments in Asia.

There was no further information. I went back to our quarters and told Mildred the news, adding my own prediction: this was the beginning of World War III. I could see war breaking out like wildfire over much of Asia—and the 24th Infantry Division undoubtedly sat right in the middle of it.

Naturally my concern at the moment was principally for the division. The 24th had a long and creditable history in World War II and had been in Japan since shortly after V-J Day. But the battle-trained veterans of the early occupation days had been whittled down by time and reassignment until they made up only about fifteen per cent of the men and officers now on duty. The division strength was down to about two-thirds of its wartime total. Infantry regiments had only two battalions each; artillery battalions only two batteries. Other units were proportionate. Equipment was all of World War II vintage—2.6 bazookas and light (M-24) tanks.

We were training, but our program was greatly hampered by the fact that the division was scattered all over southern Japan. The 19th Infantry Regiment, based at Beppu, just then was on an amphibious maneuver near Yokohama. The 21st Infantry Regiment was at Kumamoto, the 34th at Sasebo, and the artillery near Fukuoka. The tank company, the reconnaissance company, and a company of engineers were at Yamaguchi on Honshu; the signal company, other engineers, and quartermaster and ordnance units were with the headquarters at Kokura. I found a light airplane essential to visit them all. To get them together in a hurry would be a major task.

Not that it was necessary at this time. On June 26 we had new information from Korea: the South Korean Army was counterattacking and the situation looked much better than it had the day before. Perhaps this would turn out to be only a slightly larger version of the many border incidents that had occurred since the 38th parallel had been established as a dividing line across Korea.

We had several South Korean officers on a tour of duty with our division, and I began to worry about them. But when I sent a message to Tokyo, asking whether we should get them back to Korea right away, I was told, "No. Have them finish their courses, and prepare to receive another group in July."

This was going to be a short and easy war.

But by the next day it looked less easy. We received word

to prepare to meet evacuees from Korea, a job assigned to the 24th Division in a long-standing plan for action in case of any major emergency in Korea. In my experience, few of these long-standing plans ever work out as plotted on paper, but this one did.

American women and children in the Seoul area were loaded aboard a Norwegian freighter at Inchon, and it started around the tip of the peninsula. But the Communist advance to the south was so fast that the men left behind had to be evacuated almost before the ship was out of the harbor. Many of them arrived by plane well before the crowded ship docked, about noon on June 28.

Incidentally, that ship gave me my first real fright of the war. I went down to the dock to meet it, but it failed to arrive on schedule and we weren't able to find out anything about it. When it was more than eight hours overdue I thought, "Oh-oh, a Russian submarine has hit it." It was one of those hazy days when a ship could not be seen from the air, and the Japanese Coast Guard at Fukuoka refused to send out a search vessel; so I asked the U. S. naval base at Sasebo if a destroyer could be sent out to look. We finally put an American officer aboard the Japanese Coast Guard ship, and he got them to go past the harbor entrance. Outside in the fog he found the Norwegian ship hove to, with a skipper thoroughly upset by orders which forced him to wait outside Fukuoka rather than to go in to Moji, where he would not have needed a pilot. The passengers jamming the ship had too little room in staterooms or on deck, and almost all of them were immoderately seasick. It was no tragedy, but just one more confusion in a confused week.

Personally, I was especially disturbed when the incoming airplanes brought not only civilian refugees, missionaries, and military families, but also quite a number of U. S. officers and men from the Korean Military Advisory Group (KMAG). I found out later that a general order issued by the U. S. Embassy in Seoul for evacuation of Americans had somehow been so confused that these Army people thought they were included. Brigadier General Lynn Roberts, commanding KMAG, had completed his tour of duty and sailed for the United States on June 24; and the KMAG chief of staff was in Japan to see his own wife off to the States. So there was no one to correct the confusion before many of these people reached Japan.

The 24th Infantry Division did a fine job in the reception of evacuees. Officers and men worked around the clock to care for the distraught families, who arrived with nothing but a few meager belongings, and to get them started toward other points in Japan. We still had no knowledge that this job would have to be rushed, but rushed it anyhow.

That was just the start. On the evening of June 30 I received orders to go to Tokyo for a conference and started by sedan from Kokura to the airfield at Itazuki—but I never arrived. Outside of Hakata an officer intercepted me with new instructions: I was to return to my headquarters and await teletyped orders.

They came at midnight. I was to go to Korea, with two jobs: my usual division command, plus the over-all command of a land expeditionary force.

▶▶▶▶◀◀◀◀

CHAPTER II

Men Against Tanks

I have run through all of this at the risk of boring readers, because it all made some sense in relation to the first days of war in Korea. I knew quite a bit—although not as much as I thought—about the Korean people and geography; and my division was the closest American battle unit when the fighting started.

My orders specified that a task force of two reinforced rifle companies, with a battery of field artillery, was to be flown to Korea immediately and to report to Brigadier General John H. Church, who had flown from Tokyo to Taejon, in the middle of South Korea, with a headquarters detachment. Taejon was well south of the battle line and an obvious choice for a defensive headquarters. The entire 24th Infantry Division was to move to Korea by surface transportation as rapidly as possible.

Lieutenant Colonel Charles B. (Brad) Smith was picked to command the task force. No commander likes to commit troops piecemeal, and I'm no exception, but Smith was definitely the man for the job if it had to be done. He had a fine World War II record in the South Pacific and was a natural leader. So he and his 406 riflemen, plus a few artillerymen, were on their way to a landing field outside Pusan on July 1. From there, they could move by train to the front lines, then somewhere between Seoul and Suwon—the exact location depending on which Republic of Korea (ROK) Army intelligence report you believed. Meanwhile I tried to move a division, scattered near half a dozen ports, with no ships ready. It was an interesting assignment.

I myself started for Korea one day after Task Force Smith. My original effort was made in a C-54, a large four-motored aircraft, so I took along a jeep as well as various members of the division staff and my aide. We got over the airfield at Pusan without trouble, but there were stalled by a report that the mud field had been so cut up by the big planes carrying in Task Force Smith that no more large aircraft could land. So we flew back to Japan, changed to a C-45 (a much smaller plane), left the jeep and other equipment behind, and made a second try. This time we landed successfully and took off again, after a brief stop, for Taejon, where I would take over the command. It was nearly dark, but I had been over this area several times in 1948 and 1949, in a cub plane, and was sure I could recognize Taejon from the air. But when I pointed out a field to the pilot he only shook his head. If it was Taejon, the field had shrunk and no longer was big enough for a C-45.

At any rate, it was now dark and there was no lighted field in this part of Korea. We had to fly two hundred and fifty miles back to Itazuki in Japan. By the time we had something to eat, we could get only about three hours sleep, then took off once more, shortly after dawn, for Korea.

This time fog was covering that whole part of the peninsula, and we could not even see Taejon. But I was desperate, so we finally flew out over the Yellow Sea, bored down through the fog bank, then came back east, following the Kum River line and dodging mountains under the high fog, and eventually landed. I never thought I'd have so much trouble in getting to a war. But one thing was definite: I didn't need my yang-ban hat, then or later in Korea.

My first day in Taejon, July 3, I tried to get a picture of what was happening, and it was fairly obvious. The principal attack was on the main road and railroad lines, which roughly parallel each other through Suwon, Osan, Chonan, Taejon, Kumchon, Taegu, and Pusan. This was the historic military route through Korea, followed in dozens of forgotten wars, re-emphasized by the Japanese in their invasions, and now being used in reverse by the North Koreans.

To the east of this route mountains prevented easy troop movements, so there was no other great danger point except on the extreme eastern coast. The Yellow Sea protected us to the west as far south as Pyongtaek; but below that the left flank would also have to be guarded.

South Korean civilians were thronging this road south from Suwon; and unfortunately thousands and thousands of national police officers and some military also were marching south, apparently making no effort to stand and fight. What might be happening in the mountains to the east was anybody's guess, although South Korean Army headquarters, now beside our own in Taejon, repeatedly stated that their Army was fighting hard there, and occasionally brought in a captured armored vehicle or some other such token to prove their claims. But they did not seem to be able to produce any prisoners of war for interrogation.

Our own force obviously was too small to maintain adequate communications over such a large area, so we had to depend on South Korean civil telephones and telegraph for wire communications, and on radio to get our messages through to front-line troop units. General Church explained that he had ordered Task Force Smith to take up two positions —approximately one company at a road crossing at Ansong, another at Pyongtaek on the main highway. Theoretically these two positions blocked the two roads down which the enemy was most likely to come—but one company per road is not exactly a strong block, especially with South Koreans pouring past them by the thousands. All these Korean police and soldiers had their rifles and equipment, so it's no wonder that the sight of them was disconcerting to our own troops who had been ordered to make a stand.

I approved General Church's plans and asked him to set up the organization for an expeditionary force headquarters, then flew back to Pusan. The 34th Infantry Regiment had been arriving there on ships that day and was entraining for Taejon. We slept that night on the floor of a Pusan building that had more bedbugs in it than any other structure I've seen, before or since.

At this time my own organization was still scattered. G-2 (Intelligence) was at Taejon. The G-3 (Operations) section was operating from Pusan, but G-1 (Personnel) and G-4 (Supply) were still in Japan. The 34th was on the way north, but other infantry units and all support organizations were still at sea or in Japan.

On the afternoon of July 4 I flew back to Taejon. Still no American ground forces had been in action against the enemy; but there could be no doubt that it was coming soon. The positions Task Force Smith had reconnoitered in the vicinity of Osan (north of Pyongtaek) appeared to have such strength that I ordered the whole task force up there, to form one solid lump of Americans, which might help to stem the backward march of all these South Koreans. The ROK headquarters, now operating under its third chief of staff since the war had started less than two weeks before, was torn by internal strife, with everyone shouting "Communist" at one another, and everyone apparently quite willing for me to make all decisions, especially theirs.

I tried to encourage some sort of ROK stand, but most of my efforts were lost in a fog of excuses for the backward march. They were short of artillery, they had nothing to stop the enemy tanks, they had been outflanked—there was always some good reason.

I don't think they ever did try the suggestion of their second chief of staff, Lee Bum Suk, that they let the enemy tanks come through, dig ditches behind them, and thus prevent them from getting back or getting gas. At this time many of the North Korean tanks were coming through alone, without infantry support, and the trick just might have worked.

At any rate, I got my first strong contingent of American troops when the 34th Regiment arrived in the fighting area late on July 4. I ordered this regiment to reoccupy the positions Task Force Smith had left, blocking one road at Ansong and the main highway at Pyongtaek, where an arm of the sea comes up almost to the highway, forming a natural defense on the left. The north-south mountain range approaches Ansong on the right, so these positions presented a minimum of flanking problems—and Task Force Smith still was out in front, to blunt any enemy attack along the main road before it even touched this line.

The morning of July 5 the attack came. The only word I received from the 34th was that there was fighting at Osan—then that we were out of contact with Task Force Smith. At this time our communications were not reliable. My aide, Lieutenant Arthur M. Clarke, and I drove through a blackout up to Pyongtaek, where I met Brigadier General George

Barth, who had been loaned to me from the 25th Infantry Division as an extra general officer. General Barth said that he had been at Osan; but that just after he left, tanks had been reported coming down the road. After that there was no further contact with Smith. Worse, a patrol from a battalion at Pyongtaek had just moved forward and run into North Koreans, losing one man. This indicated that the Communists had somehow by-passed Osan and that their forward elements were nearly to Pyongtaek. While I was there the battalion was planning to send out a heavier patrol, in a new attempt to reach Task Force Smith, but there was no report by one o'clock in the morning of July 6 when we left to drive back to headquarters at Taejon.

We arrived just about dawn and I had an hour's sleep. Then my headquarters was filled with Korean politicians, each with a different suggestion. I also received a disturbing report that President Syngman Rhee, now at Pusan, was anxious to come back north to Taejon—which would put him in personal danger and further complicate the military problems.

Then I received one encouraging bit of information: Task Force Smith, which we had about given up as overrun and lost, was coming back to Pyongtaek. They brought out the trucks and about half of the force, but had to leave the artillery pieces after pulling the breech locks and sights so that the guns would be useless. Both Smith and Colonel Basil H. Perry, the artillery commander, were with the party which fought its way through the Communists behind them. For the next two or three days men kept dribbling in, singly or in small groups, so that our eventual losses were much less than I'd feared.

A couple of the early arrivals from the task force also brought me the first direct word about enemy tanks—how forty of them had come down the road, rolling right up to what the Americans had thought were good emplacements, and then firing point-blank into them. The fact that they had been able to see our emplacements didn't surprise me (American soldiers are anything but masters at camouflage), but the number of tanks did. Up to this time I'd been inclined to discount the numbers reported by the South Koreans, but this was reliable information. The soldiers also told me how the infantry had managed to get four tanks, and how the artillery had knocked out four others, firing in direct lane.

All in all, it was not a discouraging story. It had been the first American action, we had lost it, but the enemy had paid a considerable price. I felt better—for all of a couple of hours.

Then I received astonishing information: the 34th had pulled back south of Chonan—more than fifteen miles from the river defense line with its flank on the sea. Units that had been at Ansong were now a full twenty miles from where I had left them—without even waiting until the enemy hit them.

I learned this at four o'clock in the afternoon of July 6, and I jumped in my jeep and rushed up toward Chonan to find out what was wrong, why they had not held on the river. But by the time I got there the whole regiment was south of Chonan, most of the men having ridden back on the trucks. I should have said, "Turn around and get going now"; but rather than add to the confusion and risk night ambushes, I told them, "All right, hold tight here until I give you further orders."

When I reached my own headquarters once more I issued such orders: to advance until they made contact with the enemy, then fight a delaying action.

There is no point now in rehashing past mistakes endlessly.

I have always believed that when there is a confusion in orders, the person issuing those orders is at fault for not making himself entirely clear; so the fault in this affair was mine. But whatever the fault, the results were tragic. Chonan is a road intersection from which good routes lead to the west as well as to the south. Once we had lost Pyongtaek, we had opened up our whole left flank, defended only by some dubious forces known as the Northwest Youth Group—five hundred or a thousand dissident, non-Communist North Koreans who had been armed by the South Korean government but were not part of the regular Army. Other people had considerable confidence in them, but I did not share it—and the fact is, North Koreans harried our flank on that side from then on. There is no doubt that those Northwest Youths were bloodthirsty people who hated the Communists, but they did us very little good.

On the afternoon of July 7 I gave command of the 34th Regiment to Colonel Robert B. Martin. Bob Martin and I had served together in Europe in the 44th Division, and I'd observed his methods of commanding a regiment in combat. As soon as I had received my orders to go to Korea, I had asked Far Eastern headquarters for Martin by name. I knew Bob would want to get into the fighting, and Tokyo agreed to free him from his staff assignment.

When Martin took over the regimental command at three p.m. on July 7 I breathed easier once more. It's unfair to expect other people to read your mind, but I knew very clearly what I wanted, and that Martin was one man who could read my thoughts even before I said them out loud. He was also my very good friend.

In the meantime the 34th, following my orders, had moved north once more, setting up defense positions in and slightly north of Chonan. But that night at ten o'clock, another message came through from the regiment: the situation in Chonan was bad, Colonel Martin had gone up from his command post south of the city to straighten it out—and now he was cut off. There were no communications with the one battalion still holding the town.

I got very little sleep that night, but about four o'clock on the morning of the 8th we received word that the situation in Chonan had improved and Colonel Martin was back at his command post.

That morning Lieutenant General Walker flew in from Japan and told me that the whole Eighth Army—including Walker himself—was coming to Korea. So I no longer would have to wear the double hat of division command and force command. Together we rode up toward Chonan to see what was going on. At the 34th's command post, south of the city, we were told that there was more trouble in Chonan and Martin had gone up again. Once more they were out of contact with their own front lines.

General Walker and I pulled on north, to the top of the last rise south of Chonan, with the town about six hundred yards ahead of us, out in an open valley. From there we watched our forces being driven out.

A sweating officer coming from Chonan told us that North Korean tanks were in the town, although we could not see them. He said Colonel Martin had grabbed a 2.6 bazooka and was leading his men with it, actually forcing the tanks to turn and run, when one tank came around a corner unexpectedly and fired from less than twenty-five feet. The shot blew Colonel Martin in half. Thereafter resistance had disintegrated and now our troops were bugging out.

Now a new decision faced me. The highway below Chonan

divides: one part follows the railroad to Chochiwon and the Kum River; the other goes straight south to Kongju, then angles eastward to rejoin the other highway at Yusong, just outside of Taejon. Both routes had to be defended. I ordered the 34th to back down the Kongju road and the newly arrived 21st Regiment to fight a delaying action on the route to Chochiwon. We were fighting for time. The 19th Regiment, which had come all the way from Honshu, was just getting into a reserve position. I already had ordered the tanks attached to it to come up on the line, and they came up while General Walker and I were watching the Chonan evacuation. These were the same little light tanks the rest of the division had.

As the commander of the first platoon came up the hill, General Walker stopped him and asked, "What are you going to do down there?"

The lieutenant said, "I'm going to slug it out." You could see that the boy was certain he was on his way to death. He'd heard what happened to other M-24 tanks against those heavy Russian-built tanks, but he had his teeth clenched and was going in.

But General Walker said, "Now, our idea is to stop those people. We don't go up there and charge or slug it out. We take positions where we have the advantage, where we can fire the first shots and still manage a delaying action."

Right there on the battlefield he gave this man as fine a lecture in tank tactics as you could hear in any military classroom.

We were still losing a war, but the delaying tactics did begin to delay a little. We weren't blowing as many bridges behind us as I would have liked—leaving them intact is a very brave thing to do when you're planning on a counterattack along the same route, but when the enemy is pushing you all the time it's an expensive form of courage—but otherwise the retreat was being fought rather well.

The 21st Infantry, under Colonel Richard Stevens—"Big Six" to his "Gimlets"—did a magnificent job at Chochiwon. With its forward elements overrun by the enemy, the 21st counterattacked, regained the lost ground, and in so doing revealed the savagery of our enemy: they found the bodies of six soldiers with hands tied behind their backs and holes through the backs of their heads.

During this period Dick Stevens too gave me some anxious moments when for several hours he was well forward of his command post and cut off. Only after the 34th Infantry was forced across the Kum River at Kongju, exposing the left flank of the 21st, did that regiment withdraw in good order to Okchon in the hills east of Taejon.

On their way back they passed through the 19th Infantry, the "Rock of Chickamauga" Regiment, which had taken up positions along the Kum at Taepyong-ni on June 13. This regiment put up a determined fight along the Kum. They were almost completely enveloped and the regimental command post surrounded before the "Chicks" withdrew to Yongdong to reorganize. I've always had a soft spot in my heart for this regiment, with which I served as a captain in Hawaii in 1936-38. In the battles around Taejon, under the inspired and gallant leadership of Colonel Guy S. (Stan) Meloy, the Chicks did a lot of killing and made the enemy pay full price for the ground won. Colonel Meloy, badly wounded, came out on a tank late at night, just as I thought I had lost him.

The 34th held on the Kum at Kongju until North Koreans swung around the exposed left flank and attacked the 63rd

Field Artillery Battalion on its flank and rear. This forced the 34th to fight a delaying action, facing northwest, just east of Nonsan.

Now our front was narrowing again, and only the 34th was still in contact with the enemy. I sent a battalion of the 19th up to give them some added strength, and ordered the units in contact to try to hold along the curve of a Kum River tributary north and west of Taejon.

Various officers of the 25th Division already had been up to look over the front, and I knew that division would come to help us just as soon as they had secured a vital airfield on the east coast. The 1st Cavalry also was on the way. So I moved my own divisional command post east to Yongdong but stayed behind in Taejon myself, working out of the 34th regimental command post, located in a schoolroom. I had ordered the 34th to leave the river perimeter on the night of July 17 but countermanded those orders and decided to try to hang on to that river line.

My reasons for staying in the town were simple, although of course there can be much argument about them. (I spent a great deal of time later trying to second-guess myself about them.) But these reasons were compounded of poor communications, which had cost me one valuable position up at Pyongtaek, and the old feeling that I could do the job better—that is, make the hour-to-hour decisions necessary—if I stayed in close contact with what was happening. My staff was quite capable of operating the headquarters at Yongdong, under the direction of Brigadier General Pearson Menoher; and frankly, it was easier to get a message through toward the rear (or so it seemed) than toward the front.

None of which changes certain facts: I was forward of my own headquarters on the night of July 19; the situation was so confused that I could not even be certain we still held a solid line northwest of the city; and very few important command decisions were made at that time. Very few of the things I did in the next twenty-four hours could not have been done by any competent sergeant—and such a sergeant would have done some of them better. I have no intention of alibiing my presence in Taejon. At the time I thought it was the place to be. Three and a half years later I still do not know any other place I could have been to accomplish any more. The accomplishments, I think, would have been virtually zero in any case.

On the night of July 19 I went to sleep to the sound of gunfire; and in the morning more gunfire knit a ragged and shrinking border around the city. I am no longer a young man, and so I awoke very early, although I had been short of sleep for almost a month. I heard the sound of the sporadic firing and inhaled the odors which no one ever escapes in Korea, of rice-paddy muck and mud walls, fertilizer and filth, and, mixed with them now, the acrid after-odor of cordite from the artillery, indefinable odors of thatch-roofed houses slowly burning.

There no longer was any great doubt: my forlorn hope that the 34th could hold the line long enough for more help to arrive was growing more forlorn by the minute. Spiteful rifles of infiltrators and turncoats spat from windows at the streaming refugees. The doom of Taejon was evident to them, to the lost and weary soldiers straggling through the town (the same soldiers who less than a month before had been fat and happy in occupation billets, complete with Japanese girl friends, plenty of beer, and servants to shine their boots), and to me.

Perhaps there is a certain somber poetry to any battle, and

the phrase, fight and fall back, has a brave sound. But a retreating army is no place to appreciate poetry; and for the people doing it day after day, fighting and falling back is a sorry business. Our first twenty days in Korea had been bone-wearying and bloody for the soldiers and frustrating for me (as such a battle must be for any commander who must tell soldiers when to fall back, when to turn and fight again). Any infantry officer must at times be ruthless. Part of the job is to send men into places from which you know they are not likely to come out again. This is never easy, but it's an especially soul-searing business when the only thing you can buy with other men's lives is a little more time. Sometimes I wonder now, when so many people are so friendly and kind to me, whether they realize that they are being kind to a man who has issued such orders in two wars, and to many, many men.

But these are thoughts which come after a battle, not during it. On that morning in Taejon I remember especially the hour of six-thirty. It was then that Lieutenant Clarke, whom I had as an aide partially because he was an aircraft pilot but who had been doing exactly no flying whatever since we hit Korea, relayed a report that North Korean tanks had been seen in Taejon itself, although the battle line was still presumed to be well north and west.

This was the sort of report with which the whole division was thoroughly familiar by this time—and of which every man in it was deathly sick. There was only one difference between this report and many previous ones like it—this time there were no immediate decisions to be made, for the moment no general officer's work to be done. So we decided to go tank hunting—Clarke, Jimmy Kim, my Korean interpreter, and I. We couldn't do anything at the moment about the fact that the 34th's headquarters had lost contact with two of its leading battalions and did not know where its flanks were, or about the war in general. But perhaps we could do something about a couple of tanks.

We found them easily enough. Two T-34s had come into an intersection where the east-west road through the city meets the road from the airfield—but they wouldn't be going away again. Both were dead in the street. Behind them, one of our own ammunition carriers was burning, with much phosphorus smoke. A third tank was in a field near some housing built for dependents of American soldiers during the Korean occupation. This one appeared to be undamaged. As we approached it we received one round of high explosive, although we could not be sure of the source.

A three-quarter-ton truck mounting a 75-millimeter recoilless rifle was just backing toward the two dead tanks at the intersection, but I succeeded in getting the driver's attention and redirected him to back toward the tank in the field. But even though we reached a firing position we accomplished nothing. The gunner either was too nervous or was unfamiliar with his weapon, and none of the four or five rounds of his remaining ammunition scored a hit. The truck then pulled away, but the tank in the field still didn't move. We discovered later in the day that it already had been put out of action, although it showed no signs of damage.

This whole incident was only a repetition of an old story: we had nothing with which to fight this or any other tank. Lieutenant Clarke wrote an independent report of this day's activities and in it said that we returned to the regimental command post and ate breakfast. But I must confess I remember very little about the meal, although shortly food was to mean more to me than it ever had meant before in my life.

I do remember that after a time we went tank-hunting once

more, and this time located both a weapon and two more enemy tanks. The weapon was a bazooka, for which the soldier carrying it had just one remaining round of ammunition. The two tanks were on the same street as the two dead tanks, and behind the ammunition carrier, which still was burning. Our first attempt to get close to them ended abruptly when we began to receive machine-gun fire just over our heads, apparently coming from the turrets. We scuttled out of the line of fire and came up again from behind the buildings along the side of the street. This time smoke from the burning trailer and the protection of ruined buildings enabled us to get within ten or fifteen yards of the street, well behind the tanks. Just as we did, one of the live tanks managed to turn around in the narrow street and started back the way it had come into the town, and the other followed.

This was our day for bad shooting. The bazooka man too was nervous. His one round was fired at a range of a hundred yards but fell far short. The last tank rumbled right up to us and on past, within twenty yards.

There was nothing we could do to stop it. Some people who escaped from Taejon that day reported that they last had seen me firing a pistol at a tank. Well, they did, but I'm not proud of it. As that last tank passed I banged away at it with a .45; but even then I wasn't silly enough to think I could *do* anything with a pistol. It was plain rage and frustration—just Dean losing his temper.

After that display of disgust, all I could do was to have Clarke take a few measurements of treads and armor thickness on the dead tanks, then return to the regimental command post and call for an air strike on the fleeing enemy armor, if the planes could find it. Our withdrawal from the battle of pistol against tank was punctuated by white phosphorus shells exploding from the burning carrier and falling much too close for comfort.

But we still weren't through with tanks. Very shortly a lone tank, without infantry support, calmly rumbled through the town, coming from the direction of Kumsan directly south of us, and going up toward the front lines to the north and west. It passed between our command post and the artillery area, not firing on either one and not being fired upon, waddled all the way up to the front line, then calmly waddled back again, still not firing. In passing the command post a second time, that tanker certainly must have seen more Americans milling around than he'd ever seen before, but he just kept going.

The only deduction we could make was that this tank must have come all the way around our left flank, leaving road-blocks of infantry as he came. I think he then went up to the battle line to report to his people, "Well, I've got these boys hooked from the rear now. Come on and make your attack."

In the days before July 20 I was getting intelligence reports from Korean Army sources and some of my own Korean agents. My private agents had said days earlier that the Communists would not attempt a direct attack on Taejon but would move around it to the west and south. It was also reported that civilians in captured areas had been ordered to make thousands of suits of typical Korean white clothing, in which North Korean soldiers would infiltrate our lines at Taejon itself. Then these, plus the turncoats already in the town, would capture it without a frontal assault.

I discounted this information in preparing for the Taejon defenses; but there is no denying such thousands of infiltrators did come into town and confuse the situation. Whether the final North Korean decision to make a frontal attack was based on the failure of these infiltrators to drive us out entirely, or on such information as this lone tank could have provided, is anybody's guess.

At any rate, we decided to chase this tank with a headquarters group, in spite of our previous failures. Clarke, Captain Richard Rowlands, a division liaison officer, a ROK ordnance officer, and some casuals from the regimental command post made up the party. The latter were normally cooks, clerks, or messengers. On the way to the spot where the lone tank had last been reported we located a bazooka man and his ammunition carrier and a few other soldiers. Clarke's notes show that we killed some snipers on the way through the town; I think he's correct, because we certainly received a lot of sniper fire. I had reason again to note, as in Europe, that American boys really need to play more cops and robbers, as in the days of my own youth. They just don't know how to hide themselves any more, or how to sneak up on an objective—whether it be Willie Jones playing cop or a North Korean guerrilla firing out of a window.

When we located the lone tank it was parked at a business-area intersection, with two-storied buildings on all sides, perhaps half a mile south of the command post. The buildings were set close to the street but were not deep structures, so that the interior of each block formed a courtyard completely surrounded by shops and stores.

We approached by entering front doors of stores a block away from the tank, going through them and out into the rear-area courtyard, then into back doors of a building only yards from the quiescent tank. Immediately rifle fire splattered around us. The tankers had some sort of infantry protection now, and these riflemen had seen us. We withdrew through the stores to the courtyard, then tried to reach the street again at a different spot, but again the rifles found us.

This time I think our position may have been given away by a fat and stolid Korean woman who calmly stood on the street outside a building while all this firing was going on. One of the soldiers wanted to shoot her, but I couldn't be sure enough that she was a lookout.

Instead we went back to the courtyard once more, and this time moved directly behind the building at the corner. Only this one structure was between us and the tank. To get upstairs from the courtyard I had to chin myself on a window ledge, then clamber up. The bazooka man and I, moving very cautiously, entered a plastered room, about seven by eight feet. I think Clarke was in the next room, and others behind us.

Quietly I slipped up beside the street window and looked around the side of it with one eye–directly into the muzzle of the tank's cannon, no more than a dozen feet away. I could have spat down the barrel. I signaled to the bazooka man, who crept up beside me. Then I pointed to a spot just at the base of the cannon, where the turret and body of the tank joined.

The bazooka went off beside my ear. Plaster cascaded from the ceiling onto our heads and around our shoulders. Fumes from the blast filled the room, and concussion shook the whole building. From the tank came the most horrible screaming I'd ever heard (although I did hear its equal later and under different circumstances), but the tank still was not on fire. I don't think I'm normally a brutal man, but I had just one idea. I think I said, "Hit them again!" and pointed to a spot on the other side of the turret. The bazooka fired and more plaster cascaded, exposing the cornstalks to which most Korean plaster is stuck. A third time the bazooka fired, and the screaming finally stopped. Smoke rose from the tank. It was very quiet in the street.

This was a day in which I had no sense of time. Time got

lost. Although I hardly had been conscious of any lapse of hours since early morning, it was almost evening when we came back to the command post for the last time.

There only details remained to be decided. Colonel Charles Beauchamp, the regimental commander who had joined us only three days earlier and had brought the 34th renewed spirit and fire, had been away from the command post most of the day, trying to re-establish his communications, so I issued my orders for evacuation to the executive officer, Lieutenant Colonel Robert L. (Pappy) Wadlington, another of the old 44th Division officers now fighting a second war with me. The temporary command of the 34th had fallen on Wadlington's shoulders when Colonel Martin was killed; and Pappy lived up to all my expectations. With his supporting artillery ambushed, he had kept his outfit in hand and fought a stubborn delaying action back to the Taejon perimeter, at which time Colonel Beauchamp, an eagle colonel sent from the 7th Division, had taken over.

A counterattack force was organized from kitchen police, clerks, and messengers when an artillery commander reported that snipers were preventing him from moving his pieces and that he might have to pull the breech locks and abandon the guns, which had happened all too often in the previous couple of weeks of our retreat. But this time Major S. C. McDaniel took out his headquarters people and managed to pin down the snipers until the guns could pull away toward the rear. This young officer had come to us as a replacement, also from the 7th Division, when Major John J. Dunn, the regimental operations officer, was reported missing in action at the same time Colonel Martin was killed at Chonan. I felt certain that Dunn had been killed too, but learned later that he was seriously wounded and captured. McDaniel had taken over a difficult position and had impressed me by his ability and outstanding courage. Later on July 20 he too was captured. I've learned from returning prisoners of war that he was relentless in his efforts to protect the rights of his fellow prisoners, despite the repeated threats of his Communist captors. He was so adamant that he finally was taken away from the prison camp, and his fellow prisoners are convinced that he was murdered.

All day Captain Raymond D. Hatfield, the division transportation officer, had been worrying about his supply train. We had a rolling supply point—that is, virtually all of our ammunition and supplies were kept on a train, so that they could be pulled out fast when we needed to retreat again, as we had from front-line points farther north. Hatfield was trying to get the train out of Taejon toward Yongdong, but reported that Korean engineers had uncoupled the locomotive and fled with it.

Fortunately my telephone line to division headquarters was still open, and division promised to send a locomotive back to Taejon. Hatfield went down to the railroad yard to meet it, but soon returned, almost beside himself. The locomotive had come clear into the yards, then suddenly backed away again at full speed.

Once more we called headquarters. They told us a sniper had killed the engineer and the locomotive had been taken out by the fireman, but they would send it in once more, with a carload of troops for protection. The last I saw of Hatfield (who really belonged at division headquarters, not up here in the burning town) was when he made another trip toward the railroad yard, still refusing to leave until the train did.

I added his name to a list I had been keeping. That day I had listed about fifteen names of men to whom I intended to award medals the moment I got a chance—Bronze or Silver Stars for gallantry or heroic action. I even had a dozen actual medals—all the Bronze Stars the Eighth Army possessed at the moment—in my jeep, so that I could pin them on personally and on the spot. I knew I had been far too chary about awarding medals in World War II, and it hadn't been fair to the men. This time I wasn't going to hand them out like rations, but I didn't intend to make the same mistake over again.

Captain Hatfield never got out of Taejon. When American troops retook the town, much later, his body was found. He had been wounded, then bayoneted. I have recommended since my return to this country that he be awarded posthumously a Silver Star for heroic action. Most of the other men whose names were put on my list that day never did get their awards. I hung on to the list, but rain obliterated the names during the subsequent days and weeks. Three years later I couldn't remember them nor learn who the men had been. I saw my jeep again, under curious circumstances, but I have no idea what happened to the medals that were in it.

Just about dusk, light tanks from the 1st Cavalry Division, on temporary assignment to us, came up from the rear, and we organized a column of vehicles—the first of the regimental headquarters—to start out under their protection. But only moments after they left the schoolhouse, we heard them in a fire fight near the center of town.

Shortly afterward Pappy Wadlington suggested that it was time for us to go too. He showed me a last message he proposed to send to division headquarters, but I rewrote it because I thought it sounded, in his version, too much like asking rescue for me personally. As a substitute I wrote: "Enemy roadblock eastern exit Taejon. Send armor immediately. Dean."

In Europe I had ordered a lot of stations closed, without minding. This time I minded. If I had realized that this was the last formal order I was to issue for three years, perhaps I might have phrased it better—one of those ringing things that somebody would remember. But I didn't know then, and now I can't think of anything better to have said.

We organized the remaining miscellaneous headquarters vehicles into a rough column and started out toward the east, the way the previous column had gone with the tanks. As we pulled through the city we ran into the tail of this column, which had been ambushed. Some trucks were on fire, others slewed across a narrow street where buildings on both sides were flaming for a block or more. Our own infantry, on one side of the street, was in a vicious fire fight with enemy units in higher positions on the other side.

We drove through, careening between the stalled trucks. It was a solid line of fire, an inferno that seared us in spite of our speed. A block farther on my jeep and an escort jeep roared straight past an intersection, and almost immediately Clarke, riding with me, said we had missed a turn. But rifle fire still poured from buildings on both sides, and turning around was out of the question. I looked at a map and decided we should go on ahead, south and east, on another road that might let us make more speed than the truck-jammed main escape route. I had been away from my headquarters too long, and had to get back very soon. So we bored down the road in the general direction of Kumsan, while snipers still chewed at us from both sides of the road.

We were all by ourselves.

▶▶▶▶◀◀◀◀

CHAPTER III

The Lonesome Mountains

Our jeeps tried to barrel through the snipers' fire, but it blocked us time after time. At one spot, a truck lay partially on its side in a ditch with the driver slumped in his seat. We stopped and I ran over. The driver was dead, but under the truck were a couple of men talking to each other about surrendering. One said, "We might as well surrender. There isn't any use in this."

There were some walking wounded here too, and I filled my jeep with them, then started talking to the men under the truck. A Communist showed himself in silhouette on top of a hill, so I grabbed an M-1 and fired. I used to be good with a Springfield, but I hate to admit that I'm no great shakes with an M-1. I don't know whether I hit this man, but he dropped and the sniper fire let up a little. I signaled to Clarke in my jeep and to the escort jeep—now filled with casuals or wounded men—to go on; and the two men who had been cowering under the truck came out to join me.

I had hoped that there would be no more vehicles on this wrong road, but an artillery half-track rumbled up. I think that was the most heavily loaded vehicle I ever saw. It was so crammed with men that we couldn't get in—we just got on, hanging by precarious toe- and hand-holds.

We rumbled ahead and presently caught up with my jeeps.

They had been blocked and abandoned at a spot where the road made a slight S-bend as it approached a river and bridge. Here the Communists had set up a roadblock. Riflemen were along the S itself and at the left of the road, and apparently a machine gun was emplaced behind one of our wrecked vehicles at the bridge. Heavy fire swept the raised road, from in front of us and on the left side.

We tumbled off the road embankment into a ditch at the right for protection. Here I realized that I no longer had any weapon. I had left the M-1 on the half-track when I jumped for the ditch; my pistol had been lost somewhere, and the holster dangled empty at my hip.

Clarke was in the ditch with several other men. He had been an air officer, but now he showed infantry ability. When I asked him to make an informal muster, he counted seventeen Americans and a terrified Korean civilian who spoke English and later told me he had once worked for the U. S. State Department in Seoul.

We started crawling away from the road the Communist fire covered, around a small house, and through a bean or sweet potato field. On the way the little Korean, something of a dandy from his appearance, fell up to his armpits in a honey (fertilizer) pit and was absolutely speechless thereafter. We reached the bank of the river, well away from the bridge, and lay there in a semicircle, waiting. I remember delivering a small lecture to the men about keeping off the ridge lines, about using their halizone tablets to purify the river water with which they were filling their canteens (neither Clarke nor I had one), and about patience. I said that we'd have to wait until full dark to go on, and that patience was very important. A couple of years later, I wondered a time or two just how patient a man was required to be.

The group had only a few arms of assorted kinds. Clarke, who had been hit in the shoulder, insisted that I take his pistol. "I can't use it anyhow," he said.

Our bank of the river was low, but a mountain rose directly from the other side. Our plan was to cross here where the Communist fire did not bar the river to us, then swing over the mountain and down to the highway again beyond the roadblock. In full dark we got across, wading, and started climbing the steep, unstable slope. It was rough going. I was leading, and presently Clarke worked his way up to me and said, "We have a badly wounded man behind us."

Clarke and I went back to help the wounded man, who was hit in both legs, and Captain Rowlands, the liaison officer who had been with us on the tank hunt earlier in the day, took the lead.

I had carefully planned the withdrawal from Taejon to include the blowing of bridges and tunnels at exactly the right time. Rowlands—and only Rowlands—was to have given the word to demolition squads, but he didn't reach any communications for three or four days, so as far as I know the demolition charges never were fired. That's the sort of thing that happens to careful planning during a retreat.

Two soldiers already were carrying the wounded man. Another man staggered along beside them. At the first opportunity Clarke used his first-aid kit to bind the man's leg wounds, although his own shoulder still had not been treated.

This was sandy soil, very loose, and it was difficult for two men to carry another between them. I said, "Hell, get this man up on my shoulders. I can carry him more easily that way by myself."

But Dean is always forgetting how old he is. That one-man carry didn't last long. The soldier was too heavy for me, and

I was almost falling on my face. We went back to the two-man carry, and even then it seemed as if my turn came around every five minutes.

It was pitch-dark, and we were trying to move with as little noise as possible, to avoid stirring up North Korean patrols. The main group ahead kept moving too fast, away from us, simply because they had no way of telling that we weren't right behind them. The man we were carrying became more or less delirious; he drank all the available water and then called for more. We only hoped we knew where the party ahead was going; we kept struggling to catch up, but we had to stop for rest very often.

During one of the rest stops I thought I heard water running, just off the ridge to one side–I was sure I heard it. I started off in that direction, and the next thing I knew I was running down a slope so steep that I could not stop.

I plunged forward and fell.

A statement by Lieutenant Clarke about these events declared, in part: "About twelve, midnight, the general told me he was going down [the hillside] for water. I wouldn't let him and told him that we had seen North Koreans [by presumption] tracking us to the base of the hill, and we could assume they were still there. Also told him that there probably was a stream on the other side of the hill.

"The next day–1:15 a.m.–while leading the patrol, I found no one was following me, and no noise to the rear. So I returned to find five men asleep on the ground. I called for the general, and one of the men answered that he had gone for water. As I figured the round trip could be made in an hour, I set the goal of two hours as the maximum time that we could wait. The general didn't take a canteen or a helmet, so I assumed he was going to try to find some stragglers rather than to get water. At 3:15 a.m. I woke the men and we headed to the top of the hill, arriving just before dawn. . . . Just as it was beginning to get light, I had the men spread out and posted two as guards for one-hour shifts. I figured we'd at least be able to see what killed us, as we had no weapons. I no sooner posted the guards when I checked and found them asleep. I awoke them and asked them if they wanted to be killed. I don't remember their exact answers, but they were to the effect that they didn't care whether they were killed or not. So I stood guard until they woke up. At daylight I searched the area with my field glasses, saw that our vehicles [the ones abandoned on the road the night before] were gone, and three Koreans were sitting on top of a hill to the northeast of us. We spent the day where we were, on top of the hill. It was scorching hot. We had the shade only of a few bushes about a foot high. During the day the men almost turned against me because I wouldn't let them start off until it got dark. As it did begin to get dark we started south along the ridge until we reached a cliff at the southern end. At this point we walked around the top of a ledge, about six feet wide, and then slid down a slope. . . ."

The remainder of the statement details his party's further experiences in getting back to the U. S. lines, which they reached two days later, on July 23.

When I awoke I had no idea how long I had been knocked out, and at first didn't realize that I had a gash on my head. But when I tried to rise on my hands and knees I found I had a broken shoulder. My abdomen where I'd had an operation a year before hurt fearfully. I was dazed and groggy. I looked at my watch, which read twelve-thirty a.m.—or that's what I thought it said, although now I believe it must have been later. I was down in a dry creek bed with very steep sides; and all I could think of was, "My God, what's happened to those people up there? I don't know where I am."

I don't think I had walked more than twenty yards or so from the rest of the party, but I couldn't tell how far my involuntary run had taken me, or how far I'd rolled in my fall. I've tried dozens of times to reconstruct that run and fall in my mind, but I simply don't know how it happened. My present guess is that I was a hundred yards down the hill—not a cliff, but a very steep, sandy slope.

I heard water again, and I needed it badly. I crawled along the dry stream bottom and finally found a trickle oozing out of the rocks. I scooped out a hollow with my hands, and when it filled with water I stuck my face down in the dirty puddle and drank, not worrying at all about halizone tablets. I remember that I then started back up the barren hillside, perhaps on my hands and knees or just scrabbling, but I don't know what happened next.

I must have passed out again, because when I regained consciousness I was lying on my side—and an eight- or ten-man North Korean patrol was moving no more than ten yards from me. This was false dawn, just a faint glow over the eastern hills; but even in the improved light they failed to see me. I can't imagine why they missed me, but they kept right on going, scrambling up that steep incline like so many mountain goats, in the same direction that I had been headed.

I thought, "Oh-oh, this is the end for Clarke and the others. They're gone now." That was the lowest moment I've ever had in my life. I could see all those people on the hill being killed; and the realization that Clarke didn't even have a pistol —I had his—made me feel even worse. But there was absolutely nothing I could do about it.

I was also tortured by the thought, not new, that I should have done something about him earlier. Both Clarke and my other aide, Captain David Bissett, were married men with young children; and ever since we had come to Korea I had been trying to figure out some way to fire both of them without hurting their feelings. They were good aides and good officers, but my experience with aides and drivers for division commanders in wartime is that they are very likely to get killed. I felt I shouldn't have men with young children taking the risks they had to take. I had been able to keep Bissett at headquarters most of the time, although he was thoroughly angry with me and even had told me, "General, I don't appreciate this. Why can't I have a company?"

But I had not done anything else about relieving either of them, and now I thought, "Well, Clarke's gone; and if I don't get back to headquarters myself, Bissett will ask for a line company for sure, and probably get killed too." They were both very fine men, and I'd never been so proud of Clarke as in the last few hours when he'd been organizing that column and keeping people together.

When the North Koreans were out of sight I crawled back to the trickle of water and drank again. I was dead tired, but I thought, "Oh-oh, I can't stay here. Other people may know about this waterhole." So I crawled up into some bushes fifteen or twenty feet away from it, just as daylight was coming on, and stayed there all day, only about half-conscious. I could hear trucks and people over on the highway we had left, a lot of noise, as if the Communists might be working on their vehicles, and some firing.

As soon as darkness came I started out again, first crawling back up the hillside, then along the top of the ridge, without seeing any sign of the party I'd lost the night before or of the Communist patrol of the morning. My shoulder was useless, so scrambling up the hill was difficult; on the top I was able to stagger along more easily. Then the ridge suddenly ended in a sheer cliff. A trail zigzagged down, but it was extremely steep, almost a hand-hold trail, and I had great difficulty with it. Walking itself seemed to do something to my insides; and it was especially hard for me to get to my feet after I had been sitting or lying down to rest.

Working at it a long time, I finally managed to get down about ten feet on the trail, where it flattened out in an escarpment, a sort of shelf on the side of the mountain. The trail went along it for a short distance, then dived another ten feet down to a second shelf. These ten-foot slopes were murder to get down. I barely managed to reach the foot of the second when rain started to pour down, as I think it can rain nowhere except in Korea. It came in torrents, and I was almost overcome by the desire for something to drink. There had been no water on top of the ridge. I found a big flat rock, perhaps six feet across, sticking up a foot above the ground level. I wanted to keep going but couldn't make it just then, so I lay down beside the rock and stretched my handkerchief out on top of it in the pouring rain. When it got soaked with water, I squeezed it out into my mouth, a few drops at a time. I think I spent most of the night doing that, instead of moving on toward our lines.

I was still lying there in the morning when I heard a noise, something scrambling down the same path I had used. I got around behind the rock and pulled my pistol, just in case it might be a North Korean.

But the man who lurched into view was a young American. He had not seen me yet—he was too busy making his way down that brutal path—when I called to him. "Who are you?" I said. "What outfit are you from?"

He jumped when he heard me but sighed with relief when he got a look and saw that I too was an American. He said, "I'm Lieutenant Tabor—Stanley Tabor—from the Nineteenth Infantry. Who are you?"

I tried to get up from behind my rock but had trouble. Then I said, "Well, I'm the S.O.B. who's the cause of all this trouble."

Tabor said he had been with Easy Company of the 2nd Battalion, which I had thrown into the river perimeter to bolster up the 34th's strength. In the retreat he'd been cut off and had started walking south by himself.

We started walking again that morning, Tabor carrying his carbine and I with Clarke's pistol banging against my leg. I've enjoyed walking all my life and usually can outwalk many young people. But not on this day. I had to keep stopping to rest because of the pain under my ribs and in my abdomen. I just wanted to sit down. After each rest Tabor would pull me to my feet, and we'd make a few more yards.

I said, "You go on ahead. One person can get through a lot quicker. I'm stove up, and there's no use pooping around here."

But he always would say, "No, two have a better chance," and would refuse to leave me.

About one o'clock that afternoon we found the highway again. But it was bordered by open fields, and every time we'd try to cross we would see vehicles or soldiers of the Inmun Gun (North Korean term for "People's Army"). So we kept heading south through the brush, toward Kumsan, waiting for an opportunity to turn toward the east, in the direction of Yongdong, where I had left division headquarters.

That afternoon we stumbled into a family of refugees from Taejon, a mother and two teen-aged sons who had strung a rude tent—just a piece of canvas, really—beside a stream. None of them could speak English, but they gave us some of their rice and made us understand that we should stay out of sight under the canvas until dark. We got the idea that there were many North Koreans in the area, but none of them bothered us.

Both of us got some sleep. When we awakened we asked the family if they would guide us toward Yongdong that evening. They made us understand that this town—more than twenty miles east of Taejon—had also been captured by the Communists. The military situation, then, was in even worse shape than I had feared. We had to assume this news was true; and if it was, Tabor and I were in a bad spot. I knew it would be terribly hard to get all the way east to Kumchon, which would be the next logical place for division headquarters to move if Yongdong was lost. We would have to pass through a defile; and the hill country around Yongdong always had been full of Communists. Even in the occupation days hunters passed up this fine deer country because of the many guerrillas.

So I said, "We'll have to head south toward Kumsan, then try to get to Chinan, and east toward Taegu." In other words, I thought we'd make a big swing south, then cut to the east well below the main invasion route. This was to be my general plan for a long time.

That evening we started south again. There were no stars or other guideposts for holding our direction, and we didn't make much time. This was on the evening of July 22, and I guess my various injuries affected my mind, because the next days are more or less a blank. I know we had no food and that we did keep going, but the rest is just a haze of weariness, trying to get to my feet and failing without help, and everlastingly stumbling along one trail after another. Tabor must have kept us both going by will power, because I don't remember having any.

This may have gone on for one day or three. At last we reached a small town. I think we had turned around somehow and were heading west rather than south. This village may have been near Chinsan. At any rate we stumbled into it, and within a few minutes the whole population was around us. We asked for food, and someone brought us water with some kind of uncooked grain ground up in it. I've never seen or heard of it elsewhere. They also gave each of us two raw eggs. Two men in the crowd spoke some English, one of them well and one just a few words. The people seemed friendly, so we asked about where the Inmun Gun was, and whether they would guide us to Taegu. I offered them a million *won* (approximately $1100—the exchange then was about 860 to 1) if they would take us through. Even when Koreans speak English well, they often confuse figures, so I drew the figure in the dirt.

We should have noticed that the man who spoke better English had disappeared, but we didn't. The one who spoke less well said, "Okay, okay, come with me." He indicated that we should come to his house to get some rest, and that he would take us to Taegu in the morning. He led us to a house at the far edge of the village, where we took off our boots and entered an unfurnished room. The Korean sat on the floor with us and in his very broken English asked whom the village people should support. He diagrammed it: the Americans pushing one way, the North Koreans the other. It was all very confusing, he indicated, and I'm afraid we didn't help his confusion much. Instead we went to sleep on the floor.

Several hours later–it must have been early in the morning –we heard a rifle shot just outside the house. At the sound that little Korean never hesitated. He went out a door like a rabbit out of a box. He was gone, without any preliminaries.

Outside a voice called, "Come out, Americans! Come out! We will not kill you. We are members of the People's Army. Come out, Americans!" The English was the best that I'd heard a Korean speak.

Tabor said, "This is it," and reached for his carbine.

We didn't "come out." I said to Tabor, "Come on, get your boots on, in a hurry," and we both did. We left by another door–away from both the rifle shot and the door the Korean had used, and jumped into some high weeds right beside the house.

"I'll lead," I said as we started crawling up a little hill in the dark. "With the carbine, you can cover me better than I can cover you with a pistol. I'll be the point." I remember I also said, "I'm not going to surrender, Tabor. There won't be any surrender for me."

"That's the way I feel too," he said.

There were more shots. They heard us in the weeds and fired in that direction. We reversed our course and went right back through the village, which was in pandemonium, everybody in the street and everybody yelling. We went right through town, past those Korean civilians, but none of them did anything. Crossing back-lots and skirting around houses, we finally came out in a rice paddy at the other edge of town. These paddies are divided into small cells, perhaps thirty feet across, with high dikes between. The water was about four inches deep and the rice stuck up another four or five inches.

We dived into the rice and the water, crawling on our bellies, using our elbows to inch us forward in the old infantry fashion. Two soldiers were across the paddy on a dike; they did not see us at first. I led out in the crawling, crossing one cell, then scooting over a dike and into the next, while the soldiers—wearing Inmun Gun uniforms, I think—continued to search from their vantage point on a parallel dike.

We crossed three of these cells, with the intervening dikes. Tabor was still with me. Then I went over another dike and crawled some more, but when I looked back, Tabor was not behind me—and I was not to see another American for three long years.

During the thirty-five days I spent in the hills of South Korea several subjects cluttered my mind: food, inability to tell time of day or day of month, worry over my friends and aides, and the frantic necessity for getting back to United Nations lines with new information I had gathered about the enemy. These varied in importance from day to day, but all of them were there, all the time. So was an hour-to-hour, day-to-day concern about a pistol and just twelve rounds of .45 ammunition. Those twelve rounds were the most important in the world, because they were all I had.

While I lay in that rice paddy waiting for Tabor to catch up with me, I thought the time had come when I'd have to use that ammunition. I couldn't imagine what had happened to the lieutenant. We'd been doing very well, inching forward on our elbows and bellies, and there had been no sounds of firing or pursuit. Finally I crawled onto the edge of the paddy, where only a dike separated the rice land from a stream and a path beside it. Still he hadn't caught up.

I called, "Tabor! Tabor!" The only answer was from one of the Communist soldiers on a nearby dike. He fired at the sound of my voice. I clung to the ground and took out the pistol, getting ready to use it. I knew that I'd see the soldier's silhouette on the dike in the dim pre-dawn light before he could see me. But he must also have realized this, because he never came closer. I waited quite a long time, then called, "Tabor! Tabor!" once more. Again, shots were my answer. After half an hour with nothing whatever happening, I crawled back to look over into the last paddy cell we had crossed together; but Tabor wasn't there either.

It was almost full daylight now, and my advantage over the Communists hunting me was gone. I felt like a sheep-stealing dog, but I had to go on. I crawled along the path beside the stream and finally found some foxholes, evidently dug by Communists for a roadside ambush. I was still within hearing distance of the village, but I figured that the last place pursuers would look for me would be in one of their own foxholes. I crawled down into one, past drying watermelon rinds the former owners had thrown out from some feast they had held while waiting for somebody to ambush.

I have never figured out what could have happened to Tabor that morning. It's difficult to keep going in a straight line when you're crawling with heads down, as we were, and the paddy cells were oddly shaped, never square. He may simply have become confused and changed direction, losing sight of me, then was unable to find me where I stopped beside the path. It's also possible that he dropped into one of the drainage or fertilizer holes which are in nearly every rice-paddy cell. For a day or so previous to this, we had been arguing a little about these. Tabor thought we should come down to the paddies, using the holes to hide in when necessary; but I had vetoed the idea, insisting that the only way to get anywhere in Korea is to keep to the high ground. It could be that he merely decided, once we were separated, to use his own judgment. However, I am convinced that he lost direction while crawling.

I learned in 1953 that Tabor had been brought into a prisoner-of-war stockade at Taejon on August 4, 1950. Our flight from the village was in the early hours of July 25 or July 26, so I don't believe he was captured that day. The village people certainly would not have waited so long to turn him over to the nearest Communist headquarters for whatever reward was then being offered for lieutenants. I think he may have remained free several days after we lost each other, but no positive check is possible. He was in such bad shape when taken prisoner that he finally died, from malnutrition and pneumonia. Returning prisoners in 1953 told the story of his death to his wife, whom he had married three months before going to Korea, and also relayed his report of having been with me for two weeks in the hills. Actually our time together was two or three days, not weeks; but the story had passed through many hands before it came back to me.

I'm still heartsick about him. Perhaps I should have gone back even farther that morning in the paddies, but I don't think I could have found him. My recommendation that he be awarded a Silver Star for his disregard of his personal safety in staying with me was made after my return to this country.

No sooner had I dropped into that foxhole by the roadside than I saw a farmer carrying a little girl, about three years old, on his back. Thank God he was not coming from the direction of the village; presumably he did not know about the hue and cry for me. He definitely saw me, so there was no point in trying to hide. I tried for the first time what was to become a regular practice—when your hiding place in Korea is discovered, ask for food.

I got out of the hole and made signs. The word *pop*, made with a sharper sound than in English, means rice in Korean. I said, "Pop," and placed a hand on my stomach.

It worked. He made signs that I was to get back down in the hole and stay there, then went on. In about an hour he came back with a big bowl of rice, more than I could eat. After I had my fill I tore off the North Korean part of a map I had in my pocket (not being at all interested in North Korea just then) and wrapped what was left of the rice in it.

Then I crouched in the foxhole and took out the pistol again. When I tried to fire it, empty, nothing happened, which gave me special cold chills as I remembered my plan to use it against the soldier on the dike a couple of hours earlier. I spent the day stripping it all the way down, cleaning it as best I could of the mud and water it had picked up.

I had the twelve rounds of ammunition and the two clips. Then and later, I was torn by indecision: I'd burnish those shells every day, but I never could make up my mind permanently which was the better way to keep them. Should I have one shell always in the pistol chamber, and the other clip full—that is, carrying eight rounds—not worrying about the three remaining shells? Or should I put six shells in each clip and depend on having time to change clips in the midst of a fight? Neither system suited me, really, because neither could insure that I'd be able to use eleven for knocking out Communists and one for knocking out Dean. I figured this last was essential. Even if I could have stomached the idea personally, I knew that I couldn't afford to surrender, because of my rank. The Communists would be sure to capitalize on the surrender of a general, just as we had in Europe. They might even put out the information that I had gone over to their side, and there wouldn't be anything that I could do about it. I remembered that in Europe we had captured a German SS general who got lost in a retreat; and immediately our propaganda people had made capital out of him, telling the Germans in leaflets and broadcasts that he was just smart, he'd realized it was "a quarter to twelve" and had surrendered deliberately. That was not going to happen to Dean—not if bullet number twelve could prevent it.

I stayed in the foxhole all that day. Toward evening the farmer came back with more rice. When I showed him the rice I'd saved he grimaced and threw it away. When you want to keep cooked rice, you wrap it in a cloth so that it can "breathe." Wrapped in a tight paper, it sours within hours. I was to learn a lot about rice, and that was the first lesson.

After dark I left the foxhole and started walking again, still holding to my project of going south to get out of the way of the main troop movements, then east toward Taegu. I kicked myself for being without a compass. Traveling only at night, I could not use the sun effectively to check my direction; and the old Boy Scout system of getting a bearing from a watch was no good to me. My watch had stopped days before. Most nights the stars were obscured, and I had to go by guess-reckoning, which was often wrong. I think I made almost a complete circle during the next three nights, accomplishing nothing.

The only thing was, I did feel better. I could get up by myself now; and dysentery, which had bothered me during the first twenty days in Korea, was gone. In fact, my elimination came to a complete stop for thirty-two days. I thought

I was a medical curiosity, but when I told my story years later in a Tokyo hospital nobody was impressed. Army doctors said anything under a hundred days was nothing to brag about. Nevertheless I'm still amazed.

On the night of what I think was August 1, I started walking early. I was up in the mountains by this time. I was making distance every night, and I thought, "All's well. I'll get through."

I was on a ridge, approaching what I think must have been Kumsan, although I wasn't coming from the proper direction. I seemed to be traveling east, from the direction of Chinsan, rather from the south. That was what made me certain I must have been going in a circle. In the early evening I passed some women working in the fields. As I went by I noticed that a little boy of about nine left them and was following me. I went over a rise and slipped into some bushes, sure that I had eluded him. After some time I came out again and reached a hill overlooking the town. From my vantage point I picked out a house detached from the others and decided that when full dark came I would go there and ask for food. I had not eaten since the farmer gave me rice on July 25 or 26.

For some reason not clear now, I was quite certain the people in this particular house would feed me. But just as I got to my feet to go down and try my panhandling, a youth carrying a rifle came out and started running up the hill—running like mad. Pretty soon another came out and also ran up the hill. I thought it fortunate that I had waited as long as I had to case the town. Then at least three more youths ran out of other houses farther down the street. I couldn't tell whether they were armed, but none was in uniform. They all were heading more or less away from me. I hunched down in the bushes and was just about to congratulate myself on my hiding place when I heard a rustling behind me—and here was this nine-year-old, pointing down at me and trying to signal to the men. He wasn't more than a couple of yards from me.

I lunged at him, and I'm afraid I wasn't very pleasant. I really cussed him out. He turned and ran; and I crawled out of there fast and went the other way. There was shooting all around me, and bullets clipped the bushes above my head. Somebody yelled as if he'd been hit, but Dean was on his way.

When I'd come to Korea I had hoped I soon would be a grandfather, but I didn't feel grandfatherly then. If I could, I'd have wrung that moth-eaten little buzzard's neck.

▸▸▸▸◂◂◂◂

CHAPTER IV

The Capture

So I still had nothing to eat. I walked on through the night.

On the trail the next day I met a Korean man. Again there was no chance for concealment, so I walked up boldly and asked him for food. This time my system didn't work. He would have nothing to do with me, turning abruptly and walking away as if I didn't exist. I was worried for a while after that, but there were no sounds of pursuit. I decided he probably had told no one of meeting me. I think now this was a typical Korean act: to do nothing, to take no responsibility. If he had either fed me or reported me he would have been personally involved—and that's usually the last thing any Korean wants. I've been told that this fear of personal responsibility accounts for the fact that most Koreans will walk around a person dying in the street without making any attempt to give aid. So long as they act as if the dying person didn't exist, or the accident had not happened, they personally aren't responsible for it.

By that night hunger was beginning to be a vital problem. When I spotted some smoke rising I figured there must be a village near and I worked down toward it cautiously, remembering the small boy of the day before. It was a good thing I did. Just after I had scooted across a highway I saw at least ten big North Korean tanks rumbling through that village, heading south. This was obviously a main highway, and that village was no place for me.

I got better at sleeping by daylight and traveling by night, but I still wasn't making much progress. Those mountain trails wind around so in the ridges that you walk miles to make what is a short distance in a straight line. I was walking more easily now; although my abdomen still hurt and I couldn't raise my left arm. I wasn't suffering—except from hunger.

By this time I had changed my first objective to Chonju, even farther south and slightly west of Kumsan. My reasoning was that some South Korean officials just might be left in that town, with some sort of transport. Perhaps I could get a ride to Taegu, or even along the extreme southern route all the way to Pusan.

The ridge trails were such slow going that I began to get down on the roads more often. When I'd approach a village in the early evening or late in the morning I'd leave the road and circle around the village through the hills, although this had to be done without trails in most instances. It was frustrating and took endless time.

About three nights after my experience with the small boy I started walking in the early evening and saw a village ahead. It was still light and I should have started another circle, but I was a little overconfident and stayed on the road.

Then I met another little boy. This one was five or six years old. As soon as he saw me he turned tail and ran back to the village screaming as if his end had come.

Well, I knew what that would mean. Instead of turning off the road, I hurried after him, almost running myself. Close by the first houses I jumped off the road into a ditch and a bunch of weeds.

Sure enough, here came all the males in town. I noticed only one rifle and one burp gun, but a number of the other men had bamboo spears. They all followed the little boy back along the road to the point where he had seen me—I could see the little devil pointing out the exact spot—then spread out and began the hunt.

Fortunately for me, this town was huddled between a hill on one side and some *kaffir* fields (maize) on the other. Beyond the kaffir was a stream. I crawled through the fields to the stream, walked along its bed in the same direction I had been going previously until I was well past the town, then came back up on the road. The last I saw of that place, the men were still beating through the weeds with their guns and spears, and all the women were standing out on the main street waiting for somebody to bring me in.

I still didn't like little boys, Korean variety.

Thereafter, whenever I came on a village in the middle of the night, I just walked right through it, paying no attention to the dozens of dogs barking at me. Even when it was pitch-black I had no trouble knowing the villages were there. You always can smell a Korean town before you see it. You always can recognize the police stations too, because they're all built alike: a big stone wall, perhaps eight feet high, around a compound, double wooden gates at the front, and a twenty-foot round stone tower, like a silo, somewhere inside. Usually, I just ignored them. But one dark night when I was hiking along a rather good road, by Korean standards, someone challenged me from the shadows just as I passed the gates of the town jailhouse. He yelled one word, which must have meant "Halt!" from a spot no more than eight feet away.

I had no previous warning that he was there, and he startled me. He did more than that. He scared me half to death, and made me mad too—at myself for being careless and at him for being alive. I was so flustered that I did a foolish thing. I whirled and yanked out my pistol and walked right into him. He was just a youngster, I think, armed with a rifle that had a long thin Russian-type bayonet on it. I shoved my pistol right in his guts, hard, and he backed up. I backed him right into the gate. He was so surprised that he didn't do anything.

Just as he got inside the gate I turned and walked very fast in the same direction I had been going. It was only a few yards to the corner of this jailhouse compound. Here I turned to the left, ran along the wall all the way to the rear of the compound, turned left again along the back wall of the compound, made one more left turn, and came back to the road—on the side of the compound from which I had come originally. I waited there to see what would happen.

Inside the compound there was a lot of yelling as soon as the guard recovered enough to give the alarm, and a whole squad, some in uniform, some in civvies, poured out into the road and headed the way the guard had seen me go. As soon as I saw the direction they were taking, I walked back up the road on which I had entered the town. I'd noticed a Y fork off the main highway a short distance before I hit the town. I went back to it and took the other arm of the Y—in the same general direction I wanted but not on the highway. I never did get back to that highway again.

The only explanation I have for the guard's failure to act is that he was just rushed off his feet. If he'd ever lifted that damned rifle to his shoulder I would have had to kill him right there. But he didn't. When I thought about it later, I could see that what I'd done was a fine way to get killed for sure—but that one time the bluff worked.

I had one other close call, also in the middle of a black night. This time I stumbled into a town before I'd noticed, and again was in front of a police station. There had been a guard post in the road, I guess, and I walked right into a little charcoal fire they'd left burning. I don't know where the people were, and the only thing I could do was to keep on walking. I guess they never saw or heard me, because nothing happened.

None of the village dogs really bothered me. But up in the mountains, miles from anywhere, the big dogs kept by the charcoal burners around their huts sounded so ferocious, so bloodthirsty, that I stayed away from those huts even though I now needed food badly. Those dogs sounded as if they were quite capable of tearing me apart. I also wanted to avoid the charcoal people. Many of them had been Communist sympathizers and outcasts even in the old days, and I was afraid to trust them. I think now this was a mistake; but at the time I didn't feel that I could take the chance.

By this time my equipment was getting in very bad shape. I was wearing an oversized pair of coveralls—which I had got in exchange for my combat suit, too small for me, from a forward air observer at Okchon a few days before Taejon fell. These coveralls were quite cumbersome and bulky and had to be stripped off entirely when I forded a stream. My combat boots also were the worse for wear, and one was chafing the top of my foot badly. I had a watch that didn't work; a fountain pen that did; a pair of reading glasses; the remainder of my map of Korea; forty dollars in U. S. Korean-occupation scrip, which nobody wanted; and the pistol. I had no rain gear. When it rained I got wet. And it did rain, repeatedly and with fervor. When rain and dark combined I seldom knew where I was going for more than a few feet ahead. And when it rained during the day I lost sleep.

My hunger was becoming dangerous, but there was nowhere to get food. Up here in the mountain area I seldom found a house standing—the result of the South Korean government's prewar campaign against the guerrillas, which had consisted largely of burning the house of anyone the constabulary or police even suspected of harboring or cooperating with guerrillas. And I was afraid to go down to the villages. During the day I could see that the Communists already had organized the whole area. Labor had been impressed all over the place. Men worked in big gangs, mostly on the roads; and old Japanese or Russian rifles and burp guns had been given to a few youths in each town. These kids were swelled up with the importance of their jobs as home guards and just itching for a chance to fire those weapons. I couldn't take any more risks.

I had found out some things about the Korean countryside too. It didn't pay me to start walking early in the evening or to walk very far into the dawn. In the evenings children and dogs were all around the villages; and in the early morning old men would come out, often with small youngsters trailing along, to look at the fields. They didn't work in those early hours but just walked out to look, as if planning the day's work. And like old men everywhere, they awoke very early. If I walked in the evening or after the first flush of dawn I was in danger of meeting somebody.

I also found that I had to pick my daylight hiding places well away from villages. During the day brush- and weed-gathering parties—old men, children, sometimes women—worked the untilled areas around the towns. Few Koreans can afford wood to burn in their homes, and they use the brambles and grass for cooking fuel and to make smudge fires against the mosquitoes in the evenings. Each village at nightfall looks as if it is on fire, each a sort of little Pittsburgh under its own pall of smoke.

These bramble-gathering parties cover a lot of ground. Village children also play away from the houses, so I had to find cover far out to be at all safe.

When I didn't, the results weren't good. One morning I stopped to take a bath in a stream as I was crossing it, and when I got started walking again—this was somewhere near Yongdam—women already were coming down to the river to wash clothes. I couldn't reach good cover and had to crawl into some bushes much too close to the community laundry spot. The women were not more than fifty yards from me, and I didn't dare to sleep, fearing that children wandering away from their mothers might find me. If they did, I wanted to be awake to know it.

Across the river and back from it about a quarter of a mile I could see a village, evidently the hub of the universe in this area. Soldiers came and went from the police station, and civilians constantly were reporting to the same headquarters.

The women washing their clothes in the river had come from behind me, not across the stream, so I assumed there must be another village, out of my view but very close and on my side of the river. Three or four paths converged on the river bank where the women did their washing and exchanged continuous gossip.

I got through the day all right; but that evening one woman did not follow the paths the others had taken away from the river. Carrying a big pile of clean clothes on her head, she came up a path I had not seen before, not more than four feet from me. As she passed she looked right at me. If I had a face like hers, I could make a million dollars playing poker. There was no facial expression at all. Not a muscle twitched. She just looked and kept on walking.

I was still trying to decide whether that old girl with the washing on her head could possibly have failed to see me when my question was answered by the arrival of two young men who came from the direction in which she had gone. They walked right to my hiding spot. Again there was no use in trying to hide, so I asked for food, going through the "pop"-plus-stomach-gesture routine once more.

They answered "Okay, okay," and made signs for me to stay down, just as that first farmer carrying the baby girl had done days before.

I thought, "Boy, after a long time I'm in luck again." I could just taste that rice which would be along in a minute. Both youths went back up the path the way they had come.

The next thing I knew, I heard a terrific commotion, and rifle shots started coming over my head.

This place was an old orchard, all grown over with the weeds that sheltered me. When I raised up enough to look, I could see that in addition to the paths fanning out from the river bank, a wide path higher up paralleled the river some distance back. Beyond the path were houses, the village I had not been able to see while down in the weeds. Upstream from me was a ford across the river.

When the shooting started, so did a lot of yelling—and in the end that saved me. My two chums had brought out the home guard force in force. Men were already all around me in a big half-circle, and all the women and children in the world were standing up there on that raised path to watch the fun.

I could hear these men starting to close in toward me and

the river, but it was a funny thing. I guess I was tired or something. I went to sleep between close-ins. I'd wake up with a start and think, "Dean, you damned fool, you can't sleep this way! They'll be on top of you in a minute." Then I'd drop off to sleep again.

But finally I did wake up enough to start crawling. I faded back up the stream, beside a fill. These people had known where I was when the show started, but they handed me one telling advantage, because every time a man in the half-circle would take a few steps forward to a new position, he'd yell like mad to let everybody know where he was. That helped. Once a man yelled just as I was about to crawl toward the very spot where he was. I waited, and presently he went on past me.

It was just dumbness on their part, but the fact is I slipped through the circle. They were still yelling and closing in, but I wasn't there any more. I just got out on the road and walked away, not stopping to say good-by.

I think this date was about August 15. I made good time that night, walking about twenty miles. When I didn't have anything else to think about, I'd go back to my worrying. I still was desperate to get back to our lines and the division, but I knew my information—that there were far more Communists on the south flank than anybody thought—would be too late to do any good. I just wanted to get back into the fight.

Then I'd worry about my aides and their families, being sure in my mind that both Clarke and Bissett were dead by this time, their young families fatherless because of me. I worried about those families and my own. By this time Mildred would know not only that I was missing but that chances for my return were dwindling. I hoped that some of her friends would have talked her into leaving Kokura, perhaps going to the States or to Puerto Rico to be with June. Much later I found this was just what our friends did do, although they were not able to convince her to leave Japan until August 15. She was in Puerto Rico when I was captured.

I also found that my hunch about Bissett had been partially correct. As soon as he was sure I would not return he tried to get himself assigned to a line company—he was an ex-enlisted man and always believed that was where a fighting man belonged—but another headquarters grabbed him for G-1 work and never let him go. So he, like Clarke, survived the Korean war.

Sometimes I prayed for these people, as well as for the families of Bob Martin, whom I felt I certainly had sent to his death, Hatfield, and others I knew or thought were dead. These were actual prayers, repeated many times.

But when I dreamed it was mostly about food. I thought, "When I get back to headquarters and a lot of people are running around wanting to know what happened, I'll say, 'Now just a minute and I'll tell you all you want to know about it. But first bring me one of those fruit compotes from a ten-in-one ration. I want one of those cans of apricots or plums, in that thick sugary syrup. Then I'll tell you about it.' " I could just see that can of fruit and smell the juice.

One night I walked in the pouring rain, making wonderful time, and found a spot to sleep in some bushes on a hill across from a mill and a village. But when day dawned I realized that I'd been walking the wrong way all night long. I was so disgusted that I took to the hills immediately and walked back practically all day. I think I made up most of the distance I'd lost during that blind night's hiking.

The next night I decided to quit fooling around, trying to

follow roads or trails. I'd go right over the mountains and ridges to the east. I decided at least to stick to one plan of action. I told myself, "Damn it, you're walking in circles, you're wasting time. You've got to get back to division. You should go straight east until you hit the railroad, then follow it south—and no matter how tough it is."

Well, that sounds good, but when you start crossing some of that country it's awfully rough. The mountains average only a couple of thousand feet in height, but they come right up off sea level, not by plateaus, so you have to climb every inch of every mountain.

That same night while I was lying down to rest on a very steep trail that went almost straight up the side of a ridge, I heard a clatter. Before I even could move a deer jumped right over me. If I had raised my head, his hoofs would have clipped me.

One problem up on the ridges was water. Very few have any water on them; and where there was a stream the Koreans had tapped it with an aqueduct to take the water down to the rice paddies in the flats. Once I wasted a whole day going down to the foot of a ridge to get a drink. At other times I'd head for patches of dark foliage, hoping that they would indicate a stream or pool, but often I found none when I got there. For food, I tried kaffir stalks and grass, both of which made me throw up. It was too early in the Korean summer for many of the crops to have ripened; and I had no weapons with which to catch game—in any case, I saw very little except some pheasants, and never got a standing shot at one of those. I did find one variety of wild berry several times. This was a sort of cane berry, somewhat like the salmon berry of the Pacific Northwest, without much taste. I suppose I ate a hundred of those, all told, while I was in the mountains. Once I also found a field from which potatoes had been dug—and located four, each about the size of a walnut, which the diggers had overlooked. I ate them raw.

As I grew weaker, my stomach regurgitated even water. I kept looking for corn, and could not understand why I couldn't find any. I knew it was grown in this part of Korea. Later I discovered that in South Korea the corn is almost always planted right in the dooryards of the houses, almost never in the fields. The same is true of melons and squash, so I had no chance to get any of these. Several times I saw the rude towers which growers of ginseng root (beloved of the Chinese as a tonic that will cure virtually anything from flat feet to unripe old age, and also the principal component for a 150- or 170-proof liquor which will blow the top off your head) build around their fields for the guards. But the guards are unfriendly to practically everybody during the seven years the ginseng requires to mature.

Although I continued to pass many burned houses in the mountains, it was not until August 19 that I finally found one lone house far up in the mountains and intact. I spotted this good-looking structure in the night; but I knew there seldom was any use asking for food at a Korean house between meals. With no refrigeration or other storage for cooked foods, they simply don't have anything to eat except when the family meal is being cooked.

I flopped down in a path about two hundred yards from this house and slept.

In the morning I was awakened by another man carrying a little girl on his back. These fathers carrying small daughters were my luck charms, I guess. I asked for food—and my luck was in. He led me back to the house and the whole family came out to greet me. The man turned out to be the eldest brother, about thirty-four. The family included another married brother, about thirty-two, their wives and children, and two younger single brothers, twenty-two and eighteen.

They brought food out to me right in the yard—rice and pork fat. I don't know what happens to the lean part of pigs in rural Korea, but the only part ever served by the country people is the fat. I ate this ravenously, although I never had cared for any kind of fat (much of my youth had been spent in arguments with my elders about the amount of it I left on my plate in Carlyle, Illinois).

With signs I then told the brothers that I wished to stay there four days. I'd lost weight and was terribly weak. I said to myself, "If I can just have four days I'll be all right. Just give me four days of rest, and I'll make it." I thought I had put over the idea and that they had agreed.

These people had an unusually nice house, and I was led to a lean-to, built against the back of it. But this lean-to was filled with flies, just infested with flies, thousands of them. Nevertheless I lay down on the mud floor—and fought flies. I stayed only five minutes. Then I had to crawl to the door and throw up everything I'd eaten. This was August 20, and the food was the first since July 25 or 26. I guess the pork fat was just too much for a stomach ignored so long.

At noon the family gave me more rice and some kimchee (fermented cabbage, with garlic). Again I threw it up. All of them were quite concerned about me. That afternoon I noticed some chickens in the yard, pointed to them, and tried to indicate by signs that I wanted some eggs. The family misunderstood (the most fortunate misunderstanding on record) and instead killed one of the chickens. The result was some of the best chicken soup I've ever eaten, full of potatoes and rich with chicken fat. This I kept down. And the next day

I kept down all three meals, each of which consisted of rice, roasted corn, and potatoes.

From the beginning I could tell that the second brother wasn't enthusiastic about having me there. In a combination of a few words of Korean and sign language he kept talking about the Inmun Gun, and appeared very much surprised when I indicated I had no desire to see any members of the Communist Army. It's possible that up until that time he had thought I was a Russian, but afterward he was increasingly nervous. On the second day the two brothers brought up an old man to look me over. He was a smiling old fellow, apparently friendly, but the Inmun Gun kept coming up entirely too often in their conversation. I thought he was some old *harabachie* (grandfather, literally) whom they'd brought from a neighboring town to give them advice about me. I also thought the signs were bad. I gave my watch (which wouldn't work) to the younger brother, and my billfold (minus an insert with my identification in it) and my fountain pen to the elder brother, to buy the remainder of that four days of food and rest.

That evening the bad news came. The elder brother, still kindly, nevertheless told me I would have to go. Evidently he was afraid that they'd all be shot if the Communists found me there, and perhaps he was right. I didn't feel that any of these people loved the Inmun Gun especially, but they undoubtedly were afraid of it and wanted—like most Koreans—to keep out of trouble at any cost. The elder brother had been in Muju when our aircraft bombed that town, and he demonstrated to me how terrible it had been: "Oo—umphh, umphh, umphh!"

Previously I had asked directions to several different towns, trying not to give out too much information about where I actually was trying to go. So on this night the elder brother gave me four ears of parched corn and some rice wrapped in a cloth and led me out on a path about half a mile from the house. There he left me.

It was a black night. I couldn't see; and perhaps in reaction I was more tired than I'd been before. I'd taken only a few steps before I stepped into a hole and fell on my face. I managed to get about fifty yards farther, then just dropped down in the trail and went to sleep. I wasn't especially low in my mind, just tired.

I could tell when this man left me that he felt I wasn't going to make it. I could tell by his look that he thought, "You poor bastard, you're finished."

But I thought, "Well, you sad character, you just don't *know*. I'm going to surprise you. I *am* going to make it."

The elder brother had showed me the direction toward the main road and had said "Taegu" often enough so I got the idea that this was the proper route to that town, seventy miles away as the crow flies. But I didn't worry about it the rest of the night.

In the morning a highly important event occurred. Dean's digestion began to work again, all the way. I've always thought of this as the day of the great passage, although for a while I thought it also might be my last. I was still being happy about the whole thing when the second brother and one of the younger ones, out to gather wood, found me—and they weren't at all happy about the fact that I still was only half a mile from their house. They led me another half a mile along the trail to make absolutely sure I was headed right—and going away. We were far up in the mountains, and they took me to a spot from which we could look out and see in the distance a valley at least ten miles away, with a highway running down it. Very carefully the second brother showed me the routes—to Muju, to Chinan, to Taegu. He wanted me to get away, almost anywhere, but away. You might think this is difficult to convey when neither person speaks a word of the other's language, but he managed.

I went on alone again. Frankly I never did find the road he had pointed out. But long before I came even close to it I did find more food. As I was walking along the trail I heard a commotion ahead. I slipped up for a look—and there was a whole gang of youngsters, twelve to sixteen years old, all beating peach trees in the orchard of a burned-out house. They were whaling the trees and of course knocked down and took away all the good peaches. After they left I managed to fill my pockets with the culls—wizened, half-ripe, and the size of walnuts, but food nonetheless. Then rain began again. I spent the night in the shelter of a piece of corrugated iron which had not collapsed when the shack was burned.

After that I began to make time toward the east. I walked all through the daylight hours of August 23, ate my parched corn, and felt so good that I walked all night too. I found another orchard and again filled my pockets with peaches, rested a while, then took off again, walking all the afternoon of August 24. That evening I hit a main highway. In the woods above it I rested until it was dark enough to start walking the road. I think I made twenty or twenty-five miles that night, and the only interruptions were when I had to hide out now and then to let groups of highway workers pass me on their way home. Fifty men were in one group, sixty-five in another. I just lay in a ditch and let them go by.

Early in the morning, following the hairpin turns of the highway, I saw a big village ahead. Evidently this was a particularly good farming area, because there were stables, barns, and silos, in addition to the shacks common to most villages. I couldn't imagine what the people were raising, but I took no chances and made a big swing around the town.

But again I walked too long. Daylight caught me just opposite another village, on a brand-new, improved road, which I was sure must have been built with ECA money from the United States. I thought, "Well, these people should be as favorable to us as any Koreans, having had all this built for them." So I wasn't too much worried when daylight caught me. I just went off the road and up into some brush under chestnut trees, a spot from which I could see the village, less than half a mile away.

For quite a while previously I had been bothered by the decreasing number of our aircraft in the skies, and had long since abandoned my early dream that a plane would one day fly low enough to see me wave. For days none had been even close, although after my repatriation I learned from Lieutenant General Earle E. Partridge that he personally had spent long hours flying over the very area where I was wandering, searching for me from a light (AT-G) training plane. But he was doing most of that flying during the daylight hours when I was asleep.

While I rested under the chestnut trees my spirits were rising. I figured that I could walk the hundred and twenty miles to Pusan in ten days on the strength my two-day rest had given me. I was confident I'd be able to last through it. And there was one new wonderfully reassuring factor. Away over to the east I could hear the rumble of artillery—definitely guns, not bombing. I had not heard this since we'd left Taejon, so it was like hearing from an old friend.

"I'm on my way back," I thought. "I'm going to make it."

I slept fairly well during the morning. In the afternoon an

old man and some boys came through the chestnut grove, carrying little pint-sized sickles with which to cut brush. They saw me. Once again I worked my system, asking for food. I thought, "Well, damn it, things are breaking my way now. I've been well fed and I'm on my way back. Everything favors me, so I'll just continue to ride my luck."

The old man smiled as if we were long-time friends and gestured toward the village. I rose and boldly marched down that new highway to the first house. The village was a one-street affair, with the street at right angles to the highway, and I stopped at the house that had the highway right beside it.

The man of the house was in the back yard, making straw shoes. His wife and children were watching. I made signs for food and got vigorous and friendly affirmative nods. The woman had no rice ready but put some on to boil. While I waited for it to cook the householder went right ahead making straw slippers. When he completed one he would put it on and dance around in the yard to show me how good it was. The children laughed, the shoemaker laughed, and so did I. This was my lucky day.

Then the woman brought out the rice, with garlic beads as a side dish. It was delicious. I ate all I was given and asked for more to wrap in my handkerchief.

I left there about five o'clock, and had gone only a short distance along the highway when a short little Korean passed me, hiking along as if he were going to a fire. He got about twenty feet ahead, then suddenly stopped, waited for me to catch up, and walked along beside me without saying a word. Just to break the silence I started asking him the route to Taegu and other towns in other directions. When we sat down to rest at a bridge he picked up some rocks and in the dust marked the routes to Taegu, Pusan, and Chonju.

Although he spoke no English we managed to understand each other. I was still trying to cover up a little about where I intended to go, but I was beginning to be impressed with him. I made him the same offer I'd made back in the village before I lost Tabor—a million won to guide me to Taegu.

He sold me. I thought he understood everything. I asked him where the Inmun Gun was, and he told me they were at Chinan. He intimated that I shouldn't worry, everything would be okay—he would take me right past the Inmun Gun. I don't know how I got all that without any English, but I did, or so I thought. I was sure that's what he was trying to tell me.

We went farther down the road and came to a river where bombing had knocked out a bridge. He pointed that out, laughed as though he thought it exceptionally funny, and said, "*Pi-yang-gi*" (airplane). He seemed pleased that the bombing had been so good.

To ford the stream I had to take off my coveralls. I undressed fully. He offered to carry my pistol for me, but I didn't let him.

When we reached the far bank and I had dressed again, we climbed up the bank—and there was trouble waiting for us. A village came right to the river at this point, and waiting for us was practically the full manpower of the village, ten or fifteen men in native clothes and all armed with clubs or spears. They'd seen us crossing and were waiting for us. The man in front, carrying a club, had an especially ferocious expression on his face and motioned to me to go back, that I couldn't even go through their village.

Well, I didn't want to undress again and cross that river a second time. I pulled my pistol from the holster and pointed it at them. As I walked toward them, making threatening motions with the pistol, the whole group backed away slowly.

Meanwhile the little Korean by my side kept jabbering to them, and I had the definite impression that his talk had more to do with their retreat than my pistol. I thought, "He's fast-talking them." Still with their clubs and spears but just standing there and not doing anything about it, the whole gang let us go through the town.

Before we had gone more than a fraction of a mile a second Korean caught up with us. I realize now that this was the same ferocious-looking character who had been at the head of the village mob, but at the time I failed to recognize him without his club. He seemed to be great pals with Han, the man who was guiding me; and Han made me understand that this new chum was "okay, okay." We three walked down the road together until we reached a bend.

Han said suddenly, "Inmun Gun!" and signaled to me to get down.

I thought, "Boy, this is bad. There's something around this corner." I jumped into some bushes beside the road, holding my pistol ready.

Han went on ahead but came back in a few minutes, saying, "Okay, okay."

"This boy is all right," I thought. "This is working out fine."

We went ahead, and around the bend found fifty or a hundred Korean civilians filling holes in the road. This was a big project, really a major industry, and they all were working fast, although I saw nobody with guns keeping them at it. We walked right past, just as if we all had a perfect right to use the highway. Some of them looked up, but no one said anything or interfered with us.

When we came to another bend a little farther on we went through the same routine—the Inmun Gun! warning, Dean jumping into the bushes with his pistol, then an okay and another stroll right past a working party. This time I noticed two men with rifles, and there was an uncomfortable feeling along my spine when we turned our backs to them. But again nothing happened.

I thought, "This Han is a pretty good boy. He *is* going to take me through." But he did a couple of strange things, which should have warned me. One was walking so fast. He walked as if he were going to a fire, and I couldn't keep up with him. Finally I just sat down. I said, "All right, you people go ahead." But they both stopped with me, and Han tried to explain. He indicated that he was hungry and wanted to eat before we reached Chinan. It was getting late in the evening, and we had walked about eight miles, at full speed.

When we started again, however, we went only a short distance, then turned into a house beside the road. I understood that Han wanted to stop there for food. Once inside, they served us *sake*, but only a plate of garlic beads for food. I took one little glass of the liquor but ate all the garlic beads they brought. The people in the house wanted me to take more sake, and Han too urged it on me. I should have been warned by this. I did think, "What are these people trying to do? Get me drunk?" But my thinking didn't go any further than that.

While we were sitting in the house, and after a lot of conversation, a third man joined us. He walked along with us when we left. At the next bend we did the same routine a third time, with two men going ahead and one staying in the ditch with me. The stumbling block ahead was a small town, not a road crew. The two scouts finally came back and gave us the okay. We walked right through the town.

Just as we got on the other side of town there was some yelling behind us. I got out of sight while Han and his second friend went to talk, this time to our rear. Then Han called something to the fellow who had stayed with me (Little Ferocious, who had led the village gang), and he motioned me to come out. I did, once more putting my pistol back in the holster, then sitting down on the edge of the road. The road was on a cut above a stream, and we hung our feet over the edge. The night was warm and there was bright moonlight.

All of a sudden, around a corner from the village came about fifteen men, and somebody fired a rifle over our heads. I reached for my pistol and got my hand on it, but the little devil sitting beside me grabbed my wrist with both his hands.

I struggled to my feet, with him still hanging on, but I couldn't get the gun out. I fell in the dirt, he with me, and we rolled around in the road as I tried to get him over to the edge of the cut again, to kick him down toward the river. I thought the fall would break his hold, even if we both went over, and I'd have a chance.

But the gang had only about twenty-five feet to rush us, and before I could get this character to the edge they were on top of us. About three rifle barrels were on my head, and as we wrestled around, they kept bumping me. It was very annoying.

They were all yelling, and I suppose they were telling me to surrender, but I kept on fighting with this fellow who had a hold on my arm, and trying to kick somebody where he'd never forget it. But he never let go. I yelled, "Shoot! Shoot, you sons of bitches! Shoot!"

I remember thinking, "This is an ignominious way to have your lights put out, but this is it."

Then they were twisting at my arms. There were several of them doing it, and they weren't easy with it. They had both my arms twisted, and that shoulder of mine really hurt—but no physical pain hurt so much as the thought, "Well, these miserable devils have you as a prisoner."

They tied both hands behind me with sashcord, pulled so tightly that the circulation was cut off, then jerked me to my feet and shoved me back toward the town we'd just passed. I still thought there was no use in being a prisoner. I tried to run. I wanted them to shoot me. But I was so weak that I made only a yard or so before somebody danced up and shoved me from behind so that I fell on my face again. They all laughed.

As they pulled me up I said, "I can't walk." They kept shoving me, but I wouldn't walk. My shoulder hurt too much, and those bonds on my hands. I indicated I wouldn't move so long as they had my hands tied that way, and this must have confused them. At any rate they finally took the ropes off entirely.

Then we all marched toward the police station. Han was standing there beside the door, looking pleased with himself, and so were the other two whom I had thought were helping me. I did wish I could have one last kick at a couple of them, but there was no chance. In the station somebody searched me. I had my identification tags, some cards in the part of my billfold I hadn't given away (I still have the same A.G.O. card, which was given back to me eventually), an immunization register, and some snapshots of my son and daughter. They took all these, and one character reached into my shirt pocket. I wear a partial denture, but my mouth had been hurting so that I had been carrying this denture in my pocket.

About the only smart thing I did that night was to grab that denture, just as the searcher took it out of my pocket, and pop it into my mouth where it belonged. That denture had been painful; but I never put it in any faster—and never mind the pain. I knew that if anybody ever had time to see how much gold was in it I'd never get it back.

While they were searching me I was standing in front of a desk, and behind the desk a Korean calendar with Arabic numerals hung on a wall. I pointed to it, and one of the men put his finger on the figure twenty-five.

It was the twenty-fifth of August, my wedding anniversary.

Three years later, in September 1953, Han Doo Kyoo, aged forty, and Choi Chong Bong, twenty-four, were arrested by South Korean police and accused as my betrayers. Police said the pair received the equivalent of five dollars for turning me in to the Commies. On January 12, 1954, both defendants were convicted. Although the prosecutor had asked only five-year prison terms for them, the judge sentenced Choi to death and Han to life imprisonment. I had previously written to President Rhee, asking clemency for the two men if they were convicted, but the trial judge declared the court had not received any official notice of my request. Their defense statements indicated that they had intended to take me through to United Nations lines but ran into so much trouble in getting me past the various barriers that they decided they should turn me in to prevent my death in a hopeless fight. Having had no method of communicating accurately with them at any time, I'm simply not in a position to guess whether this might have been true. I did not feel that further punishment of these men would accomplish anything.

▶▶▶▶◀◀◀◀

CHAPTER V

A Small Boy from Texas

I spent that night in a cage—quite literally.

This object, sitting in a corner of the main room at the police station, was about four feet long and the same height, but built like the letter L—that is, the high portion was only large enough for my head and shoulders. I could sit in one position with my knees drawn up slightly but could not lie down or stand up. This was nothing they had dreamed up especially for my benefit, but equipment of much age and frequent usage. I suppose they ordinarily kept the town drunk in it on his bad nights.

I made one horrible mistake that night and learned one important lesson. The mistake was to take off my combat boots. After I'd been in the cage for a while I pulled them off. One had chafed my foot until my instep was infected and had been bothering me for a couple of weeks; also, they smelled awful. I made signs to the guards that I'd like to have the boots set outside to air. Frankly, I didn't want to smell them in my cell.

This suggestion was greeted with startled enthusiasm. If those people could have spoken perfect English, they couldn't have said more plainly, "Boots? Oh, my goodness, that's something we overlooked." They took them out of the cage, and somebody else had them on within five minutes—and I didn't have any boots thereafter. I realized my own dumbness almost immediately, but too late to do anything about it.

The lesson was provided by two North Korean Army paymasters, who arrived shortly after I was brought in. They came with bundles of won notes and spent the whole night doling out piles of money to the local officials. Each *gun-soo* (corresponding to town or county officials) evidently had provided a hundred men for work on the roads, and this was the big pay-off. The thing which struck me was that everybody was happy, and there was no resentment. These officers were just two Santa Clauses come to town, and nobody minded at all. The key to their success was an apparently unlimited supply of currency.

It was perfectly obvious to me, then and later, that the way for an occupying army to gain favor with a local population, especially a population of the same blood, is to pay well for everything it gets, spreading money around. It was easy for the Communists in this case because they had captured the South Korean government's currency plates in Seoul, and it was merely a printing press problem; but the lesson is one that can be applied to any army, including our own.

The point is, I never saw the Inmun Gun steal anything outright, although the theft may actually have been just as bad as any in the long run. When a soldier wanted a farmer's peach he always paid for it. He went out and bought it. So even when the currency turned out to be worthless, that individual soldier was not the target of the farmer's wrath.

All night long the two officers dished out the money, then folded up their briefcases and left just before dawn. Incidentally, neither of these paymasters showed the slightest interest in me, nor, for that matter, did the local officials. None of these people spoke English; and apparently no one guessed that the dirty old man in the cage was a propaganda prize because of the accident of military rank.

Han, the man who had turned me in, had come into the police station when I was taken in, and he stayed there all night. I didn't see him do any more talking. A couple of times in the early evening he smiled at me, as if he had done me a big favor. But it's always hard to tell what a Korean means by a laugh. Those youngsters who had shoved me down in the road when I tried to run had laughed, but I'm not sure it was sadism. It could have been embarrassment, or any number of things. I've seen Koreans laugh when a dog was being tortured to death. It would be hard to tell the difference between that laugh and the one Clarence Rhee used to let out when he was reading Korean newspapers to me as military governor. He was an official of the government and a patriotic man—but whenever one of the newspaper stories was exceptionally bad news, he'd laugh. I never could figure it out. It's on a par with their feeling about death: that to kill a man isn't too serious but to mutilate his body is terrible. Rhee, for example, never seemed affected by stories of guerrillas killing constabulary or farmers, but if the man's head had been cut off after death he was horrified.

So I don't know what Han's nervous little smile meant there in the police station. He stayed quietly in a corner all night, and left in the early morning. I never saw him again.

A guard brought me breakfast shortly after dawn. I was allowed to get out of the cell and eat at a table. The meal was excellent—rice, soup, and kimchee. Then I was put back into the cell and stayed there until nine or ten o'clock. When they hauled me out a second time I could see I was about to be moved. I demanded my boots—but I didn't get them. Somebody did bring me a pair of Korean rubber shoes—not mates, and both with holes in the soles the size of pancakes. They were too short, and when I tried to walk they came off. I made noises of complaint, so finally one fellow folded newspapers to make insoles, then brought some straw rope and tied the shoes to my feet.

My escort consisted of one Korean youngster, in an Inmun Gun uniform and armed with a long rifle, and a civilian carrying a briefcase. The civilian had a bicycle; the soldier and I walked. The little town where I was captured was Sangjonmyon; and we started toward Chinan, only a short distance away. But the walk took more than an hour, because my feet hurt so much that I had to stop at frequent intervals. The man on the bicycle got impatient, but the soldier was a pleasant youngster, showed no evidence of being rough, and let me stop whenever I needed a rest.

The one thing I noticed especially was that my guard was quite a hero to all the small children we met on the way. Whenever we passed a group he would say a phrase to them and the children would reply in chorus. It sounded like "Chosen-all," which I assumed must be some Communist slogan about a united Korea, because they all knew it and repeated it with enthusiasm. Often the children would start singing a marching air, which I was to hear thousands of times —the Inmun Gun song. I thought, "Boy, these Communists have done a job of indoctrinating these youngsters." They were delighted with the soldier, but not even interested in a captive.

In Chinan I was taken to a house apparently being used as a company headquarters. A cheerful young captain already was busily cleaning my pistol. He dropped that job and came over to try to talk to me. It wasn't a great success since he spoke not a single word of English. However, I could tell that he was asking if I was hungry, and when I nodded he immediately ordered up food for me—a bowl of boiled pork fat. After the walk I ate this like candy, and the captain was so pleased that he sent out for a bag of ginger cookies, which he paid for himself. I tried to share these with him and the two lieutenants also in the headquarters, but none of them would take any. So I just ate and ate; and the captain was as pleased as a child who succeeds in getting a puppy to eat. To top off my meal he brought me some apples.

Two women in uniform also were in the house, and I could see that one of them was some sort of political instructor. All the soldiers gathered, and she held a class for them. I was pleased, in a backward sort of way, when an air-raid alarm—they used a series of rifle shots and a bell—interrupted the instruction and everybody had to run for cover in doorways. I was moved to a seat in a closet doorway. The planes went on past Chinan, without bombing or strafing. When they had passed the political class was resumed.

I was moved twice more during the day, first to a police station, then to another building, which might have been a rice warehouse or garage. This was some sort of registration point, with people coming and going constantly. I was left sitting by myself in a corner, under guard, for a long time. Up in a parklike area above the warehouse I could hear drilling and counting off all afternoon, as if local youths were being drilled by the Inmun Gun in close order. It seemed like a very long time for close-order drill to last, but they kept it up. Once again I was struck by the fact that if the people of South Korea resented the northern invaders, they certainly weren't showing it. To me, the civilian attitude appeared to veer between enthusiasm and passive acceptance. I saw no sign of resistance or any will to resist.

Nobody showed any further interest in me until about seven o'clock in the evening, when I was taken out to a truck packed with Korean civilians, obviously prisoners. They were mostly men, but with some women. I was pushed toward the center of the mob, and there I wedged myself down. I had not yet learned to sit cross-legged comfortably. I put my feet out in front of me, and that was a bad mistake. People sat on my feet and insteps, others on my legs and knees. Knees jabbed into my back and ribs, which still ached, and pushed against my sore shoulder.

Very few words were spoken, none to me. Three or four guards clung to the sides of the truck, with one foot in and one out—and thirty-seven people were jammed between them. I didn't get a good look at the truck, but it was about the size of one of our two-and-a-half-ton vehicles, and may even have been one of ours. None of the people showed any emotion whatever. As we started out I saw a road sign in English: "Chonju—78 miles."

But we still weren't fully loaded. About ten miles out of Chinan the truck stopped beside a rice paddy. Across the dikes came a line of men with their wrists bound, and roped together. This single file of prisoners climbed right in on top of the rest of us. Twenty more had managed to get in when I lost count, but I think there were at least twice that number. It was impossible for every one of them to touch the bottom of the truck; they were piled on top of the rest of us like bags of grain.

The truck ground ahead again, but fortunately for us (otherwise somebody surely would have smothered) the load was too heavy. The vehicle faltered and stalled on a hill, and the guards took off some of that last chain gang. With the remainder, we bumped on into Chonju, arriving in the middle

of the night just as a flight of our bombers unloaded on one end of the town near the railroad tracks.

We were ordered out of the truck in front of the police station when the bombing started. I was singled out from the other prisoners and hustled to protection in the archway of a school or church in one of the mission compounds. When my guard finally brought me back, past a mission hospital, we met townspeople carrying two litters with a woman and a child on them. Both were bloody masses.

We got back on the truck and drove through the other end of town, passing a group of houses still smoking from the bombs while civilians poked through the wreckage, looking for other victims. I don't know what the objective of this bombing was, but the railroad, a spur line, was unhurt.

We were taken to the provincial penitentiary, which I remembered having inspected when I was military governor. (There was irony in this.) This was now an improved institution, with at least two new cell blocks. All the prisoners were lined up; and each of us was made to turn out his pockets and put all his belongings in front of him on the ground. I had nothing left except a handkerchief and a few cookies which the Inmun Gun captain had given me. While an inspecting party was working down the line I ate the cookies, and they let me keep the handkerchief when I put up an argument about it—although I was arguing in English and nobody understood a word. The prisoners were counted off in twenties, and each group moved separately toward the cell blocks. The count didn't come out even, so I was led off by myself to a twenty-man cell, the most commodious I'd ever seen in a Korean prison, with a nice smooth floor and twenty little wooden pillows lined up along one side. The guards locked the door, and I picked out a pillow.

As a policeman back in Berkeley, California, many years before, I'd made a few arrests and watched the people taken off to cells to spend the night. But this was the first time in my life that I'd been on the other end of the story. I slept fitfully.

There was no sound in the prison during the night, no weeping, no noise, from the many prisoners. Bombers came over again, and I did a little hoping that they might hit this lovely brick building, so close to the railroad yards; but they didn't even score a near miss—just a lot of racket. I could not hear any anti-aircraft fire.

In the morning the aperture in the cell door opened and a guard shoved in a little tin bowl of rice; just as I was about to eat it he indicated I should thrust it outside again, and some grass soup was poured over it. The rice might have been all right, but that grass soup was the most sickening stuff I've ever tasted. As hungry as I was, I could only pick at it.

Later that morning the first of the questions came to me. A guard handed in a pencil and a printed form, which asked my name, rank, organization, what my orders were, where I'd landed in Korea—and where was Syngman Rhee?

They already had my identification card and tags, so there was no point in trying to hide my identity. I put down my name and rank—and as for orders, I wrote: "To assist the Republic of Korea in repelling the aggressors from the North."

I knew full well that I didn't have to answer that or any similar questions, but I figured the answer would make the Communists mad—and at the moment I wanted to do just that.

After about an hour guards came and took me to the commandant's office. The commandant was rather a handsome man, wearing North Korean Army blue breeches and black boots, but a white shirt and a civilian coat. He needed a shave badly, and had the only green eyes I've ever seen in a Korean. Somehow they reminded me of a tiger's eyes. He was friendly and apologetic for having put me in a cell. An interpreter was present, a chap with long hair and in need of a shave even more than the commandant. He told me the commandant had no idea, when I was brought in, that I was an officer, but that he would make up for his oversight. He'd bring me a barber, give me a chance to wash, and secure some decent clothes. I would have to go back to my cell temporarily, but they'd prepare another room, give me better meals and the courtesies due my rank. Then he also asked a question: Where was Syngman Rhee?

This was question number one of some thousands which were to be asked, and it made no more and no less sense than most of them. Always, question and long-winded statement were closely related. The commandant said, "Your family and your countrymen are concerned about you. You must go on the radio and tell your family that you are well and being well treated, and tell your people that there is no use in continuing the war. Tell them the people of South Korea have welcomed us as their brothers. You must do this for the sake of your family and friends, and to save the lives of your countrymen."

There was much more of the same sort of thing. I said I wouldn't go on the radio, and that nobody would believe any such statement even if I did make it. I don't remember my exact answers to some of his questions; but frankly I was just indulging myself. I was trying to be as sarcastic as possible, for my own amusement, not to make these characters laugh. This was one time I didn't have to be careful. The things I'd never say normally, for fear of hurting someone's feelings, sounded terrifically witty to me now. I said I didn't have the faintest idea where the president of South Korea was; and when I was asked why we had come to Korea, I embroidered my written statement. I said we had come to help South Korea repel the aggressors from the North, who had violated South Korean national territory, that it was our duty as a member of the United Nations to assist in repelling that invasion, that the free world looked to us—I gave him quite a speech.

He said, "Well, now you can see how your forces have been driven back. So if you were released, would you continue to fight us?"

I said, "Yes, that's what I want to do. That's why I've been trying to get back, so I could fight again. I know I can do better next time, and kill more of you for the men we lose."

He didn't care for that. Finally he said, "General, you're a brave man, but you're very ignorant politically."

That ended the political part of the discussion, but he couldn't resist a little something personal. He said, "I've seen you before, general, even if you don't remember me. I was a political prisoner right in this same prison when you inspected it as military governor. But I'm going to treat you better than you treated me."

As military governor I had been technically in charge of South Korean prisons, but did not control immediate operations, which were handled by Koreans under the advice and supervision of Americans. I don't think that the treatment as a whole was bad, although some things possibly seemed worse to the Koreans than to me. I remember that on one prison inspection trip I was pleased by the number of beans mixed with the rice being fed to prisoners, but my interpreter,

Kimmy Kim, was affected just the other way. He said, "I hope I never get put in prison."

Prisons were overcrowded at that time, however, and I was very much disturbed when I found out how many people were being held for long periods without being brought to trial. In April of 1948 I had pardoned more than thirty-five hundred at one time because I found that some of them had been incarcerated for as long as eighteen months without trial, and charged only with talking against the government, or opposing rice collections. In the bad food days in Korea rations for prisoners were larger than those for civilians, because we expected the prisoners to work.

We were only partially successful in raising the standards, and we never had enough U. S. personnel to be positive that all our orders were being carried out; but we were trying. And, of course, I was responsible, as military governor, for any bad treatment that occurred. That's one of the things you accept when you take a job of that sort.

The prison commandant also gave me some information, which I believe was honest, so far as he was concerned. We had lost Taegu, he said, and the fall of Pusan to the Communists was only a matter of hours. I think the captain in Chinan had tried to give me the same information, without benefit of interpreter. The commandant was quite confident that we were being swept off the whole Korean peninsula.

I was confused. It was true that I'd seen fewer and fewer airplanes in the previous couple of weeks; but the information didn't check with the artillery fire I was sure I had heard on the last day of my freedom. I didn't know what to think.

At last, the commandant dismissed me to go to get my shower, the promised shave and haircut—and some very carefully posed before-and-after photo coverage. The interpreter said, "You'll be amazed to see the difference." I don't doubt that I would have, if I had ever seen the pictures. I wish I had them now.

Before the "after" picture was made I was given a very much patched pair of American olive drab trousers and a sun-tan shirt to replace my coveralls. The fact that both were clean made them seem wonderful, old as they were; and I noticed that the size fifteen shirt collar fit me very well, although my normal neck measurement is sixteen and a half. The barber who did the job on my hair and beard was only about fourteen years old, but he knew his business. And I was delighted to get that shave. I'd caught a glimpse of myself in a mirror that morning and had realized that I probably was the ugliest man in the world with a month's beard. From my left chin it comes out black, but is white off the right side. In the middle it's just bare.

During this washing and shaving I saw the interpreter going down a hallway—and a guard was with him. When I asked later, he admitted that he too was a prisoner. He said he had been an employee of our military government in Taejon, in an official capacity, and would be tried for having cooperated with the Americans and for being a reactionary.

"What are they going to do?" I asked. "Shoot you?"

He shook his head. "No, they're going to give me a trial. I'm sure it will be fair. I think I'll be freed, because I now see my mistakes." He added that he had been well treated in prison and that his wife was allowed to visit him. He also said that Eun Suk Koo, former South Korean chief of communications, was in the same prison; and later the same day, in a hallway, he introduced me, but we had no time to talk. All I could do was wish both of them luck.

The interpreter appeared to be quite sincere about his

change of viewpoint and gave me a considerable lecture about the fact that the future of Korea lay only in unification under communism. He also said he thought I would see the light, once I had some political education.

I was taken to a cottage outside the prison compound, where there was a U. S. white army cot with a mattress, pillows, and sheets—and where even the inside plumbing worked, rarest phenomenon in all Korea. A woman brought in an excellent noon meal, with meat, and I had some rest before I was called back to the commandant's office that afternoon.

This time five or six men in civilian clothes were present, in addition to the commandant and the interpreter. I thought I had seen some of those faces before. The questions started immediately, and the first was, "How can you prove that you're General Dean?"

I said, "I have no desire to prove that I'm General Dean."

The next was, "Why did the Americans come over here?"

Again I said, "To help the people of South Korea to retain their national integrity and to protect them from the aggressors from the North."

Then they shot a whole series of questions at me: "Why do the Americans bomb innocent women and children?" "Why do they bomb children in swimming?" "Why do they bomb farmers along the highways and kill their cattle?" I answered all these questions by saying that Americans never knowingly harm women, children, or noncombatants; but this didn't even slow up the flow of questions. The next was, "Why do Americans prey on schoolhouses and churches?"

I said, "The only reason a church or a schoolhouse is ever struck is when it is evident from the air that the Inmun Gun is using those buildings as Army installations, especially as command posts."

They wanted to know, "How do you account for so many women and children being killed?"

I gave as one of the reasons that the Communists brought military operations right in amongst civilians, into cities, and were using all sorts of buildings for military purposes.

Then my principal questioner said, "We won't discuss that any more."

These fellows also wanted to know the whereabouts of Syngman Rhee—but instead of listening to my answer, told me themselves. "You ought to know that your government has taken him to Tokyo. What does your government mean, supporting a puppet like Syngman Rhee?"

I did not answer that, so the interview ended with several of them giving me lectures about what was wrong with United States policy, accusing the U. S. of exploiting South Korea and preventing unification of the country. I think even the interpreter was a little bored.

As the civilians filed out the commandant asked me if everything about my treatment was satisfactory, and whether I wanted anything special. I said I would like some of the big peaches which I had admired in this area during occupation days. I had not been able to eat any then, because I had to obey my own order against the use of any indigenous food while the Koreans were hungry. But now I thought the peaches should be ripe. . . .

The commandant sent out for a dozen, and he and the interpreter and I each ate a peach, congratulating one another on how big and juicy they were.

On the way back to my cottage I asked the interpreter, "Who were those babies doing the questioning?"

"Oh, that was the press," he said.

This made me feel much better. Now I remembered where

I had seen some of them before—as hecklers on the edges of press conferences in the old days when I had visited here as governor. Also, I thought, "Now at least the world will know I'm a prisoner, and my family's fears will be eased."

I'm still curious about this situation. The interview was given and stories about it printed. But nothing was picked up at this time even by Communist newspapers outside Korea. Later, references to my capture were made by Tass, the Russian news agency; and I was told that I was mentioned in a collection of short stories published in Poland by a Russian writer. But for some reason none of this information seeped back across the Iron Curtain to my family.

I'm in possession of a fragmentary story that apparently appeared in some English-language newspaper in Korea as a result of this interview, but it reached me by such a circuitous route that I'm not sure of its origin. In part, the story reads:

Question: "How were you arrested?"

General Dean: "Due to the blind shootings from Australian airplanes. I lost most of my men. Furthermore, my driver was killed while we were in retreat. Therefore I sheltered myself alone into [sic] a mountain and attempted to make my way toward Pusan for approximately fifteen days in the mountains but failed and was arrested by the People's Army."

Question: "What is your last peak of aspiration?"

General Dean: "It is a painstaking resentment that I am captured by you fellows. I wish I could command my officers and men again and annihilate all you People's Army."

At this time Eun Suk Koo exchanged handshakings with General Dean and thus they consoled each other's situation. But the People's Army guard brought and offered some food including tinned goods to General Dean, however General Dean casted away these foods and made his resistance to the guards. . . .

There is more of this, which reached me via a letter, but it adds no more clarity to the situation than the above. Just how that part about Australian airplanes got in is beyond me. At the time I didn't know there were any Australian planes in Korea.

In the cottage, that cot with the mattress looked wonderful —so wonderful that I'm afraid I only grunted when the interpreter told me, "You know the warden bought those peaches with his own money? See what a kind man he is." A good supper delayed me some, but I headed toward the cot as soon as I could. This, I thought, would be the night's sleep I had been dreaming about. This would make up for days in thickets and nights in the rain.

But I was a little premature. I was restless, and every time I turned over, the cot squeaked. Every time the cot squeaked, the guard in the room would bellow at me. These guards were just youngsters, and I suppose they thought I was trying to escape; but their bellowing wasn't restful.

In the middle of the night my old dysentery started up again. The first time or two I had to get up I had arguments with the guard, but he finally desisted. I couldn't stay in bed just because he wanted me to, so I got up regardless of whether he was still yelling. Finally he got the idea and must have passed the word to the men who relieved him, because I had no further trouble. I would holler "*benjo*" (Japanese for toilet), and they understood that. Any Korean above the age of sixteen understands Japanese, although some of them pretend that they cannot. It was a required language all the times the Japanese controlled the peninsula.

I was up five or six times that night, and for many nights thereafter five or six trips were the minimum; the maximum, up to thirty-six times a day. There's one thing about Dean's digestion: it never does anything halfway—it either doesn't work at all, or it works all the time.

There was more questioning the next day, this time by a stout major general of the Inmun Gun who sat behind the warden's desk while a youngster with a sub-machine gun stayed in the room to guard him. The commandant and the interpreter also were there, but the general did all the talking, the interpreter translating for him. He was a very calm, soft-spoken man, not threatening and not ingratiating. I think the other two must have been as tired of the same old questions as I was: Would I go on the radio to broadcast? Why were the Americans here? Why were non-military targets bombed? The only thing he left out was Syngman Rhee, and I felt I probably should have reminded him to ask that too.

The questioning went on for forty-five minutes or more, but of course it was slowed and complicated by the translating. Neither of us could be sure that the interpreter was getting everything straight. This was evident when he asked me about the bombing of civilians.

I said, "We're not in the business of bombing civilians—we're too busy working on military targets."

I don't know how that was interpreted, but it infuriated the young guard. He snarled and jumped forward, pointing his sub-machine gun at me. He was so excited and upset that I laughed and asked the general, "What's the matter with him? Does he want to shoot me?"

The general spoke to him in Korean and ordered him out of the room. To me, he said, "The guard is very young, but he is moved and greatly disturbed by the barbarities which your Army has committed against his countrymen."

I still wonder what the interpreter told them in Korean.

The general might have let that part of the questioning stop there, but I wanted to get in a few thoughts of my own, so I said, "As long as we're talking, there's something I want to get off my chest. You people are not following the tenets of the Geneva Convention. Of all the men who captured me and shot at me with arms while I was being pursued in the hills, only one wore an arm band, let alone a uniform. You're fighting this war with men dressed in civilian clothes, so far as I can see."

The general's attitude toward me was that of a kindly senior trying to straighten out a wayward child, but he didn't deign to answer this. Instead he asked me if I would return to Korea to fight again if I were released.

I told him I surely would, if my country would let me, after the poor job I'd done the first time.

His reply was, "You are a brave man but very ignorant."

This was roughly the same thing I'd been told by the commandant: but the same interpreter was working, so the words may actually have been his rather than the general's phraseology.

The only thing that amused me during this interview was the realization that our names and numbers confuse the enemy almost as much as the many Rhees and Paks and Kims confuse us. Many questions concerned happenings on the east coast of Korea or involved Negro troop units. Finally I realized that this general had me confused with Major General William Keane of the 25th Infantry Division, and was hopelessly fouled up between the 24th Infantry Regiment, part of Keane's command, and the 24th Infantry Division, which I commanded. I didn't bother to straighten him out.

Actually none of this official interrogation bothered me as much as the fact that practically everybody working around the penitentiary wanted to interrogate me on his own. Every corporal or private who spoke a few words of English would try to get his oar in—when I was in the washroom, going down the corridors, or trying to get some sleep. One after another they came in, each one saying, "Rhee Syngman" or "Truman" in exactly the same tone of voice. A lot of them also asked me about Henry Wallace, on whom they apparently pinned great hopes. And one spoke a whole line. He said, "O America, America! My hopes were in America, but America has failed us."

I finally had to complain to the commandant about the constant harassment in order to get relief.

That day and night my dysentery grew worse, and the next morning a doctor came to see me. He felt my stomach, listened to my breathing, and spent most of his time giving my chest a very thorough thumping—although personally I doubted that the seat of dysentery was to be found in the chest. He left some medicine, which may have been salts and bismuth. Whatever it was, it did me no good.

In the evening the prison commandant showed up again, this time freshly shaved and in full officer's uniform. He looked so much better that I might not have recognized him, except for the green eyes. He let me know, without an interpreter, that I was to be on my way. I was given a tight-fitting American fatigue jacket. I pointed to my feet and the old Korean rubber shoes, which were all I had. The commandant looked all around—and the unluckiest guard in the prison was right where the boss could see him. This fellow had big feet for a Korean, and was wearing G.I. shoes. The commandant nailed him and forced him to change shoes with me. The pair I got were the most odoriferous shoes I've ever approached, but I could cram my feet into them. Although they were about two sizes too small, they definitely were an improvement over what I'd had before. I was ordered into a three-quarter-ton truck (United States property, naturally) with three guards and an officer. All the prison officials came out to bid me good-by like old friends. It was quite a farewell.

We were no sooner on the road to Taejon, just after dark, when United Nations aircraft began coming over. Whenever one did, the truck would stop and the guards would insist that we go fifty or a hundred yards out in the bushes or up a hill away from the road, to wait there until the sound of the plane had faded out entirely. We would remain quite motionless all the time it was above us, even though the night was black. This delayed matters, and so did our indirect route toward Taejon—which may have been taken either to avoid big troop movements or to stay off heavily bombed roads.

On the way we passed six or eight different battalions of Communist troops, all marching south. I was struck by their excellent march discipline but also noticed that only about half the men were armed; the weapons were about evenly divided between rifles with long bayonets and sub-machine guns. I could only assume that the rest expected to pick up arms from Americans or their own fallen comrades on the battlefield. There were no signs of heavy machine guns, mortars, or any artillery or tanks.

It's not a long ride from Chonju to Taejon, but we took all night to do it, losing time for the bombers and for the stops I had to request frequently. I was quite miserable from my digestive troubles.

We arrived in daylight, which allowed me one special satisfaction. At the edge of town were two tanks, both knocked out, and I was quite sure they were the same ones that had escaped unscathed from my pistol fire on July 20 but on which I had called down an air strike. It was nice to know that a few things on that miserable day had worked according to plan.

Two other tanks still were at the main intersection, where Clarke had measured their treads and armor, and a fifth was still in the field near the dependent housing area. I knew the one down between the business buildings definitely had been knocked out, so that made six in all. I savored that figure. It didn't win Taejon back by any means, but I was happy to know we had at least run up some kind of a score for the day, even while we were being run out of town.

I tried to see everything I could, but there were no answers to some questions. There was no clue about Clarke or any of the other men. Both the old regimental command post and the building which had been my headquarters, across the street, were occupied, but I couldn't tell their present use. I couldn't tell whether the railroad was operating, and saw no prisoners, but the whole town was full of adults, apparently in labor gangs, moving in the direction of the railroad. There were hundreds and hundreds of men, marching in organized groups but with no weapons except occasional shovels.

I was taken out to an old mission schoolhouse northwest of the center of town, near the airport. I spent the day sitting in the office of a man who apparently was the local commandant, although he wore no insignia. Officers up to the rank of major kept reporting to him. There was no real interrogation; but one officer who spoke some English did show up with some photographs taken of me when I had reviewed constabulary troops at Taejon in 1947. He appeared very happy to have these and displayed them to me as special prizes.

Nobody else bothered me. I was supposed to rest and perhaps to sleep, but found it difficult while sitting in a chair. I was not happy to notice that the furniture had very familiar markings—the 24th Division Medical Battalion. Twice I was served rice-and-soup meals, and in between the commandant gave me four or five pieces of hard candy from a jar on his desk.

One thing amazed me. An enlisted guard stayed in the room all the time; and whenever the officer would leave, the guard would promptly go through his desk, look through the drawers, riffle papers, and calmly help himself to the officer's cigarettes.

While he was busy doing this, I seized the opportunity to reach over myself and grab some more of the candy, putting it in my pockets. I figured that if it ever were missed the guard would be blamed, which would be just too bad.

Even when the officer was in the room, and made the mistake of laying a package of cigarettes on his desk, the guard calmly would help himself, just as he might do from his best buddy's supply, without arousing even a complaint. I found out as time went on that this was a regular practice in the Inmun Gun. Maybe it's part of the Communist theory that private property is wrong.

That night I was taken northward again, this time with new guards, a different officer, and in a jeep—which made me feel very bad. It was marked "P-5, 19th Inf"—one of our military police jeeps. Behind the wheel was one of the world's really rare drivers—and although I was comfortably seated between two guards in the back, the night was not precisely restful. I had to call for stops many times. Once, in my hurry to get out of the jeep, I caught my foot on a trailer hitch, couldn't get my hands out in front of me in time, and fell on my head in the road. Landing on that part of my anatomy meant that no great damage was done.

Another odd thing about the Inmun Gun is that the driver of a vehicle appears to be its undisputed boss no matter who's riding with him. An officer is just like any other passenger and gives no orders.

This particular driver reminded me of the drugstore sheikh of the 1920s. His long, lank hair hung down to his neck—or to his chin when it was in disarray. To get it out of his eyes while driving, he had a sure-fire system: he'd throw back his head, whirl it from side to side, and the hair would fall more or less into place—all this, of course, while he continued to push the jeep at almost the top speed it would make. Each time I was certain he was going to go off the road.

When I wasn't hanging on, waiting for the inevitable crash, I had time to notice a few more satisfactory things: where Task Force Smith and its artillery had fought near Osan, dead tanks still proclaimed the cost of that victory to the Communists; and all up and down the highway a remarkable number of tanks had been knocked out by aerial action. Unfortunately there were also several U. S.-built armored vehicles, probably those we had turned over to the ROK when we ended the Korean occupation, also burned out in the ditches.

Somehow the driver managed to stay on the road until we reached the suburbs of Suwon, where he whirled his head once too often. We hit the ditch, bounced over the debris of a wrecked tank (it sounded as if we had hit a mine), and blew all four tires. We finished the night by walking a couple of miles into town.

Suwon was badly smashed by air attacks, and two more came while we were there. They both hit at the other end of town, and I was delighted to see air activity stepping up so much.

After breakfast at a hotel the officer went away by himself, and I guess the two guards decided it was too much trouble to watch me all morning. They took me down to another building where at least thirty Korean prisoners, all civilians, were wedged into one eight-by-ten room, under guard. I was put in with them, to sit cross-legged like the silent others.

Almost immediately a young boy, twelve or fourteen years old at most, spoke to me softly in English. We were sitting close together. He told me that some peacetime American officer at Ascom City, one of our military headquarters between Seoul and Inchon, had befriended him as an orphan and had sent him to school for a year in Texas. I think the town where he had attended a junior high school was Austin, but I'm not sure. He said the officer had not been able to adopt him but had provided the year's schooling as the next best thing.

He was an intelligent-looking youngster, dressed in American schoolboy clothes. Now he was a political prisoner. I started to ask him more questions, but the guard came to the door and growled at him; and afterward the youngster whispered to me, "Don't talk to me. There are snoopers in here and they've told on me. I'll catch it now."

I managed to slip the youngster all of the hard candy I had stolen the day before in Taejon, but I had no chance to do anything else. My own guards returned, the escort officer with them, and the expression on their faces announcing very plainly that they had been chewed out thoroughly for putting me in with the Koreans at all. After only about forty minutes, total time, I was taken out again.

The youngster from Texas neither waved nor changed expression when I left. The last thing he had said was that he expected to be shot. He hoped that they would do it quickly, without torture.

▶▶▶▶◀◀◀◀

CHAPTER VI

The Battle of Ideas

I have been telling my experiences in Korea in chronological order, for the sake of simplicity, and will continue to do so; but a more logical division of these events might be by their character: a chase and capture, the battle of ideas, attack by boredom, and attack by luxury. Of all these, the battle of ideas is the one that, to my mind, has the most importance.

It began with my arrival in Chonju and the original suggestion that I should broadcast on the Communist radio, and did not end until the Communists had given me up completely, either because I was too stubborn or too stupid for their uses. In all its facets, certain curious elements were present; and perhaps some of them are important as clues to the workings of the official Communist mind.

One of the things I noticed first was that these people were much more anxious to have me say what they wanted me to say than to extract any really new or useful information. Pressure on me was greatest to agree to perfectly obvious falsities: that the United States was an aggressor; that we had exploited the people of South Korea or wished to do so; that General Douglas MacArthur had ordered Syngman Rhee to start the war. On questions of real significance—our defense plans for Japan, commitment of troops, infantry strategy or organization—they gave up when met with baldfaced lies or simple refusal to answer.

I also noticed that the questioning failed completely to evaluate known facts. It just went on and on, over and over the same lines, even when the answers could not possibly have made any difference. In September of 1950 Communist interrogators hammered at me day after day—to learn prewar plans of the South Korean Army, which by this time were thoroughly out of date, or to force me to admit certain things about the air campaign (indiscriminate bombing, for example) on which I, an infantry officer, obviously was no authority.

There was also an almost pathological insistence on getting something signed. I would not broadcast on the radio, therefore I must sign a paper saying that I would not go on the radio. I would not sign a proposed letter, then I must sign a letter saying *why* I would not sign a letter. I don't exaggerate: such things were demanded. This could not have been solely for the sake of the signature, to be transferred later to vastly different documents. They had my signature on literally dozens of documents from the occupation era, captured by them at Seoul, and I had signed my name several times since my capture. These could have been transferred to any statements they liked, without even the necessity of keeping me alive. Rather, I think that this was a business of a minor functionary feeling that he must take back *something* to show his superiors after an attempt to question or indoctrinate Dean. Apparently almost any old signature would do.

Still another tactic is the obviously planned mixture of the real with the fanciful. This may come in a questioning which starts on topics so wild and absurd or so utterly unimportant that even the person being interrogated gets bored with them, and then finds himself quite suddenly on the defensive about something quite important, not wild at all, when his guard may be presumed to be down. Or the prisoner is threatened with cold or starvation, and suffers both. Then he is told that unless he cooperates, something will happen to his family in Berkeley, California. The promise of better food brings a bit of meat into a dull and insufficient diet—and right after it comes a promise as improbable as that he will be given a corps command in a Communist army.

As I said, this verbal battle of ideas began at Chonju with my first questioning and continued almost everywhere we stopped. After I was removed from the crowded cell at Suwon, we went back to the courtyard of the hotel, where a sick Inmun Gun officer was stretched out on a bench under a canvas erected as a sunshade. I was directed to another wooden bench, and the two of us tried to sleep during most of that fearfully hot day, although I had very little success. In the afternoon a doctor and nurse came to give the Communist officer a hypodermic. Then the doctor examined me, giving my chest an especially thorough thumping, and later provided me with more medicine, which I again believed to be salts.

Late in the day we started for Seoul. We were delayed when we found that a pontoon bridge over the Han River near the municipal airport no longer was passable. We joined a long line of vehicles waiting for a hand-operated ferry farther up the river, then got across it in reasonable time because the officer in charge of me pulled his rank to get us past the lined-up trucks. I noticed that many of these waiting vehicles were driven by Inmun Gun enlisted men and were piled high with loot and loaded with women and children. These looked like families, complete with all their household goods, going back to Seoul. I have no idea where they'd been, unless they were Communist families who had pulled out of the city to avoid an expected battle and now were coming back while the Inmun Gun was busy rounding up their non-Communist neighbors for prison or execution.

I'm sorry now that I didn't pay closer attention to that ferry. A few weeks later that hand-operated job became familiar to many Americans and helped to move much of the 7th Division, my old command, across the river as U. N. Forces, landing at Inchon, drove the Communists out of burning Seoul for the first time on September 26.

We entered Seoul just before midnight. The streets were deserted. I was taken to the old municipal police department building, where a major general greeted me pleasantly and told me to get some sleep on a table, which I did with the greatest of ease.

In the morning I was served an amazing meal, carried up from the police grill. It consisted of an excellent steak, well fried; three nice fresh eggs, turned over easy; french-fried potatoes; and eight—count them—small loaves of french-type bread. I was also handed, with considerable ceremony, a can of evaporated milk, and a guard was insistent that I drink it—straight.

This was the first American-type food I saw. Any portion of it would have been sufficient for a breakfast, but I couldn't stand to see it go away again, so I ate all of everything except the bread. I simply couldn't get down more than a loaf and a half of that. I secreted the other half-loaf in my pockets, but when a soldier came to clear away the dishes he took the other six loaves with him—and I watched them go with real regret.

Then for the next several hours I was busy regretting how much I'd eaten.

The general occupying the office where I slept apparently had worked all night (if he slept, I don't know where or when). In the morning another group of civilians came in, and the general and I held what was obviously a press conference, although nobody bothered to explain it to me. Interpreting was done by an elderly civilian, whose thin white beard stuck out in bristles two inches long.

These people were interested mainly in my experiences since I had been captured, but they also wanted to know exactly *why* I had permitted myself to become separated from my own troops. I found myself angrily defending Lieutenant Clarke and my bodyguard against the absurd claim that they were to blame for my separation. I don't know why this was important to the press, but they made a great point of being critical of the men with me. They also hammered at the question of whether I had been alone in the mountains, whether anyone with me had escaped when I was captured. I had to be very careful never to mention Lieutenant Tabor. I thought he might still be at large, and I certainly didn't want to stir up any special hunt for him.

I did say quite a lot about the terrible ride I'd had between Chinan and Chonju in that truckload of prisoners. I said that it was the worst ride I'd ever experienced, that the treatment of those prisoners was brutal, but I could have saved my breath. The minute my story began to get unpleasant, the general spoke to the press; and although all of them had been taking notes steadily, they all put away their pencils. Censorship was working, with no arguments.

Then my questioners did one of those incomprehensible things which just don't make any sense, no matter how you figure them. One of them–I think it was the general himself –said, "Would you like to see Ahn Chai Hong and Kim Kyu Sik?"

I said, "Not particularly."

In prewar days these men had been South Korean leaders of importance with whom I had worked as military governor. I had liked them both and respected Ahn especially as an intense patriot and a brave man. Kim Kyu Sik was an elderly man, a leader of stature equal to or greater than Syngman Rhee's in the days of the formation of the South Korean government. He had fought that formation because he thought it would mean permanent partition of the country. A doctor of philosophy, he had headed the interim assembly. Using English, he had been an orator of exceptional ability.

I certainly had no desire to see either of them under these circumstances. Nevertheless, Ahn—obviously also a prisoner and being detained in this same building—was hauled in. He looked at me with the most shamed face I've ever seen. I said, "How do you do, Mr. Ahn. I'm sorry to see you under these circumstances."

He made no audible reply. I had always admired this man, although he was stubborn. Now he must have been terrified, because his palm was clammy when we shook hands.

That was all there was to it—and its purpose escaped me. There could not have been any doubt of my identification by this time. Perhaps they just wanted to watch us squirm. Kim Kyu Sik was ill at his home, I was told, so he wasn't brought around.

Later both these men went north to cooperate with the Communists. Kim Kyu Sik died very soon after going north, but I've been told that Ahn is now a Communist commissar of some sort. This is difficult for me to understand; but I'm sure somebody must have convinced him, somehow, that communism was the best thing for his country.

I had all the comforts of home that morning—another shave and hair trim, and a chance to wash. In the afternoon another major general showed up to question me, mostly about military matters. He made a great point of wanting to know exactly when my division had come to Korea, and I could see that he was working to prove we had moved before the United Nations gave full approval. I suddenly developed a very bad memory for dates.

When he asked about the strength of the 24th Division I decided to take a little wind out of his sails. The North Koreans were so cocky about having pushed us back that I knocked three or four thousand off our actual strength. I said we had eight thousand men, but that by no means all of those were combat soldiers—the division included ordnance, signal men, and many others. I tried to get across the idea, "You boys aren't really as good as you think you are."

He pulled out one of our tables of organization and began reading off unit sizes, but I stopped him. "Oh no," I said, "that table is only for war. We didn't expect a war, so we came under strength. I want you to remember that the Inmun Gun has not done as well as you think, because you weren't fighting the numbers you thought you were."

I had tried not to knock off too many numbers, but to make it sound just barely reasonable. I thought I was getting along quite well with all this when he threw me a real curve. He said, "Did you personally explain to your men why they are fighting? Do your officers and men know why they are fighting?"

That was a telling point, because I hadn't. I had done so when we were fighting in Europe, and in Japan had made a point of explaining personally to each replacement exactly the theory of our duty as occupation troops. But here in Korea I just hadn't gotten around to any such explanations. I had talked to most of the officers and headquarters groups, but all

I could do was hope that the regimental and company officers had done such explaining to most of the men. I remembered that at an early briefing some officer had asked me, "Just why are we fighting?" And I had said, "That's a tough question. Why do you think?"

He had said, "We're fighting for liberty," and I'd agreed that this was as good an answer as any.

I lied like a trooper to this Communist general, but I also made a personal resolution never to let that explanation detail slide again, no matter how tough the situation or how little time I had. That question really hurt me, and I hated like sin to have to look that buzzard in the eye and say, "Of course I did."

But he switched immediately from the important to the innocuous. His next question was, "How did you identify yourself when you were up front? How could people tell you were a general?"

I said, "I had two little stars on my helmet."

He said, "How did you identify your jeep?"

I said I'd had stars on that.

He asked, "Leather cushions?"

I said I couldn't remember whether they were leather.

That evening I was ordered downstairs, and the general of the Inmun Gun went with me. In front of the building he asked, "Did you ever see this before?"

There was my own jeep that old White (Corporal Malcolm D. White, my driver) had been so proud of, still with the leather cushions and the spick-and-span numbers on the front. The general presented me with my own two-star license plate and handed me my own helmet with the two stars in front and the taro-leaf insignia (distinguishing mark of the

24th Division) on the side. He said, "You can have these for souvenirs."

Then I was directed to a three-quarter-ton truck, while he drove off in my jeep. I never did get a chance to find out whether those unawarded medals might still be secreted in the jeep somewhere, but I doubt that they were.

The two major generals at Seoul were of the two principal branches of the North Korean services. The man who had welcomed me was a member of the Security Police, which in time of peace does rural police work and furnishes border guards, operating independently of the Army, but in time of war is called in for various duties, including management of prisoner-of-war camps. These people are recognizable by their green shoulder tabs. The Inmun Gun, or Regular Army, wears red tabs; and the general who had my jeep was one of these regular officers.

Now that my identity had been established definitely, obviously there was a plan to defer to rank in my case. The deference, so far as the truck ride north from Seoul was concerned, consisted of placing a wobbly kitchen chair in the exact center of the truck. I was ordered to sit on this; and a six-man guard, armed with four sub-machine guns and two rifles, found seats on the floor all around me. We headed north.

Once again the driver of the truck was the person I watched. An officer sat with him in the front seat of the truck but said very little and did nothing. The driver was boss. I always remember him as the Singing Driver, in contrast to the Hairy Driver, who had run us into the ditch below Suwon. This fellow was also a most un-Korean type of Korean: he even acted as if women were human. Specifically, he stopped to pick up a girl hitch-hiker, giving her a favored seat on his *left* side, even though the English-speaking officer obviously was opposed to the whole idea. But again the supremacy of North Korean drivers was quite evident, and the girl got in. If the people who later hinted about giving me commands in the North Korean Army really had been smart, they'd have offered me a job driving a truck. If I'm ever in that army, that's what I want to do. Truck drivers have it all over officers.

At any rate, the girl snuggled up to the driver, playing up to him in a fashion you might expect in a Western country, but hardly in the Orient. It worked. She rode all the way to the north side of the Imjin River in one of the best seats. If the officer was crowded, that was just too bad.

The guards apparently were men going home on leave. Before we left Seoul I'd noticed that they were showing each other photographs, apparently of girl friends, and exchanging addresses. Among them was a barracks-room bully, who would have had a rough time in our own Army. One of the smaller men displayed a photograph, and this big fellow not only snatched it to look at, but refused to give it back. The poor little devil did everything he could, but never could get it away from him.

The guards pooled their money—everyone seemed to have bales of it—and sent one fellow out to buy some dried fish and hard crackers. As we rode north they ate the fish, offering me pieces of it. I couldn't get this down but managed some of the crackers, which were like hardtack.

They also sang. It seemed to me that all the songs were political, in one way or another. There was the Inmun Gun marching air, and another about Kim Sung Soo, one of South Korea's outstanding leaders, which was like a hate song, or perhaps even unprintable. Another, sung with the same inflection and undoubtedly a hate song, was "E-Syngman." Koreans usually reverse the order of names, placing the family designation first. And a *single* character may be translated Rhee, Dee (or Di), or just as E. Thus this song title, although sung with the syllables widely separated, actually is only the name of President Syngman Rhee—but I doubt very much that he would have enjoyed it. There was also a song about Stalin, but I could tell that this was quite different, with Stalin being extolled. Whether they're still singing it, now that Stalin is being officially deglamourized by the Communists, I can only guess.

The driver loved to sing with them, especially those songs which concerned the Inmun Gun. This I wouldn't have minded, but each time he joined the singing he would lift his head to bay out the choruses toward the stars—and take his eyes completely off the road. Each time I was quite sure we'd hit the ditch.

We had trouble getting across the Imjin River, but finally made it through a ford. The girl hitch-hiker left us on the north side. We continued on to a town which I believe was Paekchon (just south of the 38th parallel and west of Kaesong), although it could have been another village in the same vicinity. This was a roundabout route to Pyongyang, the reason for which was not clear to me. At any rate, we stopped for an hour or two, parking in the yard in front of a police station while the escort officer went inside. I shall never forget that town, for one reason. All the time we sat there someone was screaming inside the jail. It was screaming even worse than that I had heard coming from the tank we had hit at Taejon, and it kept on monotonously. This was no child, no wounded soldier. This was someone being cruelly tortured;

and whatever they were doing to him continued intermittently all the time we were there.

Finally we went on again. The kitchen chair had not been equal to the bumps and twists that truck driver had managed to put into the road and was about to fall apart. I talked the guards into throwing it away (with the officer, who knew how to speak English but obviously didn't wish to, providing grudging translation in monosyllables) and sat on the floor with the enlisted men. Shortly I was a little sorry I had, for as soon as I tried to stretch out, all six of them were on top of me. They meant nothing by it. It was just their way with each other, but they were like a ball of puppies or a bunch of snakes, arms and legs everywhere and all on top of me. I was nauseated and weak, and this made the nightmare night even worse. The autumn chill was increasing at night, although the days still were fairly warm.

The men went on singing, and the driver went on flirting with ditches every time he raised his head to give voice. This even affected the uncommunicative officer. I said that I thought they must have searched for a week to find such a rotten driver, and the officer agreed with me. They had succeeded, he said, in finding the worst driver in Seoul.

At another time he did mention that the weather was much colder in the north, and that although the springs and autumns were beautiful, the country was too hot in summer and too cold in winter—that Korea, in fact, had a terrible climate. It was my turn to agree with him. Otherwise he volunteered no information, not even about where he had learned English, and I wasn't curious. Perhaps if I had guessed how long it would be before I had a chance to speak English regularly again, I would have tried to start more conversation.

I got some relief from that pile of snakelike humans because of my dysentery. On that trip I had to ask the driver to stop seven or eight times. There was a much longer rest from them just before morning. As we were dropping down into a long valley the driver finally sang once too often, or lifted his head too far, and ran us off the road into a rice paddy. The truck turned over. But this was a vehicle without a top, like most of them in North Korea, and we were all thrown clear. Nobody had anything land on him, but one man in the front seat hurt his ribs. He was in pain and moaned all the rest of the night.

The guards succeeded in shoving the truck back on its wheels but could not get the engine started again. I think the exhaust pipe must have been clogged. So we walked seven or eight miles to a town which I was told was named Oreo, although I've never been able to locate it on a map. I made eight more dysentery stops during the hike and I think the guard more or less appreciated them, for the officer had been marching us all at a very fast pace. He was the only one who appeared to mind the delays.

I was taken to a hotel in the town just at daybreak, was given breakfast, and spent the day there. The hotel was built around a court, and all day long the town children wandered in and out, coming to stare at me. A prisoner must have been a curiosity, and the word had got around. In the afternoon the parade became so constant that the officer aroused me and took me down to the center of town so everybody could have a look. Nobody threw anything, nor even jeered. They only stared, like people looking at a monkey in a zoo. I think I must have been ahead of the infamous prisoner marches which later covered more or less this same route.

During the day someone repaired the truck, and that night we drove on to Pyongyang, crossing a pontoon bridge to get into the city, and arriving about ten o'clock. First we stopped in front of a large building, which I was told was the Security Police headquarters (although other accounts mentioning this building refer to it as the Secret Police headquarters); the officer went in to report, while a guard and I sat outside in the truck parked under a tree. Presently another officer and two guards came out, and we were driven to a house near Liberation Park (a park that became familiar to Americans a couple of months later during the brief occupation of Pyongyang, captured by the Eighth Army on October 19 during its push toward the Yalu River). The house was directly across the river from a large airfield, and not far from Kim Il Sung University.

Here I was greeted by a very pleasant-appearing Korean in civilian clothes. He said, "I'll be your interpreter here. I'm here to make you comfortable." He did not identify himself, and later, when he did tell his name, Lee Kyu Hyun, he asked me never to use it, as he was under orders not to tell it to me.

This was a Western-style house, two rooms with a double door between them. Again there was an Army cot for me, complete with mattress, pillows, and sheets, and a couple of overstuffed chairs and some straight chairs. Lee asked me if I wanted to go to bed immediately. I said, "Show me the latrine first. The way I feel, I'll need that often."

When I got to bed there was no problem except the lights, which were ordered left on so that a guard who stayed in the room could see me at all times. Another guard was outside the house; and Lee and another civilian, who carried a pistol on his hip and was apparently in charge of affairs, also slept in the house—the man in charge usually just falling asleep in one of the easy chairs.

Breakfast was served to Lee and me together, and he told

me that he had been a professor of literature at Kim Il Sung University, but had been drafted by the Inmun Gun at the outbreak of war. He had been translating captured documents, he said, but wouldn't be any more specific. He said he hadn't seen any other prisoners before I arrived.

Later I was told that the North Koreans had captured many secret documents, both from our Embassy in Seoul and the headquarters of the Korean Military Advisory Group (KMAG). I can't guess whether the Embassy documents were important, but would guess that those in KMAG headquarters concerned principally South Korean military planning, and therefore would have been thoroughly out of date by the time the Reds got them.

I saw no Russians in Pyongyang, and the anti-aircraft fire sounded weak. I was in no position to find out whether those batteries actually were manned by Russians, as some of our people were told when the United Nations captured the city, but they could have been.

From Lee I received the first inkling of what the war meant to middle-class North Koreans. He was very much concerned about his wife and a baby born in June. He had not been able to see his wife since the war began but knew that she had no milk for the child (extremely unusual for a Korean woman) and had not been able to find any fresh or preserved milk, so was trying to raise the youngster on rice broth. She and the baby were with her parents in a village about twenty miles away, but Lee never was given leave to go to see them.

Lee expressed great surprise about me. He had been briefed on me, he said, and had been told that I was a tough, rugged individual who liked only rough outdoor sports—an uncultured type. He was amazed when I asked for something to read and promised to bring me something the next day. He also was amazed that I cared for music or painting, and could not understand how in the world anyone who believed in "pure culture," literature and the arts, could also be a professional soldier.

He managed to let me know that he had some culture. He had been to school in Japan, where he learned English; had visited Moscow; and had taken post-graduate work at Kim Il Sung University.

On that first day Lee brought me a good tan, summer-weight civilian suit, with a Seoul tailor's name on it. It fitted well, except in the waist, and I had to tuck the top of the trousers inside my belt. There was also a nice shirt, of some material like nylon. The tailoring on this was special: the sleeves were too long for my thirty-five-inch arms, but the tail was so short I couldn't keep it inside my trousers. Lee also gave me a necktie, so I was a natty-looking individual.

On the second day he brought some reading matter—a novel, *Allitet Takes to the Hill*, and the July issue of a Soviet magazine, *News*. The latter contained stories of strikes in Japan and stevedores refusing to load military cargoes for Korea, articles about a proposed international anti-atom-bomb pledge, and others criticizing the United Nations for interfering in Korea.

I read anything they'd let me read. I was interested in finding out what modern communism was all about. You can't fight something intelligently unless you know what it is. In the United States we can't afford to be so ignorant. Before I was a prisoner I didn't know what the Reds were talking about, what they meant when they said "Leninism." I had studied Marxism when it was still taught at the University of California as a political science course, but their interpretation of Leninism was all new to me. Not one officer in a thousand in our Army—and, if anything, an even smaller percentage of civilians in the United States—has any idea of what they mean. So I read everything I could. I'm an authority now on the history of the Communist party and much of its doctrine.

Just for the record, later on one of the things the Communists were always yapping about to me was "McCarthyism." All I could say was, "Who the hell's McCarthy? I never heard of him." He became a political figure after my capture.

In one of my first conversations with Lee I repeated my request to be taken to a prisoner-of-war camp, and I remember his answer very well. He said, "Oh, the men in your camps are very happy, very merry, very cheerful, happy. They're whistling and singing and cracking jokes all the time." But he did not say anything about taking me to join them. Instead he brought me a novel, *Port Arthur*, which concerned the 352-day siege of that city in the Russo-Japanese war. Possibly it was intended to take my mind off the current conflict.

On September 6 I had a very important visitor: a four-star colonel (equivalent to our rank of brigadier general) named Kim. I have every reason to remember this man, and I'm sure I could pick him out of any crowd. I know the way he fumes when he is angry, the unctuous approach he uses when he's trying to wheedle, the manner in which spittle foams out of his mouth when he's threatening—yet I find it difficult to describe him. Perhaps it's like trying to describe someone very close to you. You find yourself thinking, "Well, she just looks like June," or, "Well, he's just an ordinary man." For quite different reasons, I feel somewhat the same about this Kim: he's just an ordinary Korean, although I'm quite sure that I'll be able to reach out a beckoning finger when I see him again. And I'll be waiting for that day.

Not that he was unpleasant at first. Quite the contrary. He was friendly, kindly, interested in my welfare—and left me a thick folder of alleged copies of statements by American prisoners of war. These statements all concerned a resolution, said to have been approved at a mass meeting of prisoners, calling for American troops to cease fighting. Some eight hundred typed signatures were attached, many of them names of officers and men I had known in the 24th Division. Quite a few were men I thought had been killed in the fighting.

The resolution was wordy, but the general idea can be conveyed by the opening statement: "We were brought here under the assumption that North Koreans had started the war; but we found out after we arrived that the war was in fact started by the South Koreans, who were the aggressors and have been for some time."

Colonel Kim's request (I give his rank each time I mention him in order to avoid confusion with many other Kims, but this indicates no special respect on my part) was simple: I should sign the petition and go on the radio to notify my family that I was alive and to tell the people of the United States that we should stop fighting. He said, "Now I'll give you time to look these over and to think them over."

Also in the folder was a long statement allegedly signed by Philip Deane, a British war correspondent captured by the Communists in the early days of the fighting. This was highly critical of Americans, discussed his own capture, and quoted some U. S. sergeant as saying that we had been too busy bringing post-exchange supplies to Korea to take time to tell our soldiers what the war was about, and that we had sent troops in to fight without proper preparation. It also lauded North Koreans for their care of prisoners and the wounded. I didn't know what I was supposed to do about this, so I did nothing.

The next morning we moved again, this time to a church building in the village of Sunan, about sixteen miles north of Pyongyang. Even before we left the house, the rug on the floor of my room and some of the furniture had been taken away; and when we reached the church these already had been set in place by the pistol-toting civilian and a truck crew. The church was divided by a rough board partition, full of cracks and knotholes, at the chancel. In the portion of the church where the congregation normally sits, the guards—some twenty or twenty-five men—were housed, without furniture, sleeping on the floor. The chancel area, about twelve by twenty feet, was for me; and here were the rug and furnishings from the house near Liberation Park. Directly behind the chancel was another partition, and a room about seven by twenty feet, where Lee slept. Beside the church and only a few yards from it was a small Korean-type house that was used as a cook-shack; there was no provision for heat or cooking in the church building. The two structures sat in a grove of chestnut trees, and the chestnut crop was ripe.

One guard was always in my room, and the light burned constantly. Lee told me that we had moved because of the increased bombing of Pyongyang, including the use of anti-personnel, air-bursting bombs. I had noticed that for two or three days previously, bombing had been more frequent than before, most of it by small propellor-driven planes and some jets working over the airfield. Often the jets would get in before the air-raid warning sounded. Our house was shaken, but none of the bombs hit especially close. Lee told me, however, that the bombers were destroying the city. He was worried about his own family and friends, especially about his father, who was still living there. On the day we moved he told me, "Yesterday the bombers hit the section where my father is. I hope he wasn't killed." Apparently he had no method of getting any direct information.

I failed to mention that before we moved another doctor had come to see me, given my chest one more good thumping, and left some powders for me to take. My digestive troubles had increased, and I was fast growing weaker. I don't think I weighed more than a hundred and ten pounds when I was captured (my normal prewar weight being about two hundred and ten), and ten days of uninterrupted dysentery certainly hadn't allowed me to gain any of it back again.

When the very polite and kindly Colonel Kim came to see me again, a day or so later, he insisted that I take a walk with him. I tried but simply could not keep going after fifty or a hundred yards. So we stopped at a point from which we could look down over the valley surrounding Sunan; and while we sat there he gave me a lecture on the virtues of communism.

He wondered if I had not noticed a vast difference between South and North Korea. I told him that although I had been traveling only at night, and could not see much, the farm houses in North Korea looked much poorer to me and that I thought the people lacked comforts of life which farmers in South Korea took as a matter of course.

That didn't please him at all. He pointed out a housing project being constructed near Sunan as an example of what communism was doing for the people. He also said that although we might talk about communism, using the term loosely, North Korea actually wasn't a true Communist state, because people could still own their own homes and there was sanctity of private property. The only feature of true state socialism, he said, was that all land was owned by the state and had been so subdivided that each man now farmed his own, paying nothing in the way of rent or taxes except one-fourth of his annual crop. No landlord could exploit another man by having his land worked for him; all large industries and public utilities such as railroads were owned by the state; women had full equality with men; and industrial workers had priority at state-operated food stations. I should, he said, see the light and realize how wonderful all of this really was. It was a long, exhaustive lecture, and I was exhausted. And I thought mostly, when I thought at all, about my digestive tract, which did not feel good.

We finally went back to the church for lunch. It was delicious—there was even boiled beef, the first meat I had seen since I left Seoul. After lunch the colonel asked if I had signed the petition asking our people to stop fighting. When I said that I had not, I could see he thought he had wasted his boiled beef.

About September 10 Colonel Kim came back again; and this time all he wanted was my signature on a couple of long written statements, which he said were precisely the same things I had told him in conversation. One was to the effect that we were making a mistake by fighting in Korea, battling not only North Korea but actually fighting against South Korea's interests and desires too. The other was even more simple: Syngman Rhee was no good, a rascal, a crook, a senile old man, a thief who looked after only his own personal interests.

Somehow all I could remember about our previous conversation was what he had told me, not what I'd told him—and certainly not these statements. But the colonel made everything exceptionally clear. "These," he said, "represent my minimum requests. If you sign these, you'll go to a prisoner-of-war camp immediately—and you won't be tortured."

Well, that insertion about torture wasn't exactly a reassuring note, but we didn't get anywhere that day, although he spent most of the afternoon working on the problem intermittently. His pushing wasn't constant, but it was wearing as hell. He didn't shout or scream, but he wasn't quite the kindly friend he had been previously—except for a few minutes, when he suddenly asked whether I liked to drink.

I said, "No. I seldom drink any hard liquor. I do like a little something—sherry wine, perhaps—before dinner, but that's usually all."

This confused him a little, I could see; but he wasn't stopped entirely. "Then," he said, "all you have to do is to sign these statements, and your troubles will be over. Sign, and you'll be taken to a nice house in the country. It's a fine house, and you'll have an easy and pleasant life, just living there until the war is over. Nobody will be shooting at you, and you'll be in no danger of being killed. Also, there will be plenty of fine sherry wine to drink."

He embroidered that house-in-the-country picture quite a lot, but I think he was a little troubled because he couldn't stock the cellar with scotch or vodka.

For two more days the colonel stayed at the church, alternately being persuasive, dangling in front of me this hope for a lazy country life with a bottle of sherry, then shifting over to the crimes being committed by the United Nations in the war—mostly, the bombing of schools and churches.

Here I think I should digress a moment to explain statements that must be made in the rest of this book. During the next three years I had a true worm's-eye view of our air war. Obviously, being unable to see much or to move far, I was in no position to evaluate the effects of bombing as a whole. I could see only what was right in front of me, I knew only the effect of bombing on a few people, with whom I had direct contact. So when I say that bombers missed or hit an apparent target, or that bombing increased the hatred which one of a thousand Kims had for the United States, no over-all criticism of aerial warfare is meant or implied. The importance of an individual miss—or a single person being confirmed in his communism as a result of bombing—can be judged only in relation to thousands of such bits of information. The fact that a bomber did miss, or a man did lose his wife and children, must be told, however, in order to understand what happened to the people around me, and how they thought.

But no one should forget that for three years those jets and bombers in the skies were my only link with my country. In all that time there was no sweeter sight to me than the vapor trail of a Sabre or the fiery fall of a MIG, no sound lovelier than the solid whuummp! of a salvo of bombs falling just over the next hill. Those were my people working, and I cheered them, every one.

At Sunan, however, it did seem to me that there was a good deal of bombing being wasted on the roads when I could still hear switch engines chuffing up and down on the undamaged railroad. The noise of those locomotives, coming after a flight of bombers had left, hurt me, personally; although of course I merely had to assume that the railroad actually had not been hurt. For all that I know definitely, they may have been chuffing up and down on the only bit of track left to them, and accomplishing nothing.

During this time bed was still the greatest thing in the world to me. My cares all seemed to drop away if I could get back to that cot and sleep, endlessly.

About eleven-thirty one night Colonel Kim spoiled it. He came storming in, got me up, and wasn't in the least friendly any more. "Now," he said, "I want you to sign this request to stop bombing our innocent villages."

I said, "Nobody will believe it, if I sign anything like that. If I could get back to my own people, however, I certainly would advise them to concentrate more on military targets. I'm sure those are the orders, but sometimes there are errors. I'd like to get back so that I could tell them."

He kept on arguing, insisting that I sign a statement. I was very tired and sick, but I don't intend to alibi—I merely got what seemed like a brilliant idea at the time, but less so later. I said, "No, I won't sign a statement, but I *will* write a letter to General Walker, if you'll get it delivered. I'm sure you can do that, the way your people infiltrate. I'll bet you could send somebody down there and hand it to him, by hand. I'll write a letter to General Walker, right now."

My belief that the Communists could infiltrate almost at will had a good deal of early evidence to support it. In the first hours of the war I was shown Communist handbills, clear down at Pusan, which were being used to frighten workers on our airfield. Thousands of these, which read, roughly, "You'll die, you dog, for helping the Americans," were put in the hands of these Pusan laborers even before the battle line had moved south of the Han River, at Seoul. And all the while I was with troops, we were harassed constantly by roadblocks and snipers who went around our lines or right through them as infiltrators, with a minimum of difficulty.

I guess that letter from Sunan was a silly thing, but I did write it. I wrote along these lines:

Dear General Walker: Unfortunately I was captured on the 25th of August. It was a physical capture. I was overpowered on my attempt to get back through the lines. [I did want both General Walker and my own son to know that I had *not* surrendered.] I've been well treated but I'm anything but happy at being a prisoner of war. I urge that you impress upon the Air the necessity to confine our attacks to military targets. William F. Dean.

I don't think I ever would have written this letter if I had been fully awake. Afterward I was much troubled by it. I thought those damned fools just might put it through, and if they did, I only hoped that General Walker would understand what I was talking about—that I wanted more and better bombing, not less of it.

As I've said, almost any signature would satisfy these people. This letter stopped Kim's harangue; and as I was going back to bed the interpreter, Lee, said, "All Korean people will love you for this." But so far as I can learn, they never did anything with it. Don't ask me why.

I have thought many times of this letter. I have no alibi for having written it; but I certainly want to emphasize that I keenly regretted having done so immediately after the deed. In fact, the following days were a veritable nightmare because of my reviling myself for having so written. One of the most difficult problems for a prisoner is that of maintaining his judgment. You have no one on whom to test your ideas before turning them into decisions. A thought, which normally you would discard as soon as you saw that it affected listeners adversely, balloons in your mind until you are sure it must be exceptionally clever. And sober reflection, which might show it up as being both foolish and dangerous rather than clever, just isn't possible under prison conditions. Of course I'm sorry I wrote that letter. It did no good and might have done great harm.

But this night was just a starter for Kim. He was there almost every day after that, and the mask of friendliness was gone. Paraphrased, what he had to say again and again was, "I've got you now. You can't back down. I'm going to discredit you. You've lost all dignity, so you might as well sign anything I put in front of you. You signed one thing, so I've got you. I've never lost on a man yet, I've never failed to obtain my objective, and I've had them tougher than you." Often this harangue was delivered just after he'd shaken me awake in the middle of the night.

I signed only one thing more for him, however, and again I thought that I was being real cute. Kim had been after me about the alleged hatred of South Koreans for Americans and wanted me to sign a prepared statement that we should withdraw from the peninsula. I was feeling very cagey, so I said that I wouldn't sign that, but I would write one similar to it. In my own handwriting I made another statement. As nearly as I can remember I worded it:

> The United States has lost favor in the eyes of South Koreans, who have seen their own nationals from the North win apparent military successes in the South; and this has given them a national consciousness. Many South Koreans through fear have outwardly manifested hostility to all Americans; and if we drive only to the 38th parallel, it will be only a matter of time until we have the same problem again, because the seeds of communism have been planted in the South. I base this observation merely upon my experiences when I was harried for thirty-five days in the mountains.

Again I attached my signature—and with it, an invisible hope that if the statement ever reached anybody who mattered, he would be able to see that I was trying to urge our people to come north of the parallel, not to stop at it, at the same time covering the thought with enough meaningless words to confuse the Communists.

At the time I thought this note was really quite clever, and Colonel Kim was obviously so pleased that I hoped it might work. He went away, carrying that statement like a treasure, but was back a couple of days later, fuming mad. I guess he had showed it to somebody who understood the English language well enough to see what I was trying to do. Kim said I was a running dog of Wall Street, and various other things. My statement was no good at all and would do great harm. He was displeased with me.

On the night of September 14 he got me out of bed again and ordered me taken to Pyongyang, while he departed in another vehicle. The truck which carried me stopped first at a building near the river, where an officer did some complicated telephoning before my guards took me any farther. I judged that this was to set up final arrangements for what was to come later, but was told nothing. While we were waiting there, Lee pointed to some nearby buildings, which could have been factories or some sort of dormitories. He said, "That's where the American prisoner-of-war camp is." He did not elaborate, and of course I saw no prisoners in the middle of the night.

Later we went across town, to the same building where I had waited when I first was brought to Pyongyang, the Security Police headquarters. Here, to my astonishment, a sentry actually saluted me, although I was in those summer-weight civilian clothes. I was taken to an enormous room where a lieutenant general was seated at a massive table. He was introduced to me as General Pak (although from later information I believe he actually was Lieutenant General Pang Ha Sae, head of the Security Forces). The general invited me to sit down. He said he understood that I had refused to "cooperate" (whenever I use this word, I'm referring to the Communists' term, not one of my own choosing), but he was sure that I would cooperate with him. He wanted, he said, to know three things: What were American intentions in the Far East? What secret weapons did we possess? What was the plan of maneuver for U. S. Forces in Korea?

As I think about it now, there may have been a special reason for that last question, on September 15. The tide of war was turning and U. S. Marines and soldiers were either landing at Inchon or steaming toward it in the flanking amphibious assault that broke the back of the North Korean Army in 1950. As the minimum, North Korean intelligence must have guessed that something was going on and must have been highly curious about the location of a couple of divisions they knew to be in the Far East but hadn't seen on the southern battle lines for a while. So I don't wonder that the general wanted to know our plan of maneuver. As a matter of fact, I was curious about it myself, but for obvious reasons rather glad I didn't know just then.

I told him that I didn't have any of this information, but succeeded only in bringing on a harangue, which was broken only when I had to excuse myself to go to the latrine. This was one activity with which none of my interrogators ever felt inclined to interfere.

The gist of what the general had to say the rest of the night was that I was completely at their mercy, they were going to try me as a war criminal for things I had done as military governor in 1948, nobody would know what had happened to me because the American newspapers and radio already had reported me as dead, and they had "trained operators" who would make me talk, whether I wanted to or not.

Finally he said that he would give me a few minutes to think things over. I was taken to an anteroom and given a cup of tea. I was so very tired I went to sleep sitting there. Lee said I snored.

After a few minutes I was awakened and led in to see the general again. When I said I had not changed my mind about talking he was angry. He said, "You won't talk?"

"No."

"Then you must sign a statement saying *why* you won't talk."

I said that would be all right with me. On a paper I wrote:

Fortunately I do not know the information you seek. But even if I did, I would not give it to you, because by so doing I would be a traitor to my country. So help me God. William F. Dean.

Lee, the interpreter, captured later by American forces when they took Pyongyang, said of this incident: "General Dean disclosed nothing. He was given two days to change his attitude and reminded that the American press and radio had reported him dead, so it was left to the Communist people to dispose of him as they saw fit."

▶▶▶▶◀◀◀◀

CHAPTER VII

Colonel Kim and Friends

Once again, my signature for the general at Pyongyang seemed to get him off some sort of hook, and they let me go back to Sunan, where another doctor came to see me. He struck me as having more sense than the previous medical visitors. He did give my chest the usual thorough thumping, but he also took some specimens and asked me what our doctors would do in a similar case. When I told him sulfathiazol, he nodded his head knowingly—at least he'd heard of the medicine. He put me on a *chook* diet—chook is rice cooked until it is soft and gummy, with lots of water in it. Nobody likes this, and I was no exception, but it was all I got for days.

Then the delightful Colonel Kim came back. He was still wondering if I would cooperate, and I signed another note saying that I would not, that I had not changed my mind, that I had no information and would not give them any if I did.

Kim went away, but that night—September 16—returned with three other officers. They set up a table in the room where the guards were sleeping and for hours pored over papers. Colonel Kim came into my room once to tell me, "Well, tomorrow we're going to interrogate you. I have trained assistants who are going to get what we want to know."

I thought the next day might be tough, so I went to bed and got some sleep.

They started about nine o'clock in the morning, after spending a couple of hours getting their papers in order. There were three interrogators working in shifts: two lieutenant colonels, Choi and Hong, and a Major Kim, just to confuse the name situation. A second interpreter, Tal, came along to spell Lee.

The interrogation took place in my room. I sat on a straight chair (which had been hand-made by somebody who hated the human race and wanted to make all members of it uncomfortable) facing a table, with one of the interrogators on the other side. The interpreter also sat in a straight chair, at one side; and a guard usually stood, holding his sub-machine gun. When Colonel Kim came in now and then to see how they were getting along, he'd loll in one of the easy chairs. The room was icy—I would guess the temperature at about thirty-three degrees above zero—and the Koreans all wore heavy overcoats. I started out in my summer suit, and sock-footed. In all Korean houses the removal of shoes is a prerequisite to polite entry. To me, it was even more important to have my shoes off, for my infected left foot had not been treated and was now the size of a small balloon. My weight loss had left no padding on my hip bones, and when that home-made chair became unbearable I would sit on both hands, which also swelled to twice their normal size.

Lieutenant Colonel Choi began the questioning, using a prepared list of inquiries, mostly about military matters. The session lasted four hours, broken only when I had to go to the latrine, at which times a guard accompanied me.

Choi started easily, and typically. Who, he wanted to know, had been the assistant commander and the artillery commander when I had the 7th Division in South Korea in the autumn of 1948? I asked him if he had not read the newspapers. Those names had been in them, numerous times, but I couldn't remember them, certainly, after such a long time.

Incidentally, Colonel Kim had prefaced the actual interrogation by giving me a small and informative lecture. More than forty members of the South Korean Assembly, he told me, had come north voluntarily and were now enrolled in the Communist cause. Furthermore, he had absolute proof that the war had been started on the orders of General MacArthur. This "proof" consisted of a typed statement, allegedly made by a man (whose name I don't remember now) who had been in the South Korean government as one of the various ministers. The statement declared that he (the statement signer) knew Syngman Rhee had gone to Tokyo early in June and had received orders to begin the war, to invade North Korea prior to July 1. I repeat these claims endlessly and to the point of boredom because these were essential parts of the Communists' carefully prepared "proof"—for the benefit of their own people rather than the international community—that South Korea had started the war. Through tiresome and endless repetition of such trash, they probably did succeed in convincing most North Koreans that they were fighting a defensive battle.

Colonel Kim also showed me a photograph of John Foster Dulles, standing in a trench with U. S. officers and South Korean soldiers and pointing to something out of the camera's range. This, said Kim, was further proof. Dulles was pointing north, telling the South Koreans where to attack, giving instructions for the invasion.

I don't remember what I said to all this. I'm sure it wasn't important, because to this day I don't know exactly why you go about refuting absolute absurdities or lies so bald. Once the lie or the absurdity has transcended the whole realm of reasonableness, there simply is no reasonable answer.

Kim also made a great point of dates. North Koreans, he claimed, had done no fighting until June 26, although the ROK troops had invaded North Korea on June 25. I didn't know what I was talking about, he said, when I gave him the date of June 25 for the start of the southern invasion. Well, for a while I just listened to this, but finally he made me lose my temper. I said, "Now listen, you can do a lot of things, but to try to tell me, a military man, that a six-pronged invasion, including amphibious operations, was nothing more than a counterattack is just plain dumb. As far as the South Koreans being ordered by us to start the war, the whole idea is absurd. Nobody would conceivably order a war started when all the top officers were out of the country. You may take me for a damn fool, but I'm not that silly."

Nevertheless, he continued, then and later, to spend hours trying to convince me the South Koreans had started the war.

Lieutenant Colonel Choi spent a long time on the 1948 organization of the 7th Division. I don't know whether he didn't realize that American general officers seldom stay in any one division job two years, or whether the questions were merely a warm-up. But the answers could not possibly have made the slightest difference in the fall of 1950. He also wanted me to tell him the names of the Republic of Korea chiefs of staff (there had been three in about the same number of weeks at the start of the war), ROK division commanders, and the location of ROK divisions at the time I was captured. Some of this information I actually did not have; and about the rest of it I developed a convenient lack of memory.

Then we moved to tack number two. Choi told me how

aggressive ROK division commanders were, how all of them but one had a Japanese Army background. He proceeded to name each division commander, each corps commander, and the various chiefs of staff, telling me what they had done for the Japanese, where they had served. He gave me a detailed dossier on every man, including his relatives and what jobs they held. The information was complete, even to the fact that Lee Heung Koon, one of the South Korean generals whom they apparently hated with especial fervor, had as a young lieutenant taken a blood oath of fealty to the Japanese emperor.

These were things far beyond any information I had ever had about the South Korean generals. Why he wanted answers from me when he had seemingly complete records in front of him is a little hard to understand, but we spent hours on this line of inquiry.

Then he shifted gears. What secret weapons did we have? Were we going to use the atom bomb? What would be our target? (Obviously they were scared to death that we might use it.) How did our airplanes home on a target? How did they find their way? What types of planes did we have in the Far East? How many airfields in Japan? (He knew about a good many I had not known were in operation again.) The questions went on and on, and I almost wore out those vocal cords which form the words, "I don't know." I was tempted to manufacture a few secret weapons just for his benefit, but resisted. The trouble with that sort of lying is that we might actually have some of the things I dreamed up. In war things happen very fast. So I said nothing, although I could have created some dillies out of my imagination.

We stopped a few minutes for lunch, and then Lieutenant Colonel Hong took over. He was a big, well-built Korean, weighing perhaps a hundred and eighty pounds. Hong was a labor specialist, and I learned from his questions that he had been in Seoul, helping to organize strikes and sabotage, when I was military governor. He boasted that he had never been to second school (meaning high school) but was nevertheless a well-read Marxist, knew the Communist Manifesto by heart, and could quote the Geneva Convention (on the treatment of prisoners in war and allied matters) by paragraph. When I protested that as a prisoner of war, under the Geneva Convention, I could not be questioned except about my name, rank, and serial number, he stated, quoting paragraph so-and-so, that in special cases prisoners could be required to give further information. I was a special case, he said, because I was a war criminal, so he could question me about the 1947-48 acts that had made me one.

I was getting fairly well accustomed to this title of "war criminal." Both Colonel Kim and General Pak had used it earlier; and Pak had added that as military governor I had been responsible for the deaths of "many patriots." I could have said that most of those killed might have been patriots to him but were also murderers and wreckers, but it hardly seemed worth while at the time.

Hong's questioning started with the massacre of policemen and their families at Taegu, a 1946 event that had been one of the low spots in our early occupation of Korea. About this he wanted to know who was to blame, why some American officers in the area were transferred—all the details. I couldn't be of much help to him. In 1946 I had been in Leavenworth, Kansas, and Korea still had been only a remote spot on the map to me.

From that episode he went through virtually every event up until the time the war started, with special emphasis on the wave of railroad sabotage that had disrupted our communications in February 1948, when I had been governor. In each case he obviously was trying to put the whole onus on the military and on American officials—especially me. We went over and over the guerrilla campaign on Cheju island, the South Korean Army mutiny, and the railroad strikes that had occurred while I was in Korea; we also went over and over things that had occurred before I came or after I left. Why had I sent troops and police to Cheju-do? Why had I imprisoned railroad and streetcar strikers? Why had I arranged the elections of 1948 in the manner I had?

During this session I permitted myself to argue occasionally; on military matters I had said almost nothing. But Hong's absurdities succeeded in making me angry—among them, more about the United States ordering the war started. Again I stated, "That's nonsense on the face of it. Even if we ever planned to do anything that silly, we certainly wouldn't do it when our troops were all over Japan on maneuvers. If we were going to start a war deliberately, which we never do, at least we'd be ready. We wouldn't have to scurry around after it started in order to get ships to carry our army to the fighting."

At last we had twenty or thirty minutes for supper. I was eating as well as the rest of them, but never had much time to do it. I don't think they were deliberately attempting to make me sick. It was just that they had no hospital facilities or decent medical treatment, and very little food. Actually I think they believed they should get me well, so that they could get more out of me.

In the evening Major Kim took over, with the best-prepared notes and the most searching questions of the three. He concentrated on questions concerning the economics of South Korea—why we had not built more industries, why we brought in food for the Koreans rather than more instruments of food production, why we hadn't constructed fertilizer plants but were exploiting the country.

I said once, "That's just your opinion."

He immediately became wildly angry. "You're not cooperating! You're toadying to rank. You're very nice when a colonel talks to you, and not too bad when a lieutenant colonel talks, but you won't cooperate with a mere major."

The techniques of the questioners had one thing in common. A question frequently consisted of a statement, paragraphs long, followed by three words: "What's your opinion?"

For example, Major Kim spent hours telling me about unemployment in the United States, the defects of capitalism and so-called free enterprise, the ills of our country.

Finally, tiring of this, I said, "Have you ever been to the United States?"

He said he had not.

I said, "And you're trying to tell me about things I was born and raised with! I know more about the political structure of the United States than you do, and more about conditions than you do. You're young. When you grow up, maybe you'll learn something, but I'm old enough to be your father. Talk about being ignorant! You're the ignorant one." I didn't tell him, "I can sing louder than you," but I suppose I might as well have done so.

He jumped up. "I'll have you know," he said, "that I have my doctor's degree, and I got it by writing on the political and economic situation of the United States. I was a professor of economics at Kim Il Sung University, but the Inmun Gun thought so highly of my ability that they made me a major when the war started."

Perhaps I would have been more impressed if my hands

hadn't hurt so much from sitting on them, and if I hadn't needed to go to the toilet just then. I went.

Major Kim kept it up for his full four hours, and he had information that made some of the questions hard to answer. He had an annual report from the Chosen National Bank and referred to it frequently. He would say, "Here in 1938 there were so many *chung-bo* (equivalent to a hectare, or two and a half acres) under cultivation, but in 1948, when you were military governor, there were so many less. Why was that? Here you talk about feeding the people, but you have less land under cultivation and more people unemployed. You come over here, you bring the people food, but you make paupers out of the population. You didn't give them work, didn't establish any industry, or give them the means of production. The reason was, you wanted to import your own matches, your own cigarette lighters, your own pencils. Here in North Korea we make those things for ourselves. What is your opinion?"

He was a smart boy and he had enough facts to make a fairly good case—especially when I was sitting there with nothing to refer to, no figures to compete with his.

But finally he too wilted, and Lieutenant Colonel Choi came back, fresh as a daisy, with more questions about military matters. The interpreters had a rougher time than the interrogators, because there were only the two of them; they had to work shift and shift.

As I relate this, I can't be sure just which questions were asked in which session, or the exact division among the three questioners; but I do remember that Choi emphasized questions about the air war a great deal. Why did we have fields on Okinawa? What was our objective? Obviously he thought I was the most stupid general officer he'd ever encountered.

Finally I said, "Well, you were lucky. So far as division commanders are concerned, you were fighting the second team when the war started. But we'll have the first string in presently—perhaps we do now, for all I know—and then it'll be a different story. You have to remember that all American generals are not as dumb as I am. You just happened to catch the dumbest."

I got Hong's attentions again in the middle of the night, then the special ministrations of Colonel Kim, who interrupted the questioning for an hour to reprimand me for failing to answer questions. I still was not cooperating. While he talked my teeth were chattering, and this seemed to annoy him. I also was shivering.

The colonel said, "What are you shivering for, making your teeth go that way for? Are you cold?"

I said, "Yes, I'm a little chilly."

"This isn't cold," he said. "This isn't cold at all. Take off your coat. Take off your shirt. Take off your trousers and your undershirt. I'll show you what it means to be cold."

I ended up in my shorts. The temperature was still thirty-three degrees.

Then Choi went back to work. After an hour, during which Colonel Kim departed, Choi also was annoyed by my teeth chattering, because he said, "You may put on your undershirt." I could see the pattern now. Choi was to be the kind person, my only friend during this endurance contest, while Colonel Kim (who had already shouted too much to pretend to be kind now) would play the part of the meanie. It's an old police interrogation technique that has whip-sawed many a criminal into a confession.

The undershirt felt wonderful, even though it was only a cotton T-shirt, and I was allowed to keep it on until Colonel

Kim returned an hour or so later. Then I went back to shorts only once more. I didn't get the T-shirt again during the entire questioning.

There were breaks for meals—when I got nothing to eat except soft and watery chook, which left my mouth filled with white flakes, like alkali—but the Choi-Hong-Kim, Kim-Choi-Hong-Kim succession never stopped for sixty-eight hours. The only other breaks I got were when I'd yell "Benjo," and run for the latrine outside the church. A guard always went with me, to see that I didn't loiter; and usually they lived right up to their orders. One enlisted man was a little kinder than the others, and when he was along I could steal a few seconds outside to stop and pick up chestnuts that had fallen from the trees. I ate them on the spot while he conveniently looked the other way, or hid them behind the cushions of the overstuffed chair in my room.

Then Colonel Kim called a halt, after using the last hour himself to give me information. This consisted of his opinion that I would not cooperate, that I was a dog and a robber, "and," he said, "I'm going to treat you like a dog." He ordered the guards to take away the medicine, which had seemed to be doing me a little good, and to move my cot out into the guards' big room, where it was left in the middle of the floor.

Colonel Kim said, "No more washing. You can't wash, you dog! You can have one blanket and sleep over there in a corner on the floor. We're going to let you have some rest, but you'd better think it over and realize that you must cooperate. You want to remember that it's getting colder. If you fail to cooperate, we not only won't give you any clothes, we'll keep you outdoors."

I'm not sure whether this was the time that he threatened

to have my tongue cut out, but he did at one time. I said, "Go ahead and cut it out. Then you won't be able to make me talk." After that I heard nothing more of that particular threat.

I had no trouble getting to sleep on the smooth boards of the floor. During the sixty-eight hours I had been allowed no sleep, and the guard would yell at me or kick me with his bare foot if I dozed in the straight chair. But I had been asleep only a few minutes when somebody tapped me with his foot until I awoke again. The awakening was for breakfast, which consisted of more sticky rice and an apple. I slept most of that day and that night, rolling off the bare floor onto the rug when the guard wasn't watching too closely.

The next morning at eight, here came the boys again. Hong was the lead-off man, and Exhibit A was an alleged captured South Korean government report of the suppression measures taken against guerrillas and Communists in 1949, including the burning of forty thousand homes, the slaying of large numbers of guerrillas and sympathizers, and the loss of many police officers and soldiers. Also, he had a large photograph of one guerrilla's head, impaled on a pole. What, he wanted to know, was my conclusion about that?

I didn't have any. I had been in Japan that year.

Then we shifted back a year, to Cheju-do and photographs taken of me with anti-guerrilla leaders there. Guerrillas had constantly hampered our occupation government and the new South Korean government on this island off the southwest tip of the peninsula, and the isolation of the place made control quite difficult. When I was governor I sent both constabulary troops and police detachments there to try to restore order; but for a time it seemed to me that they were fighting each other rather than the bandits in the hills. On an inspection trip, Colonel Rothwell Brown discovered evidence that civilian women had been killed without trial, and I sent a summary court-martial officer down. He tried several policemen, who were given prison terms of twenty-five years each.

At another time I went to the island myself, taking the leaders of Korean constabulary, police, and civil administrations just to make sure they did issue orders which would stop the bloody confusion. Even with this effort the election of 1948 was badly botched (the only place in Korea where frauds were completely obvious) and ballot boxes were stolen and would-be voters intimidated. As a result, I was forced to declare the election void on the island, and to order it held again.

After the South Koreans took over their own government trouble continued on the island. In October 1948 the 14th ROK Regiment was ordered to embark from Yosu; instead, mutineers killed many of their own loyal officers and started to take over that part of South Korea, at the extreme southern tip of the peninsula. Immediately other ROK forces, led by Brigadier General Song Ho, were sent to quell the mutiny. There was a bitter battle; and after the loyal ROK had won it, several of the mutiny leaders were executed summarily. Others escaped into the mountains and headed up guerrilla units, which continued to harass the South Korean government up to the war, then started cooperating with the Communists from the north.

Hong and Choi, at Sunan, went over and over these events, trying to prove that I had ordered executions and had been responsible for the entire mess. I got tired of all this conversation and said, "Well, you're wasting your time trying to get me to admit responsibility for things that happened when I was military governor. It's your language, not mine; and you have all the names and the figures. I can't possibly put up a factual defense, having nothing to work with, so go ahead and shoot me. I never sanctioned the killing of any soldier or civilian without trial; but if any were killed without trial, in the final analysis it was my responsibility. Anything that occurred while I was military governor I was responsible for. Why don't you just shoot me? Don't wait and go through the farce of a trial."

This wasn't exactly bravery, in the ordinary sense, because I was quite certain that nothing I said or failed to say would make any difference—I was sure they were going to shoot me anyhow.

Once more they shifted the emphasis, to the national elections of 1948. The top exhibit was a series of photographs of police officers lining up men and women, presumably to force them to vote. The photos probably were from one of the isolated border towns from which we had received reports of this sort at the time.

But so far as I was concerned that had been the only free, secret-ballot election in Korea in four thousand years, and I was proud of the way it had been handled. I had organized local committees, made speeches telling the people of the importance of voting, held endless conferences. For the election period itself, I had stopped all military government work and sent out more than a thousand people to visit all the different voting areas, making sure that just such incidents as these did not occur, that no one was forced to vote. We did not have the personnel to keep someone at each polling place all the time it was open, but we covered all the major spots and at least visited practically every other spot.

During the preparations and the election itself some eighty-two policemen and sixty election officials had been killed, and there had been fires in polling places and other property damage—but on the whole it had been a free election, held by a people who did not know anything about elections. The killings and the burnings, I felt, had almost all been done either by Communists or at the instigation of Communists who were ready to do anything to prevent the new government from being organized—just as later they were willing to start a war to prevent it from functioning.

In the questioning, these boys at Sunan weren't interested in any facts other than that I had been responsible for holding an election, therefore for all the official deaths. I remember Choi saying, "Why do you think these officials were killed? Because the people wanted to vote? No, it was because they were being forced to vote."

I began to have some idea, in these hours, what the term "war criminal" can mean—which is anything the people applying it wish it to mean. And I could talk all day—about the fact that eighty per cent of the people registered and ninety per cent of the registered voters cast a ballot, or about any other figures I wished—without making the slightest impression.

Oddly enough, in the middle of a session in which I was being called a robber and a running dog of Wall Street, one of my interrogators—Hong, I think—paid me a sudden compliment.

"One thing we have to admit about you, though," he said, "and that is that you never violated Korean womanhood. You're a thief and a murderer, but you never had a concubine." Apparently their excellent prewar intelligence system in Seoul had interested itself in all sorts of details.

It was also Hong who informed me that it was only a matter of time before the United States would be Communist, and he read off a list of the principal offices of the Federal Bureau of Investigation and their territories.

This sort of thing might ordinarily be dismissed as common knowledge, but it did frighten me a little. Several times I had been warned that I should be thinking about my family, who might not be as safe as I imagined in Berkeley, California. Both General Pak and Colonel Kim had warned me that if I didn't start cooperating, something unpleasant would certainly happen to Mildred or to my children.

As the second interrogation continued I began to notice a few amusing things. One was a sure way to make the interviewer—any of them—hit the ceiling. So many of these questions actually were long statements, harangues, and the only real query was at the end: "What is your conclusion?"

I'd just say, "I have no conclusion," and the interrogator would blow his top. He'd worked a long time over that complicated statement, and he hated to waste it for just one measly little four-word answer.

The questioning did not go on steadily. There were periods of an hour or two when the interrogators were out of the room, but they didn't do me much good. My hands were swollen to ham size, my hip bones were like two boils, and sitting down at all was continuous misery; but I still had to sit there as if being questioned. If I nodded the guard would shout or kick me with his bare feet. And in these silence periods I always had trouble in getting the guard to allow me to go to the toilet. I'd say "Benjo," but frequently he would shake his head in a negative. I couldn't have that, so I'd just go out anyhow. That left him no choice but to come with me or shoot me, and I guess he'd have been in the soup if he shot me.

In that church at Sunan I became so acclimated to continuous cold that I grew a whole new set of ideas about comfort. And ever since I've been home I want the windows wide open when other people are shivering. I freeze out all my friends if I'm not careful.

Sometime during the second interrogation Colonel Kim came back to take an active hand. He said, "You say you have no knowledge of America's intentions in the Far East, you have no knowledge of the plan of maneuver, you have no knowledge of secret weapons. But you do have knowledge of the defense plans for Japan. You could not possibly have held the positions you've had in your Army if you didn't know these defense plans."

He worked on that for two or three hours, yelling, storming, and asking the same questions over and over. While he was at it I just sat there. Once he screamed, "You're sleeping with your eyes open!"

That was a good one. The interpreter had trouble with it, but I got a small chuckle anyhow. I wished I were doing just that.

After Kim got all through that time, he said that he was getting tired and if I didn't start cooperating soon, they'd take measures to see that I did. Up to now, he added, they had not done anything to me that our own intelligence officers didn't do. He was just using our own CIC methods.

The other three interrogators were tired too, so they let me go back to sleep on the floor—without my blanket. I was keeping track, just for my own satisfaction, and they had not done so well: it had taken only forty-four hours to wear out the three of them, plus Colonel Kim. This was about four a.m. I slept on the floor most of the day and was looking forward to another night's rest. I felt I wasn't in too much trouble yet. I'd had experience in staying awake before. During a New

Year's Eve attack in Europe, in 1944, I worked four days without sleep, and I knew I could do that well again; I thought, "Well, if they get over five or six days, I'll probably just go to sleep in spite of them."

This Communist army life was not all gravy for the enlisted men. Whenever they were awake but not actually on guard, they spent their time doing their Communist doctrine homework or holding classes. Sometimes even the duty guard would be working on his papers, copying something while he kept one eye on me. They copied by the hour, and most of them got paper for the work by stealing it calmly from the desk in the interpreters' little room behind my own. They also lifted any cigarettes anyone had been careless enough to leave on a desk or in a drawer. For entertainment they practiced throwing rope bonds on each other, getting so they could tie a prisoner's hands tight enough to cut off the circulation in a few seconds.

I did not get that night's rest. About nine p.m. I was awakened. Nobody said we were going to dance again, but I got the general idea. Major Kim came on stage, then Hong, then Choi, but they all showed signs of running out of questions. I would be left alone with a guard for hours, still having to sit in that uncomfortable chair and being kept awake, but at least not having to listen to any more of those fancy arguments. Whenever they'd think up a new question or one more way to ask an old one over again, one of them would come in and work on me for a while.

Now and then they'd vary the procedure by giving me another lecture about the American War between the States, reminding me how much the United States had resented British aid to the Confederate States, and what a furor there had been over a British threat to interfere.

"This," they said, "is our civil war, not yours. We're not attacking America, we're not bombing America, we have no designs on America, and yet you come over here and interfere in our civil war. You're fighting in our house." That was a constant refrain.

In this manner we passed the night, the next day, and most of the next night—thirty-two hours. About the second midnight Colonel Kim took over once more, for what was to be the last interrogation. He was in a standing-up, table-pounding mood, and got himself so worked up that phlegm flew out of his mouth. Tal, whom I liked because he just translated in a monotone, like a machine, never mirroring the shoutings and rantings of the interrogator, was the interpreter.

Colonel Kim was talking about the murder of innocents by our aircraft when I broke in, "I've seen atrocities committed by your troops worse than anything you've mentioned. I've seen our men captured, then murdered in cold blood while they had their hands tied behind them, at Chochiwon. And I talked to a lieutenant who saw your men drive prisoners ahead of them, to try to get others to surrender—then shoot them when we opened fire to repel an attack."

This so infuriated Colonel Kim that he yelled, "Close your eyes! I'm going to spit in your face."

I should have said, "Spit, you creep, and I'll knock you on your ——." But I just wasn't up to it physically. I said, "Close my eyes? Go on and spit! You've been spitting in my eyes for the last half-hour."

I don't know how the interpreter told him that, but it must have been accurate. I thought Kim was going to have apoplexy.

He said, "All right, this is the end. We're going to torture you."

▶▶▶▶◀◀◀◀

CHAPTER VIII

A Gun That Wouldn't Fire

Colonel Kim leaned back. "Do you know," he asked, "how we torture people?"

I said, "No."

He described a process in which water is forced into either the mouth or the rectum, under pressure. The latter, he said, "forces everything in you, everything, to come out through your mouth. It's very sickening."

I said, "That sounds good to me. The shape I'm in, you won't have to use much pressure. I think that'll kill me quickly. That sounds all right."

He had been fuming, but now he spluttered. "Sometimes," he said, "we drive bamboo splinters up under the fingernails and then set fire to them."

The setting fire didn't sound too bad to me, but that business of driving the splinters hurt just thinking about it. I laughed at him, but perhaps the laughter was a little forced. I was fearful he might be telling the truth.

"Also," he said, "we have electrical treatments. The building where we use these, our laboratory, is just a mile from here, and in the morning we'll take you there."

It was almost morning.

He said, "You know that you're dead? Your own people think you're dead, so we can do anything to you that we want to do. Under torture you'll probably die, but not before you've given us the information we want. We will get that. You probably won't live but your death won't be too fast for you to give me the information I want—in detail. I've never failed yet. Do you want to write a last message?"

I said, "No."

He said, "Then you must sign a statement that you do not want to write a last message."

It was another one of those foolish things. I said, "Okay, I'll write a last message. I'll write a last letter to my family."

He gave me paper and a pencil, and I wrote:

Dear Mildred, June, and Bill, I was physically captured on 25 August and have been a prisoner of war ever since. I did not surrender but was physically overpowered. Before I was captured I wandered in the hills for thirty-five days, without food. As a result I am terribly ill and do not think that I will live much longer. Therefore this is my last letter. June, do not delay in making your mother a grandmother. Bill, remember that integrity is the most important thing of all. Let that always be your aim. Mildred, remember that for twenty-four years you have made me very, very happy.

That was all.

When it was translated for him Colonel Kim said, "What? Why do you say that you are so ill? That you're going to die? Why don't you tell them we're going to kill you?"

I was a little out of patience. I swear too much, but perhaps this time it was justified. I said, "Why, you dumb bastard! I know you'd never send out any letter which said that. If I'm going to write a letter to my family I want them to get it. I didn't write that for your benefit. I wrote that so my family would know I was dead, and what I was thinking about. You're so damn dumb! Now you can kill me and it'll never be held against you. You've got everything you want. I've stated that if I die it's by natural causes."

He just looked at me. He looked at me as if I were the most stupid individual he'd ever seen in his life. He said, "All right. In the morning we'll go to the laboratory," and he stomped out.

Remarkably, a guard had brought back my blanket. I rolled up in it, in the corner on the floor, and after a little while scooted over on the rug, where it was a tiny bit warmer.

One guard always walked a post outside this church building and another always was in my room, each of them armed with a sub-machine gun. But they had one extra gun, one of those regular sub-machine guns with a circular ammunition drum. Through cracks in the partition between my room and the guard's room I had noticed that this extra gun always sat in a corner between the wall of the building and the partition, on the side opposite me. The only furniture in that guards' room was my cot, which had been left there when Colonel Kim ordered it taken away from me. The guards all slept on the floor. In my room several straight chairs still remained, the table, and also the two big overstuffed chairs, although I never had a chance to use them. When no officer was present, a room guard frequently flopped down in one of them. Sometimes he dozed.

This morning while I was lying on the floor I thought, "Well, this is the day. If they take me up to that torture building, I'm so weak that I might say something, I might tell them something before I die. I've got to get that gun."

This was not a new idea. Previously I'd made vague plans that when I was strong enough I would try to get it, somehow, for an escape attempt. But at this time I couldn't have made a hundred yards even if nobody interfered with me. I thought, "Well, that's out now, but I've still got to get the gun. I've got to knock myself off, and fast, before they torture me." The trouble was, you see, I did know the defense plans for Japan.

The guard in my room slumped down in the chair and obligingly went to sleep almost immediately. That left the twenty guards in the other room. If they all went to breakfast in the cook-shack next door and the guard on duty still didn't waken, the time would be ripe.

About five-thirty a.m. they all trooped out. Colonel Kim, Choi, Major Kim, and Hong all slept in the cook-shack—or so I thought. The interpreters were in their own room, with the door shut. When the guards left I slid quietly out of my blanket and started crawling.

At Taejon months before I had examined one of those guns with the drum magazine. Clarke had taken a captured sample apart and together we had succeeded in reassembling it. I felt I was quite good with that double-triggered rig. I thought, "When I get it, I'll fire one short burst out of the window in the general direction of the cook-shack. If old Colonel Kim's on the ball he'll come fogging out of there to see what it's all about. The second burst will get him. Then I'll stick the muzzle in my mouth and finish the job—but I'll have Kim's company when I go. I wouldn't want to miss that."

As I crawled to the door between the two rooms I glanced up at the sleeping man in the chair. I could get only a partial look at him. But I was startled. The man sleeping there looked like Hong. I thought briefly, "Is he doing some of the guarding now?" but didn't take time to make sure. I went on around the partition and reached the corner, passing close to the cot on the way but not being able to see on top of it from my crawling position.

I got the gun in my hands and came up to a kneeling position. I tried to pull the bolt back, but it jammed. I kept working at it, but must have made some noise.

There was a bellow behind me. From the cot—not the chair—the one-hundred-and-eighty-pound Colonel Hong swung down and rushed me. Instead of sleeping on the floor of the cook-shack where he belonged, like any good member of the proletariat, this big capitalist-thinking character had grabbed an opportunity to sleep on a soft mattress.

I swung the gun. There was no time for Colonel Kim now, but I could still get Hong—or could have, if I had solved that jammed bolt. Hong was a brave man. He charged right into the barrel of that gun—and the damned thing still wouldn't fire.

Hong hit me from the front, my room guard from one side. Then there were Koreans all over me, although I don't know where in the world they all came from. In seconds it was finished. I couldn't move my arms or legs, and then I was being marched back into my own room. Nobody beat me, however, or did anything else after they had overpowered me. I was seated in the straight chair, and was still sitting there when Lee, the interpreter, came in, his face blanched. The first thing he said was, "Why, General, you would have killed *me!*"

I said, "No, Lee, I didn't want to kill you. I wanted to get that son-of-a-gun Kim, and myself. They said they were going to torture me this morning, and I didn't intend to be tortured."

Lee hadn't been there when Colonel Kim was ranting, so I don't know how he was so sure, but he said, "Oh, they didn't say that. They will never torture you. General, you must never take your own life. There's always hope. But I'm very much afraid you would have killed me, General." He went away, shaking his head.

I never saw Colonel Kim again. I can only speculate about whether he was somehow disgraced by my suicide attempt (that would have been *too* bad); whether he simply gave me up as hopeless; or whether, somehow, he was bluffed. I do hope he didn't drop dead. He and I have a few things I still want to discuss, and I'd hate to think that there won't be another chance.

They left me sitting in the chair, for once without breakfast, until midmorning, when Lieutenant Colonel Choi came in. Guards took the drawstring out of my shorts—the only clothing I had—and removed from the room everything else with which I might conceivably have harmed myself—string, my knife and fork, everything. Thereafter I ate with a spoon, which was removed immediately after I laid it down.

Choi said, "I want you to know that there is an increased guard, both here and in the village. You're to be tried for armed insurrection. How did you happen to do this? You were trying to escape, weren't you?"

I said, "In my condition I don't think I could have. I wanted to kill Colonel Kim, and then I was going to kill myself."

He said, "No, you were trying to escape. That's armed insurrection."

He called in a guard—and it was the one boy who had been kind to me, the one who had allowed me to pick up and hide chestnuts. Choi said, "Was this man asleep when you went out?"

I said, "No. Colonel Hong was asleep in that chair when I went out." I still thought this, at the time.

He said, "No. Colonel Hong was on the bed in the other room. He's the man who took the gun away from you. This is the man who was on guard and went to sleep."

If I hadn't said already that Hong had been asleep in the chair, there might have been a chance to cover up for the kindly guard, but now the fat was in the fire and there was nothing I could do. I said, "I don't know anything about that. I just crawled out there and got the gun. I don't know who was on guard or who was sleeping. But whoever the man on the bed was, he should be commended. You tell your chief that he's a brave man, because if I could have made that gun work he wouldn't be talking now."

The poor little guard was led out. I can only presume that he, my friend, was shot for being asleep.

That afternoon a lieutenant showed up to take direct charge of the guard, which had been run by sergeants before. In the evening Choi came in once more, and his attitude had changed. "Colonel Kim has gone," he told me, "and I'm going to have charge of you. You're a sick man and we're going to make you a patient. Before we do anything else, we must make you well."

I got chook for dinner again, but other things went back to the pre-interrogation system. My cot, sheets, and blanket were brought back into the room, and I was allowed to sleep or get up as I chose. My clothes also were brought back. The next morning another doctor came to see me and gave my chest another resounding thumping. The only explanation I can give for this standard procedure by all Korean doctors is that they see so much tuberculosis, they just automatically assume any patient must have it. He left some more medicine for me, and I went back to bed again.

Choi was a changed man from then on, kindly and friendly. But on October 1 he said, "As a personal favor, will you write a letter for me? I'm leaving tomorrow night, and I'm supposed to get some information from you. Will you write what you think you could improve if you were to be military governor of South Korea again? What do you think you did well? Also, your personal opinion of Syngman Rhee. This will be a personal favor to me so my superiors will think I've accomplished something; and if you do it, I assure you that you'll go to a prisoner-of-war camp right away." This had been my reiterated request.

It never was a matter of more than technical interest in North Korea, but the Geneva Convention sets up definite rules for the treatment of all prisoners—adequate food, clothing, and reasonable care. A prisoner may be questioned legally only about his name, rank, and serial number. Officers, says the Convention, "shall be treated with due regard for their rank and age." Where possible, orderlies shall be provided for officers who normally would have them in their own armies. The holding power is required to provide advances against military pay—in the case of general officers, classification number five, the local equivalent of seventy-five Swiss francs—approximately eighteen dollars—per month. Nothing is said specifically, however, about the size of camps in which they shall be held. On this one point, about which I made the most complaint, the Koreans technically were within their rights. So long as I had a prison-camp address, and the camp was in a place providing reasonable safety for me, the Convention did not require them to house me with other prisoners. Needless to say, however, I never saw anything like the required pay or orderly service, and whether my treatment corresponded to my age and rank can be judged from the details of it.

On October 2 I wrote two notes for Choi. In the first I said that I was proud of our record in agriculture, the rehabilitation of cotton and silk mills, the production of paper, the building up of railroad and shipping lines.

I did not write then, but might add now, that I would do a couple of other things. The first would be to emphasize to our own people the terrific harm done by thoughtlessness. Through all the questioning and my many subsequent conversations with intelligent Koreans who had chosen communism after knowing something about our government in South Korea, ran one refrain: they resented being called "gooks," and the slighting references to their race and color more than any of our policies, ill advised or not. Again and again I was told that this man or that one had come north because he had decided he never could get along with people who called him a "gook," or worse, among themselves; because he resented American attentions to Korean women; or because he hated to see foreigners riding in his country in big automobiles while he and his family had to walk.

When I was governor a Korean newspaper, in a friendly news story, once called me "the general who walks," because of my habit of walking to the office—for exercise, not political effect—nosing around the streets of Seoul, and hunting for pheasant in the hills south of Yongdong-po. At the time I thought the title was amusing; but before I left Korea in 1953 I realized that walking had been one of the best things I did in that job and much more effective than some of my carefully planned activities. If I were governor again I would certainly walk more—and so would a lot of other people in the American part of the government. And use of the term "gook," or its many equivalents, by Americans, would be an offense for military punishment.

On this day, however, I wrote no more about what I would change. To satisfy Choi's request about President Rhee I wrote: "I feel that he is a devoted patriot and lover of his country. He is a man who has devoted his whole life to a free and united Korea; and everything he does, he feels is in the best interests of his country."

These notes satisfied Choi, who departed the same day.

So did I, about ten p.m., in a great hurry. I got to take my two blankets, but the guards were in such a great hurry that they wouldn't even let me rescue my extra pair of shorts or a spare handkerchief, which were hanging on a clothesline outside the building to dry after being laundered.

Our vehicle was a small truck. Besides the passengers it carried a couple of iron safes, which had nothing to do with me except as nuisance value, for they constantly banged against my knees. Tal went along, a lieutenant, the driver, and three guards—U Eun Chur, Pack Chun Bong, and De Soon Yur. (These spellings, and many other transliterations of Korean words in this book, are phonetic, subject to varying interpretations.)

As we prepared to pull out, Lee said, "Good-by, General. Don't give up hope or try to kill yourself. You must live, and everything will be fine again, and you will see your family once more."

Of the two interpreters I liked Lee the less, but I think I may have done him an injustice. He shouted at me when the interrogators shouted, ranted when they ranted, but this may have been only to impress the Korean officers. Lee went to Pyongyang on October 10—this I learned much later—and surrendered to American troops when they took the city nine days later. Under interrogation he told a straight story of his experiences with me and gave American officials the first detailed word that I still was alive. I believe now that he was trying to help me all the time, even when he urged me to manufacture stories to tell the interrogators during those long questioning sessions. I'm rather ashamed that I doubted him.

I said good-by to him in front of the church that night. I should also have patted each of those chairs and given a really fond farewell to the mattress and cot. These were the last pieces of Western furniture I was to see for a long time.

We moved north in the truck, along with convoy after convoy of other trucks, all running at night and in a hurry. Traffic jams were common, and some of them, particularly near Sukchon, monumental. Nothing had been said to me about any change in the military situation, but anyone could tell that something had happened. This was a retreating army, getting out fast. I noticed the especially heavy traffic coming from the coastal areas, and now know they were pulling out in fear of another amphibious attack, such as the one made at Inchon.

It's not far to Huichon, about a hundred miles, but we were thirteen hours getting there. And on that cold night I was struck by the actual tenderness of the three guards, especially U Eun Chur, the senior sergeant, in trying to keep me warm by holding a blanket over my shoulders.

That trip was the first of many so similar that it is difficult to remember them individually; and U's kindness was almost my first experience with the many-sided, kind and cruel, inventive, clever, stupid, resilient, unpredictable Korean character. The Koreans I speak of are not the politicians or military commanders, but the farm hands and soldiers, cooks and prison guards, fine chess players and terrible watch-repairmen, the people who make communism possible. A good many things happened to me in the next months and years, but nothing more important than my opportunity to know these people as I never could have done in a lifetime as an uncaptured general. It may almost have been worth the three years.

The outstanding single characteristic of most Korean country-town hotels and ordinary Korean homes is that they have *no* furniture. I mean that literally. The Japanese run to pint-sized tables and low-slung lacquered cabinets, and the Chinese love screens and carved chests. The Korean does without any furniture whatever.

In Huichon that next day I slept in a Korean hotel, on the floor; and for most of a thousand nights thereafter I continued to sleep on floors—sometimes on concrete or clay with flues imbedded in it, and hot to the touch; occasionally on matting over wood, the typical Japanese-style floor; much of the time on hard-packed dirt.

The typical house of North Korea is a two-room structure with a kitchen. One room, about four by eight feet, is built below ground level, and one whole side of it is taken up by a sort of covered fireplace, open on the room side but topped with a flat clay or concrete cover, broken by three holes for cooking pots. Flues from the fireplace lead under the raised floors of the other two rooms, each about eight feet square, before the smoke escapes through a chimney. The kitchen is equipped with rice bowls and a stone water jar, in addition to the three cooking pots—one for rice, one for soup, and the third for water. One room may contain a closet, but nothing else. The walls are mud, reinforced with corn stalks; the roof is carefully thatched, the inside sometimes covered with paper

—and in between live the big Norway rats, happy in their burrowing place except when rains run down their tunnels and soften the paper underneath. Then the rats often fall through into the human living quarters, to the mutual upset of both parties. There may be a window or two, but rarely any glass.

In such houses, which varied only in minor details, I lived three years. More important, in such houses the people of North Korea live all the time. On those floors they sleep, eat, work endlessly, and pore, hour after hour, over the texts of communism: the works of Stalin and Engels and the devil's mixture of fact and fancy, half-truth and outright lies, that spreads the infection. That concoction is beautifully prepared for just such people, with thousands of years of hunger and back-breaking toil in their backgrounds, cold and sickness and death as constant companions, and not the slightest conception of ease or comfort such as we know.

One of the guards who left Sunan with me was De Soon Yur, and he was with me until a few weeks before I was repatriated. I came to know him well. If I were to try to change the mind of this convinced Communist and could bring him to the United States to accomplish it, I'm not sure that I'd bother to show him government buildings or legislatures at work, or even courts in which the accused has a chance for justice. Rather, I'd take De Soon Yur first of all to an American supermarket and walk with him past a hundred-foot meat counter. I'd like him to see in one minute more meat—*kogi,* in his language—than he has seen in his entire life. I'd like to take him to a Petaluma, California, poultry processing plant (the squawking and bloodiness wouldn't bother him at all), where he could watch a trainload of chickens come in, then go out to market. I'd like him to see the milking machines in a modern dairy, Kansas wheat elevators and an Iowa cornfield, a big knitting mill and a thousand sheep in a band.

I'm not sure that the *processes* of democracy would impress him or even interest him especially, for De Soon Yur is a practical man. If I could show him the *products* of democracy—this man whose father and grandfather were hungry, and who knits beautifully because he must, in order to have a new pair of socks or gloves—I think I might unmake a Communist very fast.

What I am trying to say is that a glowing ideal is hard to sell to a hungry man eight thousand miles away. What we need for Korea is something to compare favorably to the Communist promises of a hectare of land without excessive rent, rice without too much millet in it, or a pencil produced in a factory right in his home town.

However, I was not thinking of these things that day in Huichon, or that night, when we walked a few blocks to a Korean-Japanese house—that is, one that had both a room heated by an *onder* (under-floor flues) and one with no heat in it but *tatami* mats on the floor. This room could have been heated by a charcoal-burning *habachi* or a stove, but I saw very few of either of these conveniences in North Korea.

The night before, Tal again had assured me that we were going to a POW camp; now I asked about it once more, but was told, "I have been instructed to get you well and to restore your health. Then you will go to a POW camp. But first I must do everything in my power to get you well."

All this time I was unhappy at being kept away from a regular camp; but after I came home and read about the things that happened at those camps, I realized that I should have thanked my lucky stars that I was not in one of them.

I never lived as badly as the men in them lived most of the time.

I still had my two blankets and carried them from the hotel to the house myself, as my only luggage. My guards had only one blanket each but always slept in their clothing, which consisted of long cotton underwear, two or three pairs of trousers, and an equal number of shirts and sweaters. I was amazed by the layers of home-knit clothing they wore under their uniforms, which consisted only of trousers and a coat, with green tabs on their shoulders to show that they were members of the Security Forces, and a big T to show the rank of master sergeant—which virtually all of these and later guards were. Shirts were various, and so were shoes. The whole outfit could be called a uniform only by courtesy.

Tal seemed to be in charge of the group, although a lieutenant also was present; and while we were at Huichon he bought food with a lavish hand—chicken, hog liver, beef heart, eggs, and greens, in addition to the inevitable rice. We had no beverage (nor do most North Koreans) except *suhn-nuhn*, which is water boiled in the rice cooking pot after the rice has been removed but before the pot has been scraped. This is full of browned rice fragments and has a pleasant flavor. A bowl of this, taken with great slurpings of enjoyment, is the typical ending for a good Korean meal. If you ask for another bowl, you're looked at as if you were a pig.

I was too ill to enjoy much of the food, and disappointed the woman cooking for us when she prepared what was an obvious treat—sweet potatoes. In Korea it's always whole hog or none, so for that meal we had nothing but sweet potatoes. Each serving was six big ones. I had difficulty in eating two of the smaller ones, but I noticed that each guard ate his full six.

We stayed in Huichon ten days, and I about decided that this life as a prisoner was not too bad. The interpreter let me sit on a sunporch, in a spot where I could get the direct rays of the sun, which was warm in midday, even though this was October and the nights were becoming more and more chill. I'm a sun devotee, and this was real luxury to me. A doctor came to give my chest another thumping; he noticed that my hands and feet were swollen and suggested that kidneys might be at the root of my physical troubles. He lanced my infected left foot, heretofore untreated, and sent me some medicine, a salve, which cured it quickly.

To relieve boredom during the days I killed flies. I picked up each of the dead carefully, for we slept and ate on that floor.

Then a major visited us, and in his wake came two of the restrictive orders that I was to get to know so well. Apparently the guard had complained about the fact that I didn't sleep well at night; also that people might see me when I was sunbathing on the porch. Orders were issued that since I couldn't sleep well at night I must not lie down at all during the day—and this was enforced for more than eighteen months. I was also ordered to stay off the sunporch and forbidden to stand up inside the house. For eighteen months I could not stand up except to go from one spot to another, as my physical necessities dictated, or on order.

Housing already was at a premium in North Korea although the home-grounds war was just beginning in that area. But the Communist theory against private property fixed everything—simply by making every private home a public place to be used as needed. Soldiers moved into homes with families, or by moving families out. Travelers were billeted by police order wherever there was a square foot of space not actually being occupied by somebody else. I think the woman who cooked for us may actually have owned the house we were in; we were billeted there with no permission from her. In the middle of one night the household suddenly was increased by the arrival of a grandmother, two younger women, six children, and a major acting as escort for these families of some high government officials (whose names I never did learn). They all crowded into the Japanese room of the house, while my guards, the interpreter, and the lieutenant helped to occupy mine. Remember, this was about eight feet square. Previously I had been able to sleep over the warmest flue; now I was lucky to get room enough to lie down.

During the daylight hours I noticed that one or two United Nations light aircraft were almost constantly above us, as if on patrol; and during my last day at Huichon an air strike plunged down on the railroad area. The interpreter was in the center of town when the raid came. When he returned I asked him what the planes had been aiming for.

He said, "The railroad."

I said, "What did they get?"

"One car in the streets," he told me, "one house on a corner, and two women about four hundred yards from the railroad."

After the air strike trains continued to run.

That evening I heard a call which was to come frequently, "*Pahli, pahli, pahli!*" The rough translation is, "Hurry, hurry, hurry!" I packed up, which consisted of rolling my blankets, and presently the entire household except the cook walked to a police station, where we waited four hours until the same truck that had brought us to Huichon picked us up again. The women and children in the major's party also tried to get in. There simply was not room, so finally we pulled away without the grandmother, a two-year-old girl, the interpreter, the lieutenant, and one guard. The major, two guards, the driver, and I were the only adult males. We joined the jam of northbound traffic, which was steadily growing heavier. This was a retreat, fast becoming a rout. At midnight we headed for the mountains to the north.

Our truck was a very high vehicle, open-topped, loaded with luggage as well as the assorted human cargo. The cold was bitter, and I wrapped a blanket around my back to keep warm. After about two hours we came to a stop, blocked by a traffic jam ahead. We were halfway up a very steep mountain grade, with a two-hundred-foot drop to the right of the road. The major, the driver, and one guard walked ahead to investigate the delay, and the other guard stepped off the truck. I decided to rearrange my blankets around my shoulders. To shift position I stood up and stepped on the front seat, some seven feet from the ground. Then I yanked at the blankets behind me—and jerked my own feet right out from under me.

I pitched forward, could not free my hands, and landed on my head in the gravel. I rolled and went over the top of the cliff, grabbing for anything—and one scrub tree was where I needed it. I hung on, and the tree held. When I looked up I was about six feet from the top. A river was two hundred feet below.

Everyone on the truck began yelling and screaming, and in a moment U Eun Chur and the major both leaned over the brink. U reached down, and I scrambled partially up with his help. When the major reached down I assumed that he too would help me, but to my amazement he began slapping me around the head.

I swore at him, "What in the hell do you think you're doing?" I really spoke sharply, and it seemed to help, even though he didn't understand English. He stopped slapping me and gave me a hand until I got back on the road. My head was bleeding, but I was more scratched than anything else—and I wanted to kill that major with my bare hands. But again I just wasn't strong enough to try it. Instead I got back on the truck; and after a long time we moved ahead once more.

Since no one spoke English I had to wait until the interpreter rejoined us, five days later, to find out what in the world that major thought he was doing. The interpreter then explained, "He just lost his head and was very sorry. He thought you were trying to commit suicide, and he would have been very severely punished if anything had happened to you."

This occurred on the morning of October 13. In the early light I saw men in padded uniforms marching south along the road. They carried cooking utensils suspended from poles on their shoulders; and I'm quite sure now that they were Chinese troops. The location was about twenty miles north of Huichon.

Along the way I could see that the war was moving north almost as fast as we were. In a long valley leading toward Kanggye, a provincial capital, several villages were on fire, and aircraft were overhead frequently. Each time they appeared the truck would stop under a tree or beside an embankment, waiting until they passed. Thousands of civilians walked north along the highway; and from by-ways came whole cadres of unarmed youths, marching in military formation under the charge of a soldier or two, carrying pistols. It looked like a mass mobilization of every male between the ages of fourteen and fifty.

The escort major grunted in satisfaction every time we passed one of these groups, but when we saw the smoking villages his curses were quite clear, even though in Korean.

We stopped in Kanggye only for orders apparently, then drove on toward Manpo, reaching Choesin-dong, a suburb, that same day. Both Manpo, an industrial town with several large lumber mills, and this suburb, which is a railway junction, lie on the Yalu River, the border between North Korea and Manchuria.

My impression that the families with us were of some importance was bolstered when we were assigned billets. They were taken to one of the largest houses in this little town. Below the big house was a row of smaller places, perhaps built for railroad employees in the Japanese era; and I was taken to one of these. U and Pack, my two guards, went along. We were shown to a one-room house, with inside measurements of no more than six by six feet. The room was one of the filthiest I'd ever seen; and although it had a floor, I think the soil outside was cleaner. Part of the six-foot square was occupied by a closet, and the three of us used the rest for sleeping. Apparently our arrival had moved out a woman and her two-and-a-half-year-old child, because the child continued to crawl in and out of the room, and the woman cooked for us and once or twice came to get something out of the closet. A young man also stepped over us while we were sleeping and from the closet got out the uniform of a second lieutenant in the Security Forces. Rank may have its privileges in the North Korean Army, but they don't include keeping a roof over your wife's head. The guards borrowed some of the lieutenant's cigarettes while he was changing into his uniform. When they asked him for a light he gave it to them, without complaint.

I don't know where the woman and child went to sleep, but assume it must have been in one of the other row houses. She was still around the following morning, but made no move to feed us. After a long argument one of the guards went down toward the center of town and came back with some cooked pork fat and some sort of sweet roll, such as are served in Germany.

I had been thinking about escape, of course, and thought more and more about the possibilities as the North Koreans moved farther back and more of our planes appeared. But the hard fact was I still couldn't hope to get anywhere. Even the hundred-yard walk from the truck to the house had been enough to leave me panting, my heart pounding with exhaustion. On the way I had to rest several times. Still separated from an interpreter, I could only guess what was going on. My most important thought was, "Well, this is still all right, just so long as they don't start interrogating me again. I can't use any more of that Colonel Kim."

Oddly enough, there did not seem to be any great jam of refugees against the Chinese border. Roads had been thronged with families all the way from Huichon; but in the Manpo area I couldn't see that the population was terribly swollen.

After three more days in the six-by-six pigsty we moved to a house in Manpo proper, about three miles away. The officials' families got a heated room, but the guards and I shared a Japanese room, without even a habachi. Our breakfast that morning was the last of the food we had brought north in the truck, so Sergeant U went into town almost immediately. He spent most of the day trying to buy some rice. Finally he came back with a twenty-five-pound sack of it, and some garlic and pork fat. We had dinner about ten o'clock that night.

In each town and each new house we acquired some different woman to do the cooking—that is, to boil rice and make a vegetable soup without meat stock. Once in a while we had a few ounces of meat or chicken; but no matter what the food is, the North Koreans always prepare it the same way—cut into small chunks, boiled until all the flavor is gone, then liberally laced with red pepper.

I appreciate that these different houses, being all much alike, can mean little to a reader; but each is identified in my mind with some peculiarity or event. The first Manpo house had a window from which I was permitted to look because it was so situated that no one outside could see me. I noticed from the window that a Russian civilian family was living across the street—a woman, a ten- or twelve-year-old girl, and a man who must have been somewhat important, because he had a Korean company-grade officer as driver of his jeep. On entering Manpo I had also seen three Russian officers strutting on a street; and in another apartment (or, rather, large room) of the house we occupied, I had a glimpse one night of a whole group of Caucasians. These certainly were not Americans, so I assumed that they too must be Russians.

In three days the officials' families moved out, and we were able to grab the room with the onder. This ages-old prototype of modern heating systems always surprises Westerners when they first realize how long the Koreans have used the principle we consider new. But surprise wears off, and the vagaries of the onder begin to wear on your nerves. Very few really draw properly, so often more smoke drifts in from the kitchen of a Korean house than goes under the floor to create heat. Most onders have two or three flue systems; and almost always one system works far better than the others.

Stoked with grass and brambles, most onders are fired only

during the cooking of meals. For an hour or so, just at dinner time and when you are going to bed, there is stifling heat, which becomes almost intolerable in a tightly closed, crowded room. As the night wears on, the floor cools off, while the air outside becomes frigid, until in the morning and through the day there is very little difference between the zero temperatures inside and outside.

At this house in Manpo the heating system was just about average, and so was the crowding. Two lieutenants joined the guards and myself in one room, and a captain moved into the cold spot we had vacated. In our eight-foot-square room four people slept while one squatted on guard duty, at which the lieutenants cheerfully took their turns, under command of Sergeant U.

Here an exceptional event took place—I got a bath. There were great preparations for the occasion. All day long the two guards carried water in buckets to a large Japanese-type wooden tub in a little bathroom, and a big fire was built in a sort of stove under it. I assumed that the bath was for me and, with no interpreter present, tried to make them understand that it should not be too hot—I wasn't a Japanese and therefore didn't want to be parboiled.

My assumption was a little premature on a couple of details. When I finally got to go into the tiny bathroom, a lieutenant went with me (perhaps they thought I'd escape with the steam), and I learned to my sorrow that this was not to be the hoped-for immersion bath, or Japanese-style self-cooking session. The Koreans do it differently. We soaped down, using some of the very hot water scooped from the tub, and then got some of it cool enough to wash the soap off. But when I made motions to get into the tub, I found out that wasn't kosher. You just soap and rinse, and that's all.

Also, the lieutenant borrowed my bar of soap and used most of it. It was a highly disappointing evening.

I never did find out what real business these officers had in Manpo, but I judged that all of them had recently been in Seoul. Each had loot of some sort—U. S. .45s, cigarettes, six bottles of penicillin, which they gleefully displayed to one another. Seoul was repeated again and again in their conversations.

A couple of days later a woman lieutenant joined our little party and moved into the room with the captain. This should not be interpreted as anything more than a necessary arrangement. The North Korean Army seemed about as devoid of sex as any group of young men ever could be. I have no explanation for their apparent lack of interest. None was in possession of the calendar art which goes along with most armies (even the Japanese), and there was apparently no talk about sex.

The lady lieutenant brought with her a collection of American silk dresses, cosmetics, and a bottle of fine French perfume, of which she was especially proud. She should never have displayed her loot there. While she was present all the guards were quite friendly, but the moment she left the house one of the enlisted men went through her luggage like a terrier until he found the bottle of perfume, which he proceeded to use on his hair as you might use hair tonic. He kept on pouring until his hair was wet and the bottle half empty. The place smelled like seven beauty parlors compressed into one.

The woman lieutenant looked familiar to me, and I kept trying to figure out where I could have seen her. No one spoke any English except one tall lieutenant, who had injured a leg jumping out of a truck during an air raid; he also was suffering from a bad case of hypertension, which made him jerk continually. He surprised me one day by using his entire English repertoire. He looked at me, grinned, and said, "Fine, okay."

On October 17 my dysentery suddenly left me. I was virtually normal for one whole day. Then my kidneys went haywire, and thereafter that little detail of necessity occupied much of my thinking and a great deal of time—a trip every fifty minutes, zero weather or not.

About October 20 the interpreter, Tal, appeared. He had waited two days at Huichon for transportation, then had walked all the way north. He gave the woman lieutenant a chance to ask something that apparently had been bothering her too. She said, "Do you remember ever seeing me before?"

The question made everything fall into place in my mind. I remembered that day at Chinan, the captain who had bought me a sack of cookies, and the political instructor who had tried to hold classes for soldiers while our airplanes were overhead. This was the same girl. She was delighted when I remembered her.

At this period our food consisted of rice, soup with occasional bits of meat or chicken in it, and Chinese cabbage tops cut into a sort of green salad. There was no kimchee, which annoyed the Koreans more than it annoyed me. The cook was good, and thoughtful of my needs. When she discovered that I couldn't eat salad with as much red-pepper seasoning as the others liked, she would give me a special portion before putting on the pepper. I was getting used to the food and found myself eating more than half a large bowl of rice at each meal; in prewar days I couldn't have eaten a quarter of that amount. But we lived well only for a short time. Guards spent hours each day trying to buy enough food, and they no longer could supply enough for three meals. So we went down to two a day.

We moved once more, to a larger house in Manpo; and De Soon Yur, the guard left behind in Huichon, rejoined us, after having walked fourteen days, carrying his own and another guard's luggage. Tal technically stayed with us, but was sent away on frequent and mysterious missions for a day or so at a time. He may have been translating for other prisoner interrogations at some of the POW camps in the area. Once he returned to ask me for information about the X Corps of the U. S. Army and Major General Edward (Ned) Almond. I didn't know that the X Corps had been reactivated and was delighted to have that information.

This news made me feel better, and so did the general attitude of the people around me. It was apparent that most of them thought the jig was up. From the presence of the officers who had been in Seoul I judged that our forces must have cleared that city on the way north, and from the way they acted, I thought we must be moving fast.

An even more definite indication of the way things were going was provided by one of several English-speaking Koreans who came to the house, stayed briefly, and departed. He waited until a moment when he could not be overheard, then whispered to me, "Could you walk seventy-eight miles?"

I knew precisely what he had in mind, and that he was thinking of his own fate as much as mine. I didn't care in the least, if he really meant it. I said, "Seventy-eight miles? I can do that on my head. I can crawl that far." This might have been just boasting, because I still was very weak.

He was the one who finally shook his head. "It's very cold," he said. "Much snow." While I protested, trying to help him screw up his courage, he talked himself right out of the idea, and the opportunity to escape never came so close again.

That walk would have taken me to United Nations lines, but within days the Chinese struck in force and the great Eighth Army retreat to the south began.

▶▶▶▶◀◀◀◀

CHAPTER IX

A Trip to Manchuria

On what turned out to be the night before we left Manpo, I was taken for a quarter-mile walk across a soccer field, to a house without close neighbors. A brand-new cook was already preparing dinner when we arrived. Also awaiting us were the lieutenant left behind at Huichon and an English-speaking civilian. The captain who had been sharing a room with the lady lieutenant moved with us but left the lady behind. The big lieutenant with the tic also came along. We were a happy group, living in an eight-foot-square room. The girl cook, who turned out to be a sergeant, moved right in with the rest of us. It was still possible to lie down, but we either rolled over in concert or not at all. The lieutenant with the jerks, however, found this a trifle confining. He opened the door of a closet and slept in there.

The civilian, before we went to bed, told me that he had hiked all the way from Pyongyang. "It was tough," he said, "but I didn't mind. I'm glad to do anything for my country." From his tone I had the definite impression that he didn't think it would be possible to do things for his country much longer. The show was just about over. (On October 26 American Marines landed at Wonsan on the east coast of Korea.)

The next morning I got additional evidence of the same

sort. Here came the "pahli, pahli, pahli" call once more; and the captain, noting that I was still wearing summer clothes, offered me a pair of long woolen underdrawers. I figured he must know something and accepted them promptly. In a tearing rush my guards and I set out for a government building a few blocks away, then waited there. "Hurry up and wait" as a cardinal principle is not restricted to the American Army. These people were used to it too.

Trucks were parked in a courtyard, and drivers stood around a big bonfire in the biting cold, but I was not invited to join this warming circle. We acquired a new captain as tour-party director, and our luggage was put into a truck. Three of us sat in the front seat and a guard hung on the running board, just in case I might feel like jumping out.

There must be a million Kims in Korea, but the Captain Kim who now had me in charge was a churlish, English-speaking lad, whose standard answer to any question was, "It's immaterial." I asked him where he had learned English, and he admitted that he had gone to school in Kokura, Japan, my old headquarters; thereafter I got no information. He had no insignia, so I asked his rank. He said that was immaterial. So was his name, and he did not care, he said, if I merely chose to call him "Hey, you." He was a very pleasant fellow.

We drove to the Yalu River, and the captain showed a pass to guards at each end of a pontoon bridge. Thousands of people were lined up on the Korean side, waiting to cross, but our pass got us through the mob and we rolled across the bridge.

On the west side of the river I noticed immediate differences. Here were vendors with whole cartloads of meat, more than I'd seen in months, and other vendors hawked a sort of corn fluff, just as a delicacy. Mule-drawn vehicles were common. Uniforms were difficult to distinguish accurately under the many coats, but they were different from those worn in Manpo.

I asked Captain Kim if this was the first time he had been in Manchuria and got a straight lie for an answer. "This isn't Manchuria," he said. "This is just a Chinese section of Korea, like your Chinese section of San Francisco."

I said, "Then what was that river we crossed?" The captain didn't bother to answer. I was well aware that my transportation into a neutral country violated the Geneva Convention, but I was in no mood to protest about it even if there had been any chance to protest. "This," I thought, "is good. On this side of the river my chances for getting away are at least triple what they were in Korea."

We drove a few miles to a town, which must have been Chian, and stopped in a sort of hotel. We passed through a kitchen where a mule was walking around and around, turning a press that squeezed out those lovely corn fluffs. Our accommodations consisted of a shelf, about six by six, where four of us slept while one guard remained on duty. I think the hotel had formerly been a stable, and we were in one of the stalls.

That night we had an excellent Chinese dinner served from the kitchen, complete with pork cut up and cooked with lots of gravy, rice, and soup that had some meat stock in it. This was a real delight to me; and although this was my first offense with chopsticks I managed to get all the gravy served to me.

But there's no figuring Koreans. They didn't *like* this wonderful food, and the next day set up an elaborate arrangement for getting Korean food—the usual watery soup, rice, and no meat—from some other place. I had to sit there and smell those wonderful Chinese dishes being cooked in the next room—without being able to get any of them.

However, I had to pass through the kitchen several times during the night. Each time I slipped over to the press, grabbed a handful of corn fluff, and stuffed it into my mouth. I felt like a small boy sticking a finger into the icing of his mother's cake. The mule, fortunately, worked only during daylight hours, so I didn't have to argue with him.

With four of us sleeping and one on guard on that stall-sized shelf, there wasn't much room. And the captain turned out to be a pinwheel sleeper. All night long that bird pivoted on his head, kicking first one of us, then the others in rotation as he spun around, without ever waking up. The only person not miserable was the squatting duty guard, who was thoroughly entertained.

It was now October 28, and the weather was bitter cold. But Chinese flies have that little matter whipped: they all move indoors. The hotel was a black mass of them. They crawled over our faces as we slept. When one of the guards was sleeping and I was awake, I quite often saw flies wander in and out of his open mouth at will. Frequently they fought us for our food, so it wasn't unusual to have a spoonful of rice flavored with fly. If I had had a swatter I could have killed a thousand with one blow.

The next day the captain recognized that I needed something to do. He lent me, temporarily, a book called *The History of the Communist Party in the Soviet Union.* But presently he thought he should be studying it himself, so he took it and left me with his one other volume, a conversational dictionary in Japanese and English, which had been written by someone in Kyoto, Japan, and was concerned with teaching

Japanese how to order meat or groceries in English. I read it avidly.

We stayed in Chian until the night of October 30, with me sitting the whole time on the shelf—and absolutely nothing happened except that Captain Kim bought a big sack of peanuts. I can remember how wonderful those tasted.

The Korean reasoning in taking me to Manchuria can only be surmised, but to me the most logical explanation is that they intended to use my rank as a bargaining point in whatever peace negotiations might occur. They could not afford to kill or lose me, and even were forced, in the heat of the military rout, to take the chance that the Chinese might demand my custody once we were across the border. I was kept in Chian the shortest possible time. The moment their military situation improved I was hauled back east across the river.

That trip, made in a jeep in the midst of a snow and sleet storm, was bitterly cold. I was crowded into the middle of the back seat, and one of the guard's suitcases, with very rough corners, kept bouncing against my shins. This was more painful than it sounds, and I finally said, "Stop the jeep."

Captain Kim, riding in front, said, "What's the matter?"

I said, "This suitcase is cutting my shins something terrible. I'd like to stop and pull my feet up above it, or something."

He said, "That's immaterial."

Well, you can take that sort of thing only so long. I said, "The hell it's immaterial! Stop this jeep right now." I pulled back my fist as if I were going to hit him.

When I think about it now I can see that almost every time I tried a real bluff it worked—shoving the sentry when I was a fugitive in the hills, trying to kill Colonel Kim, now this business of threatening to hit the captain, who could have mowed me down with one hand in my condition. Perhaps if

I had been smarter I'd have tried more bluffs and either acquired more concessions or disproved the theory.

But at least I did get the jeep stopped and that suitcase off my shins. We proceeded to the bridge, at the end of which benches and temporary kitchens were set up. I couldn't decide then whether these were for Chinese troops coming in, or refugees, or prisoners of war. I was constantly on the lookout for some sign of prisoner-of-war camps, but never saw any.

As we drove into Manpo the snow and sleet continued. And at a corner I glanced up a side street. Men were marching there in the snow, their heads bent, their gait that of the very weary. I saw them only for a moment, and then we had gone past. Though I looked back frantically I never got another glimpse of those other American prisoners, plodding through the night. I can't even swear that they were Americans, but I don't think I could have been wrong, even in that single instant.

I was taken to a house in a cluster of three or four, well out of the center of Manpo; and when we moved into a room next to the kitchen the family that owned it had to crowd up in the one other room, away from the heat. During this period I was always interested—for obvious reasons—in the latrine facilities of any new quarters. Here they were unusual. The approach was over a raised catwalk, hazardous with ice, and the facilities themselves were directly above the pigpen, a sort of raised perch visible from all directions and open to the winter winds out of Manchuria. Fortunately for sensibilities, no pork was served to us during the three days we remained at this house.

On the night of November 2 we moved again—walking across a soccer field. I was a little confused about the locale and wondered how many soccer fields there were in North

Korea. When we arrived I found that it was the same place in which we had been the night before we went to Manchuria. The girl sergeant-cook, E Sun Koom, and the very pleasant captain who had given me the woolen underdrawers, were still there. He was just sitting down to eat an evening snack of some raw meat, greeted me like an old friend, and invited me to share it. Although I'd never eaten raw meat before, this tasted fine, especially the bits of liver.

We stayed put for ten days. From this house I could see out one window, and watched while a Russian civilian and two Korean general officers, with a large coterie, discussed locations of anti-aircraft positions on the hills behind us, then developed a cleverly camouflaged petroleum and oil dump in a fold of the same high ground, piling brush over the stored drums until they were unnoticeable even from where I sat, close to them.

I also grabbed an opportunity during this time to tell Captain Kim, who stayed with us at night, that I wanted to walk outdoors, for exercise.

He said, "You can't walk in the daytime, because somebody might see you. We don't want you to be seen. We'll arrange for you to walk at night."

But I never got that walk. A night or so later there was a violent argument outside, which sounded to me as if Chinese were involved in a dispute about quarters—and I think I was right, because we moved, on the night of November 12, to a large apartment house, in which we had one room with an onder and another that had been a tatami room until the matting had been torn off. Now the floors were bare, unheated. The room with the onder had paper windows, which let in some light; but almost immediately the guards pasted newspapers over them, to conserve heat, and made the room quite dark. The onder, as usual, didn't work too well and was fired only at mealtimes, so the room was cold most of the time.

Here we remained until January 12, 1951. It was bitter cold, Christmas was just another day, and the food steadily deteriorated. I sat on the floor, crawled on the floor, and slept on the floor. Much of the time no interpreter was present. Planes bombed the area, but with less and less frequency. I guessed at the course of the war by the numbers of Chinese troops I could see occasionally. (As I learned later, the Chinese entry into the war in October had by this time changed the whole character of the fighting. United States Marines and soldiers had to fight their way south from the Yalu River on the east coast, finally evacuating their battered units from Hamhung on December 24, 1950. Meanwhile, in the west, the Eighth Army was driven back rapidly, losing Seoul on January 4, 1951.)

Once Lieutenant Colonel Choi, of the Sunan interrogation team, came to see me, with more questions to be asked through the same interpreter, Tal. He was fairly pleasant. He wanted to know where the 1st and 3rd Divisions of the U. S. Army had been stationed. I told him that I had no idea—our divisions moved frequently and I had been out of touch with these two since 1947, and I asked him why he wanted to know. He said a radio broadcast had identified them as divisions being sent to Japan as occupation troops, replacing units fighting in Korea. Actually the 3rd Division already was fighting in the X Corps, in eastern Korea, while the 1st remained in Europe, where it had been for a long time.

I also asked Choi for information about the course of the war, but he wasn't helpful. "You won't give us any information about these divisions," he said, "so why should I tell you anything?"

He seized the opportunity, however, to ask if I had now seen the light and might be willing to cooperate—but almost in the same breath asked a giveaway question: Was it true that we were landing two Japanese divisions in Korea?

I told him that I had no information on this, but that of course there were enough trained Japanese soldiers easily to fill two divisions, so it was possible. I was struck by the expression of outright terror which crossed Choi's face. Hatred of the Japanese is beyond belief in both halves of Korea, but so is fear of the small soldiers from the islands.

Otherwise Choi was on the evasive side. I complained that I wanted to take calisthenics daily, and he said, "How much exercise do you want?"

I told him thirty minutes a day.

He said, "That's too much. You can take ten minutes."

When I complained about not being allowed to stand or to walk around the room he said he would have to "take that up with a higher authority." I asked if there was not some arrangement for dispatching letters to prisoners' families through a neutral country—there must have been some sort of a form letter so that I could at least tell my family "I am well" or something to that effect.

Choi said he knew of no such mail arrangement, but that if I wished to write a letter to my family he would see that it was mailed. I wrote, with a borrowed pencil and paper (I was not allowed to have any of my own), a completely innocuous letter, saying that I was well. Choi put it in his pocket, where it may be yet, for all I know. It never was delivered.

He also had one more request before he left—he wanted my woolen underdrawers. They were his, he said, lent to the captain who had lent them to me. So I returned them, and lived in summer-weight underclothing for the rest of the month.

Except for this visit my days were much alike. I lived with, but did not particularly help, the every-fifty-minutes kidney trouble. I sat with my back against a mud-plaster wall and refought many times the twenty-day campaign before my separation from my division. I worried about my family and their finances. Frankly, I had never considered the possibility of becoming a prisoner of war. I hate to admit it, but I knew very little about what could be expected from the holding power, or even about my status with our own Army while a prisoner. I'd always thought that anyone reported missing in action was presumed dead after forty-five days and his pay stopped. So I worried about this, needlessly, much of the time I was a prisoner.

And over and over again I planned a dinner. This would be served on my first night of freedom. It would include prime ribs, an artichoke, a small baked potato with cheese on it and a good-sized hunk of butter, quick-frozen peas, a big helping of head lettuce with french dressing, ice cream, and a huge cup of black coffee. Those were the most lasting items, although I used up days in considering and rejecting other components.

But I didn't mind the time. Thinking about food helped to keep me warm. So did the massaging of my bare toes, hour after hour. We always were without shoes inside the house, as in any other Korean house, and I discovered that my feet seemed to keep warmer without socks. The temperature hovered around zero, inside as well as out.

I was permitted to wash once a day and worked out a system so that I could get a partial sponge bath out of a single basin of warm water by using a handkerchief as a washcloth. But it was complicated by the fact that the washcloth, when

I laid it down beside the pan of water, always froze before I could pick it up again. I had no idea water could freeze so fast.

Most of the time I watched the Koreans, which wasn't hard, because ten of us sometimes were living in the one eight-by-eight room. Captain Kim departed early in November, and after that the senior sergeant, U Eun Chur, was in charge and kept them all busy. One man always watched me, at least one off-duty man always was away trying to buy food, and all of them spent a great deal of time studying Communist doctrine, copying page after page in notebooks that were checked by superiors now and then. *The History of the Communist Party in the Soviet Union* was their principal text, and I always wondered how many of them understood the chapters on dialectic materialism. They appeared to be memorizing it, as children might study a primer. U held almost nightly review sessions, and each man was called on to recite. Occasionally he or some other guard would go away, apparently to attend more formal classes, then come back to give a complete report on what he had been told. These things were obvious, although we did not speak each other's language.

Some attempts were made to teach me—guards trading me Korean for English terminology. A typical lesson consisted of a guard filling a rice bowl with bits of paper, saying, "*Ipsumida*," then demanding, "American?" I would say, "Full." Thus I learned Korean terms for full, empty, and other common situations—with some startling results. *Ipsumida*, I learned subsequently, also means "I had," or "there is"; while *opsomida* means "I do not have," "There is less," or "gone." De Soon Yur would ask me, "Sohja empty?"—meaning, "Has the major gone?" "U full?" meant, "Is (Sergeant) U here?"

Generally these people treated me kindly—within the framework of the restrictive rules. I could not stand or lie down in the daytime and got my ten minutes' calisthenics in the morning only under the frowning disapproval of U; but most of the time I was treated more or less like a member of a big family. I ate what they ate, including the occasional treats someone brought in. I was equipped no more poorly than the others.

These people had no thread, no nails, very little cloth of any kind, few needles, and no leather. They unraveled old knit clothing to make new things, laboriously twisting the thin yarn strands together by hand in order to make thicker skeins. They resoled their own shoes and mine (somewhat later) with slices of rubber and fabric cut from old truck tires.

Socks in Korea are not darned but patched. The guards all patched their own until patches were on top of patches, and I learned to do the same with mine. But I never tried what I saw—one guard patching another's socks while they still were on the feet. The one being patched wasn't worried, but the whole process looked hazardous to me.

Once while I was watching U he must have misread my interest as disgust or scorn, because he suddenly held up that sock as if he were going to throw it away and yelled, "American! American!" I was sure he resented the fact that he had to patch that sock, whereas an American soldier would merely toss it away. But he had misunderstood my expression. I was just wondering how in the world you could ever get any American, soldier or civilian, to be half that frugal.

De Soon Yur, the most kindly of the trio of regular guards, was exceptionally odd in appearance. Above the waist he was built like a middleweight, but his legs were those of a twelve-year-old child. He was the shortest one in the group and looked as if he had been mismatched at the belt. He also had the shortest fingers I've seen on a grown man, but he could do incredible things with them. He could thread a needle in the dark; and when anything unusual, from fixing a partition to carrying a heavy bag of rice, had to be done, he was the one who accomplished it. U Eun Chur was the old Army man, and an authority on Communist doctrine. Pack, the youngest and the brightest of the trio, was notable because the girl-cook so transparently thought he was wonderful. She shared her cover with him when we slept and gave him money when she finally left. But in spite of her perfectly obvious interest Pack never did anything about it except to carry her luggage to the railroad station on the final day of her stay.

None of these men ever had any time off, and none received more than an occasional letter, although both U and De had families. The only variety in their diet or mine was a very rare helping of soy beans, roasted, or, in the evening, a bowl of *pop-kay*, which is the browned rice that clings to the sides of the cooking pot and tastes vaguely like toast.

Of this last I never got a full share, although they shared almost everything else with me. But pop-kay was special, and it never was a case of reaching into the bowl and helping myself, as the others did. Rather, the guards would gather around the bowl when E Sun Koom brought it in; and Pack or De would break off a piece of the crusted rice and hand it to me, while I sat in a corner. For some obscure reason U resented this and often would grab the bowl and make a point of giving me none, or would growl a protest when one of the others handed me a piece. This didn't affect them; but once I got up on my pride when he made an especially noisy protest and for five days refused what was offered. Then I realized I wasn't hurting U in the least, and pride gave way to hunger. Thereafter I took what they handed me, like a little child not permitted to approach the dinner table.

E Sun Koom always was kind to me, making sure that I got my full share of everything, including her indifferent cooking; she washed my clothes without complaint and sewed cotton batting between my two blankets when the cold became so unbearable that I couldn't sleep. Only one thing about her annoyed me. Each day, after cooking and eating breakfast, she would wash outdoors, then return to our room with her hair damp, sit cross-legged on the floor facing the dim light, and take out a rather elaborate toilet kit, which included a bottle of pink hair cream, a popular American brand, to pour on her hair. Then she'd comb, and glycerine would fly off the comb into my face as I sat behind her. I wasn't allowed to move, so all I could do was duck or put up my hands as shields. The guard on duty always had a real nice laugh.

When E Sun Koom was to leave us I wanted to give her some present to show my appreciation for her kindness. Buttons were the only thing I could think of, or had. Everyone was short of buttons for his clothing and continually stole them from each other. So I pulled the six ornamental buttons off the sleeves of my suit coat and gave them to her. She seemed pleased and grateful, but several days later I saw Pack sewing those selfsame buttons on his own clothes.

The girl sergeant was replaced by a civilian woman, Pyun, as cook, and the meals promptly improved. I prefer rice cooked in the oriental manner rather than as Americans cook it, and the way Pyun prepared it was better than any other rice I had in Korea. It had a special fluffiness all its own. She could even make that Chinese cabbage or Japanese radish (*daikon*) soup taste good.

Pyun was in her twenties, had a really beautiful face and

more figure than most Korean women. But her hands were those of a day laborer, scarred and blunt. She had smashed the fingers of her left hand somehow, losing the fingernails and acquiring a bad infection. To my consternation, she squeezed blood and pus from these fingers every night, after a hard day's work, and had no medication except mercurochrome. I learned eventually that she was the wife of a North Korean colonel who had been involved in some defalcation before the war and had been demoted to private as punishment. But he worked very hard, the guards explained, eventually got another commission, and rose again to major. Their story had a tragic ending. In 1951 during the same week the major was killed in action and Pyun died in a bombing raid on a highway.

At Manpo she lived like the rest of us. That is to say, we tried to keep warm, were kept awake at night by rats gnawing in the ceiling or in the next room(where they had regular rat battles), and were kept busy, in any off-hours, hunting the hard-shelled lice, or cooties, which infested our clothing. These beasts loved the seams of clothing, and the only effective way to kill them was between the fingernails. All of us spent hours on the hunt. The colder the weather became, the more of them moved in on us.

For the guards the life was hard and easy, in differing details. They all liked to sleep until nine or ten o'clock in the morning, which made me unhappy because I normally awake early, and that hard floor was no place on which to loll and dream after awaking. But they worked almost without supplies, receiving during this entire period issues only of canvas shoes (in midwinter) and some heavy canvas from which they had to hand-sew duffel bags. I was allowed to make one of these for myself, and carried it for the rest of my captivity. I also was issued some winter underwear, a vitally important item, on the last day of November. You remember things like that.

There was no regular source of information about the war, even for the guards. When U would come back from one of the study sessions he attended, the house seminar talk would include names of Russian satellite countries and sometimes of the United Nations, so I presumed they were being briefed on world events. But there was no newspaper and no radio. I had heard a radio in the interpreters' room at Sunan (once I heard the phrase, "This is the Far East Network," before it was turned down hurriedly), but we never had another that worked.

We also had difficulty in keeping time. U was entitled to an issue watch, and he received four different ones. But neither he nor the other guards could stand to let it go uninspected. As soon as he would bring one home they would get their heads together over it, take off the back, then start investigating the works, lifting out a wheel or two. Sometimes they would manage to get the wheels back, but none of the watches survived the treatment for more than five days. I never could understand how the men knew when to relieve each other on guard duty.

One thing about the Koreans still arouses my curiosity. Everywhere I noticed their fine teeth (perhaps I was more interested than most because of my father's profession as a dentist), but never received any adequate explanation for their excellent condition, which is in such contrast to the mouths full of gold-covered cavities common in Japan. These people were great tooth-brushers, spending half an hour a day using a dry brush with lots of toothpaste on it. I was told once that the kimchee in their diet was responsible. Certainly their dentists can't take much credit. In the three years I was a prisoner several of my guards at one time or another had teeth extracted. I honestly believe the teeth were knocked out rather than pulled; and every patient ended up with a dry socket, excruciatingly painful for weeks. This appeared to be standard procedure.

Although I was allowed but two sponge baths at Manpo, in addition to those I managed with the little washbasin of water, the guards did a lot of bathing. They made a habit of doing their daily face- and neck-washing outdoors, stripped down to the waist even in the coldest weather. Koreans have told me that in the old days Japanese guards attempting to single out Koreans trying to cross on the ferries to Japan without permission would ask suspects to wash. If the suspect washed the back of his neck he was thrown off as a Korean and an impostor, because Japanese never wash there. I do not guarantee the accuracy of this story at all.

Many of the things I had resented so much at first became less important in my mind as I watched the Koreans dealing with each other. Actually I think they are generally less unkind than completely inconsiderate—of the rights of a prisoner, of a pig whose meat they believe will be better if he is killed very slowly, squealing for hours, or of each other. To them, I was just an animal to be fed and kept alive. It didn't occur to them that I had feelings.

For example, when one of them is looking at anything—a photograph, a book, a trophy—and another becomes interested, the second man, with never a by-your-leave, just grabs the object in question and looks at it himself. Perhaps while he's looking a third may arrive, and the process is repeated, still without any sign of an excuse or any interval for one person to finish with his inspection.

Or if a roomful of men are sleeping and the guard on duty feels like singing, he may burst into loud voice—and nobody complains. At Sunan I had resented more than almost anything else the guards' habit of kicking me with their bare feet to keep me awake. But that is their way of dealing with each other–the kick is a good method of getting attention, nothing more.

I also noticed that if one man was busy reading or sewing, and another spoke to him, no answer was forthcoming. The first might say, "Pack!" half a dozen times before Pack would deign to reply, "What?" (or a Korean word that sounds the same). When men go on duty or report to a sergeant they always salute, but the noncom or officer saluted replies, if at all, only with an expression of extreme disgust on his face and a grunted word. Many times I thought, "Boy, if that happened to me when I saluted somebody he'd be a long time getting another salute." But in that army this was standard.

These were the people around me at Manpo, and this their life, and mine, except for one detail.

That was the lone diversion, a game called *chong-gun* (general officer) and similar to chess. It differs mainly in that the pieces are moved on the intersections of lines rather than on the squares, and several pieces have slightly different capabilities. The equivalent of the king and certain added guards may not leave a restricted number of squares. Knights move two intersections in one direction and the third on a diagonal. Pawns are not exchanged when they reach the far side of the board but move thereafter at a right angle.

Off-duty guards began playing this game soon after we reached Manpo, having made their own pieces and a rough board. For several weeks I watched until I thought I understood the game. Finally I challenged U, who seemed to be the poorest player. I was beaten at first, but I began to get interested and played regularly with the vociferous help of many kibitzers. In chong-gun, kibitzing is highly vocal, includes suggesting moves or objecting to them, also the moving of pieces by a kibitzer, who repeatedly reaches over a player's shoulder without permission. Players themselves also are free and easy—if one makes a play, then sees that his opponent is about to exploit an opportunity he has created, he hurriedly yanks the piece back.

I gave a fair account of myself as a chong-gun player until the night Colonel Choi and Tal visited me early in November. The next day a guard shook his head when I got out the chong-gun board and challenged him. The other two also refused to play me, so I finally set up the board, intending to work out moves myself. U, in a growling mood, took it away from me. Although I still knew only a few isolated words of Korean, I understood perfectly that there was to be no more chong-gun for me. Colonel Choi had prohibited it.

Sometimes I could watch while the guards played, but often one of them sat—apparently deliberately—with his back to me so that I couldn't even do that.

There were frequent air raids during this period, and each time we had to take cover in a crowded air-raid shelter, which I reached by jumping through the one window that would open. The shelter was used by a number of people, including a really beautiful Korean woman lieutenant, who apparently worked in some headquarters nearby, and whose good looks I had very little chance to appreciate. Two Chinese sentries, another woman and two children, and all of our household crowded into that little shelter—and my guards, for some reason, always brought along their duffel bags and suitcases. They seemed to be more interested in getting their possessions protected than in getting protection for themselves. All of us crouched, by order, so we really were packed in.

As 1950 ended, however, the raids were lessening, while the number of night trains pulling out toward the south increased. None of this made me feel any better, and I was losing hope. I had counted on an autumn push of the United Nations Forces to come all the way to the border. Anti-aircraft fire also was increasing in our area, including some obviously from heavy guns. Evidences of military disaster for the enemy, which I had seen only weeks before, had vanished almost entirely.

On January 12 I heard the familiar "pahli, pahli, pahli." Once more I put on all the clothes I had, rolled my blankets, and prepared to move—with no idea as to whether it would be across the street, to the next block, or a hundred miles.

It was a hundred miles south, and more. We first went back to Choesin-dong. On the way U covered my head with a blanket every few minutes, just as we approached some spot where bombing had done important damage. He acted as if he were trying to keep me warm, which annoyed me thoroughly.

I finally said, "Doggone it, if you're trying to keep me from seeing, tell me so and I'll get my head down. But if you're trying to keep me warm, let me do it myself." Of course he understood not a syllable of all this.

At Choesin-dong we stopped only for supper and to get cotton-padded clothing for each guard and for me—trousers, coat, and a cap with ear muffs. This was distributed by sizes, and I was mildly amused when the best cap in the allotment, really a fine number with special buttons on top, turned out to be the one that fit me but none of the others. While we were fitting out, the guards chattered to themselves and to me said repeatedly, "Seoul, okay? Seoul, *chosumneida*?" They really thought we were going to Seoul, and so did I.

We were directed to an open, topless Chinese-made truck, already loaded with two big drums of gasoline and twenty-five officers with their luggage. Nine of these were women. The truck was so crowded that both Pyun and De Soon Yur had to be left behind.

The only thing uniform about trucks in the North Korean Army is that none of the starters ever works, and this one was no exception. But somebody finally wound it into life and we started south—with a driver who really was unusual in that he drove in a reasonable manner. U insisted that I sit cross-legged in the middle of all that crowd, while he stood up, which I wanted to do, alongside the gasoline drums. Someone pressed weight on each of my knees, some woman officer's knees hit me in the middle of the back, and other knees shoved against my sore shoulder. Every time I moved, this woman behind me screeched as if I were torturing her. She made quite a lot of noise about how I was abusing her. Fortunately for me and my kidneys, that first leg of the trip lasted only two hours and was broken once by a trouble stop. We spent the night in a Korean house, where a farm family moved over to let seven more people sleep.

But sleep didn't come to me. The temperature outside was six below zero. The house was terribly cracked, and the biting wind swept through. I noted with astonishment that the farm family had only light clothing and one big cover of some sort, under which they all slept. A little boy, three or four years old, was naked when he stepped over us to go out once during that sub-zero night; except for the runny nose common to virtually all small children in Korea, he showed no ill effects when he came back in and snuggled under the common family coverlet.

One of the officers who had been on the truck with us spoke some English. He said to me, "See, these poor people cold. Your airplanes make them cold." I gathered that he had been a resident of Seoul when I was military governor, and remembered me.

The next morning, when there was an air raid on a nearby town—I think it was Kanggye—we could actually see the house cracks widen as the bomb blasts shook it. The officer spoke bitterly to me. "See," he said, "your airplanes kill innocent farmers and make children suffer."

Again, as when coming north, we traveled only at night, and the second night was much worse for me than the first. My position on the truck was even more jammed, I could not get the truck to stop when I asked, and I was thoroughly embarrassed. When we did stop again, at dawn and near Huichon, my feet (I was still wearing for trips the two-sizes-too-small shoes given me at Chonju) were freezing. When I tried to walk a few dozen yards to a house I fell repeatedly, as the composition shoe soles glazed. In spite of my ills and falls, I remember well the breakfast we were served there—the kimchee was still frozen when it came to the rice bowls.

That night when we were ready to start I had a terrible time with the shoes. Outdoors I couldn't get them on at all; but a captain objected violently when I wanted to bring them inside. After twenty or twenty-five minutes of tugging I finally stuffed my feet into them—and we were off on another nightmare ride.

It was a wild and miserable trip, first through the ruins of Huichon, then past the site of a recent battle. Even in the dark I could see some of our 105-millimeter artillery pieces and a few light tanks still standing where they had been knocked out, or in ditches; also a few artillery prime movers and two or three Russian tanks. Villages through which we passed were in shambles.

Riding south, the officers talked among themselves, and I gathered that they already had been assigned, some of them to posts in Seoul, others to Mokpo, in extreme southwest Korea. I figured we must have been pushed far back a second time. I thought I myself would surely be taken as far as Seoul, and I hoped that we would get there soon. I thought, "I know that country. If I get loose I won't have so far to go to get away."

We continued southward until we were stopped at a road intersection by an officer who gave orders that I was to be taken off the truck. U and Pack, the officer, and I started out on a side road on foot. The night was very cold and the ground icy. I fell again and again. They were disgusted with me and bawled me out in Korean. Angrily I shouted back at them that if they had let me walk when I had asked for exercise I would have been able to stay up now. But I'd lost control of my limbs. I really cussed them out and they evidently cussed me out, but neither side knew what the other was saying.

We went on, walking and falling, for more than a mile, and at last reached a house that seemed to be in use as some sort of an office. And here was Captain Kim, the boss of my Manchuria junket, whom I never had learned to love. Nor did I now, although he was delighted to tell me some news: United Nations troops, he said, had been decisively defeated all along the line and the few we had left were surrounded, so it would be only a matter of days until all of them were killed. He said, "We have many airplanes now, our own airplanes flown by Koreans who have been trained; and it is only a matter of a few days until there will be no more Americans on the

Korean peninsula. Your own press and radio proclaim that this is another Dunkerque. What do you think?"

I told him I didn't believe the situation was nearly so bad as he painted it; that if it even approached his description the American people really would get angry, and that he'd better be apprehensive about what would happen when we put our full forces into the field.

He asked about my health and left the building. I've never seen him since.

▶▶▶▶◀◀◀◀

CHAPTER X

People, Cold, and Flies

I expected to resume the trip to Seoul any moment, but my guess was wild. I was fed but otherwise ignored until the next evening, when Major Kim—of the Sunan interrogating team—took us on another walk, back over the same road we had traveled the night before. I fell even more frequently than on the previous trip, so finally Pack offered me the heavy open-work straw shoes he was wearing. I wasn't happy about exchanging with him, but in his footgear I could at least get traction, although my feet were freezing. At last we reached a small village, which I know is near Sunan but never have been able to locate exactly. In a house there, we were taken for a single night to a room that contained, curiously enough, four beautiful brass-bound chests, but no other furniture. The other wing of the house was occupied by a platoon of Chinese soldiers. They paid no attention to me, and my guards kept me carefully out of sight most of the time.

We had no food all day, but in the evening Sergeant U returned from a junket with some pork fat and *dough*. This is pronounced just as it reads but refers to a steamed rice cake, prepared by soaking ground rice for a day, pulverizing and rolling it into patties like potato cakes or rolls, then placing it in the top of a kettle of boiling water, with straw added to keep the rice above the level of the water. It tastes precisely like flour and water, and for a long time I thought that's what it was. The Koreans consider it a first-class delicacy.

This was the beginning of my worst year—a year of two houses, two caves, many flies, malaria, a succession of odd guards, and terrific boredom—all within a three-mile radius. This was the year the North Koreans appeared to forget about Dean almost entirely, and I had difficulty myself in remembering who or where I was, and in maintaining any sort of sanity.

The house I lived in for some months consisted of the usual kitchen plus one room about eight by twelve feet. Eventually the room was partitioned so that I had a section eight feet by four, or slightly narrower, with an open door to the larger section but no light except what filtered through a paper window or came around the end or over the top of the sixty-six-inch-high partition. Most of the time the kitchen was unused; food was carried to me and my two guards (who for a time were having to stand watch and watch) from a house next door. Food wasn't plentiful, and I noticed that the mention of kogi in the guards' conversation became more and more frequent as the amount of meat we had to eat became less and less.

As soon as we moved in I decided that the house, which was on the edge of a village, had been used as a battalion or regimental command post by American Forces. Telephone wires still ran to it, partially obliterated American names still were scratched on the mud walls, and I found a broken shaving mirror with part of a soldier's serial number still visible on the wooden back. These few remnants of a lost campaign did nothing whatever to ease my state of mind, which was steadily growing lower. The house was small, cold most of the time, and gloomy with half-light. After the first four days I never got out of it. Very rudimentary plumbing arrangements were made for me in the kitchen—again so that there would be no opportunity for anybody to see me at any time.

On January 27 De Soon Yur, the short-legged guard, arrived, having walked more than a hundred and fifty miles from Manpo in below-zero weather, carrying two bags of his own and a suitcase U had not been able to get on the truck. He showed few ill effects, although Pack, riding with us, had frozen his toes. Blood and pus ran out when he squeezed them, and eventually he lost the nails, but he escaped infection or permanent injury. These small men are tough, no matter what else you may think about them.

De appeared glad to see me, and I felt as if an old friend had returned. But no sooner had he settled into the guarding routine than we were upset by the first of a series of personnel changes. An officer appeared on January 29 with two new guards—Kim Song Su and Pak (as differentiated from Pack). Pack told me, using signs for shoulder boards and the word *pure* for stars, that he and De Soon Yur were going to officers' school. De left that same night, and Pack a day later.

The two new guards were the most friendly I had seen, and sometimes would let me borrow a pencil when U was not present. But they continued to enforce the general orders—not standing, not lying down, in the daytime. I slept behind the partition, with a guard sitting in the doorway where he could watch me constantly. At first U insisted that I do this sleeping with my head toward the door; but after great argument—and their own inconvenience in stepping on my head a couple of times when they wanted equipment from the bags stored in my room—I finally was permitted to shift ends, so that at least the light by which the guard always was studying his Communist theory would not be directly in my eyes. This difficulty in effecting any change in routine, no matter how minor, was typical of my treatment. I don't think it was unkindness. They just liked the status quo, whatever it happened to be.

The partition did some good, however. I had not been getting the promised calisthenics; but with this to shield me (and the guard on duty sometimes dozing or reading) I managed to get in a few movements daily. I had to be careful, though, to do nothing that required raising my hands above the partition, or someone would yell and stop me. Sometimes I could get in twenty or twenty-five different exercises while they assumed that I still was sleeping on my straw mat.

Somewhat later I did get permission to walk for ten minutes a day—inside my own little room. I counted off this space carefully, and one day when a guard let the time run over a little I managed to get in twenty-five hundred yards of walking by taking four steps in one direction, then four in the other, on a diagonal.

When we first came there I was required to sit in the guards' room all day. Later this became too crowded, so my required seating was in the doorway between the two rooms. When they were especially afraid that people coming to the door of the house might see me, I had to sit in the dark end of my own little closet. I had nothing to read, but could not have read in any event. There wasn't enough light.

I took advantage of the two new guards and their kindness about the pencil. The first time I succeeded in borrowing one I found a scrap of paper and drew out a calendar, which I hid in my summer clothing hanging on the wall, along with the pencil.

But only a couple of days later U staged one of his surprise knock-down-and-drag-out searches, to which he was addicted, and found them both. They were taken away from me, and he really bawled me out. I couldn't understand his Korean but had no trouble with the tone. The tone said I had done something horrible, and he wasn't going to have any more of it.

Thereafter my only calendar was under the sleeping mat. In the dirt I would scratch the date each morning, wiping out the one scratched the previous day and hiding the new number by adjusting the mat over it. In this way I kept track of the days for almost a year, and was pleased and proud that at the end, when I had a chance to check, my date was correct.

Inside the house virtually nothing else happened; but outside there was a nightly drama. The village was apparently the center of a Chinese staging area. Many troops were around us all the time, and I could hear frequent firing of American machine guns and M-1 rifles on a range somewhere nearby, as if newly arrived troops were being given opportunities to fire a few rounds each with captured weapons. Chinese manned some light anti-aircraft positions near us, and their mule-drawn transport frequently creaked along outside. Now and then I could hear the dit-dah-dit of a radio from one of the wagons. My guards occasionally came back with new equipment, which they obviously had obtained in trades with the Chinese; and quite often I could hear Chinese women soldiers, who laughed a great deal, talking to the Koreans outside the house.

At night this friendliness disappeared. Quite obviously the Chinese were accustomed to using whatever houses they could find as billets, and they wanted to use ours too. But the Koreans had definite orders that no one was to see me, so there was a stalemate, which involved endless arguments, usually after midnight and often loud and violent. After a few weeks of this U must have complained, because an officer appeared with four new men—De Han Gool, U Bong Song, Kong, and Um. This made seven guards, all sleeping in one eight-by-eight room (less the one always on duty), but somehow they managed. With all this new help U set up a double guard—one outside the building, one watching me on a twenty-four-hour basis—but the increased strength was to combat the Chinese, not me.

I think the Koreans were very much afraid the Chinese would demand my custody and hang on to me if they ever found out where I was, and my rank. (This had been obvious at Manpo, and I also saw later evidence that the custody of officer-prisoners was a disputed point between them.)

The arguments, however, continued, and one night became so violent I thought they might start shooting each other. All the off-duty guards grabbed their weapons and ran out. I dressed hurriedly, planning to take a little walk away from there when the fight started—but it never did. I took off all the outdoor clothes again and went on with my exercises.

I had last seen a barber just prior to my interrogation at Sunan in September 1950. Of course I was not allowed to have a razor, so once in a while a guard would shave me, using ordinary hand soap for cream and a straight-edged razor, which was also used to cut paper and trim toenails. This was always an ordeal, and I was delighted that it averaged only once every seventeen days. Pack, who sometimes shaved me, just pulled the whiskers out; U, when he did the job, twisted them off, taking an average of two hours to do an excellent job. I'm an old twice-a-day shaver, but I didn't even want to think about it here.

As workmen, the Koreans veered between doing the impossible and doing the ordinary in an impossible way. Their carpentry was slap-dash, full of cracks and holes, and likely to fall down at any time. They're sledgehammer mechanics, and never measure anything if they think they can get by without it. They'll work and work to make a substitute for something scarce, such as nails. Whenever they had something to fix, I'd see one of the men wandering around whatever building we were occupying, wearing a wild look and searching all over—under the eaves, in the rafters, along the edges of the floor—for something he could use as a nail. I saw one of them take a piece of old American wire, carefully straighten it, and cut it off into nail lengths with an ax. But when he was through with that job he threw away what wire was left, with no frugality whatever, no thought of the next job he might have to do.

But the same men were capable of extraordinary handwork, as illustrated by Pak, one of the new guards. He had acquired a cigarette lighter and wanted to make it fancier by fitting the end of a rifle cartridge shell on it. While I watched—much too close—he carefully removed the projectile from the cartridge, took a nail, and prepared to detonate the cap in a crack in the floor by pounding with a rock. I complained so violently that he finally went down to the kitchen, but still used the same system. Of course nothing happened to him, although I would have blown off a finger if I'd done it.

A day or so later I saw him worrying because Kim Song Su's watch had no crystal. Pak found an old electric-light bulb, and as tools located a penknife blade, a rock, and an ax. With these he cut a watch crystal from the light bulb—and it fit perfectly.

Try it sometime.

Only a few weeks after De Soon Yur and Pack had gone away, supposedly to officers' school, they returned to guard duty, but I never was able to find out whether I had misunderstood in the first place or whether their plans had been changed. Language difficulty left me in the dark whenever explanations were complicated. By the same token, I was sometimes confused about just what I was eating. Once, when we had gone about a month with no meat or fish, the guard arrived with something he proudly called *kah*–and I got the idea that it was unborn calf. It was months before I learned that this quite tasty meat had actually been dog.

During most of the winter months our diversions were three–song sessions, chong-gun, and air raids. To vary their study routine the guards spent an hour or two in the evening singing in chorus the usual Inmun Gun and patriotic songs, and sometimes one would sing for the others what apparently were old folk songs of his home province. Several of the men had excellent voices, and I enjoyed it.

The chong-gun was resumed shortly after we came south, when one of the guards sketched another rough board. I still was not allowed to play but generally could watch and got a fairly good idea of the players' abilities. I also noticed one thing: De Soon Yur was a good player, and also clever. Against a really tough opponent he had one special trick. He would make a tentative move with his *sung* (elephant), then take it back again. All players made such tentative moves, but De made his count: the sung never went back to the exact spot from which he had moved it. Instead, it would end up on a spot from which, two or three moves later, he could make an effective attack. Apparently none of the other players noticed this, but I stored the information away for future reference.

The air raids were the most frequent break in our routine. Our Air Force apparently was aware that this valley had special importance, and they worked it over, day after day. A lot of the attacking planes were light propellor-driven craft, which came in so low I thought they might take the roof off the house. I wasn't sure of the main objectives, but later found we were close to an important railroad junction, which probably got the most attention.

In our immediate area, a dozen miles north of Pyongyang, there seemed to be no heavy anti-aircraft, although I thought I heard 40-millimeter guns. As the raids increased they got on the nerves of the troops around, and everybody fired something—burp guns, rifles, small machine guns. The air would be full of lead flying in all directions. I often wondered how many casualties that wild and indiscriminate firing must have caused among their own people.

For me the air raids meant little. At first we did nothing; later the guards dug a shelter, a trench with a long log-and-earth covering; one end of it was actually in our kitchen, the other outdoors. It was so shallow that when I was rushed there I had to crouch in the mud. When the raids came eight or ten times a day this got downright tiresome.

On March 3 I had my first official visitation of the year, from a three-star colonel, who neglected to take off his shoes when he entered the house—a serious insult in any Korean or Japanese house—a major, and an officer-interpreter.

The colonel, who did most of the talking, again told me that our forces were being driven south and were surrounded. What did I think? I said I thought we must not be doing too badly, because I had been told two months earlier that we were surrounded. So if we still were fighting, it was quite a record.

The colonel also wanted to know what I thought about pillaging and rape by our troops. He said, "Your men not only raped young and single women but they raped married women, pregnant women, and little children, and it was sanctioned by your officers."

I said that was an outright lie. Officers of the United States Army do not sanction rape. There are bound to be isolated cases; but in those cases the man is subject to court-martial. I myself had approved death sentences imposed by courts-martial in rape cases.

Suddenly the interpreter spoke up on his own. "That's not true," he said. "I know you've had rapes. I worked for your Criminal Intelligence Division, and I know you had troops at Inchon who committed rape and didn't get the death penalty when found guilty."

I've never been able to learn the name of this particular turncoat.

The colonel also wanted me to remember my place. "You've lost all your dignity," he said. "You must quit trying to act like a general. Here you are, a prisoner, but even the guard complains that you try to act like a general. You're no better than a dog. Stop trying to act superior to the guard."

He went on to more questions: Why did I think the Chinese "volunteers" had come in and were fighting us?

I said, "Because their master told them to, because Stalin told them to."

This made them all chatter. The interpreter finally said, "If the Soviet had wanted to attack they would have attacked when your troops went to the very border of the Soviet Union, but not a single Soviet soldier entered the fray. Therefore the Soviet would not order anyone else to fight. The reason the Chinese came in is the same reason that you would take action if there was a burglar in your neighborhood. Our Chinese brothers saw robbers in their neighbor's house, and that is why they came to our assistance."

Well, none of this was much fun, but at least I had learned about the United Nations eastern stab to the Yalu River, which was news to me. The visit came when my morale was low and my mood bad, and I took the opportunity to do some beefing of my own. I demanded to be taken to a POW camp, to be given paper and pencils, to be allowed to stand up, to get more exercise, and to get outdoors. Previously I had made such requests just as requests; this time I was half-sick and irritable, so I made demands. Not that they did any good. The only answer I got was that these matters would be taken up with "higher authority." Then my visitors trooped out.

I was mildly amused to notice that word about my attempt to kill Colonel Kim must have spread. These three cookies lacked confidence in themselves and kept two special guards with sub-machine guns at the doors all the time they were in the house. So far as I could see, there were no changes as a result of the visit.

On March 6 I became very ill, with severe pains in my right side. I couldn't eat anything and ran a temperature. Presently a doctor came to see me; he spoke no English, brought no interpreter, and there was no noticeable effect except that the guards permitted me to stay on my sleeping mat during the days until about March 15. The sickness had passed by then, but I was terribly weak, and my morale hit a new low. In my mind I had been prognosticating strategy of the United Nations Forces, and my guess-day for a major attack was March 15, when I thought I should be ready to make a break through the lines. But when the day came I couldn't have walked a hundred yards, let alone carry out an escape, even if the attack had come within hearing distance. Actually, Seoul did fall to United Nations troops on March 18, but the advance ended on the 38th parallel, well south of me.

My morale continued to sink. Finally I realized I had to do something about it, get something to think about. So I started working simple algebraic problems in my head and playing mental anagrams—how many different words can be made out of the letters in the name Sacramento? Washington? San Francisco? Having no paper, I kept score in my head and obtained simply fantastic totals. I had no way to be sure I was not duplicating, and someday I want to sit down with a dictionary and verify my totals.

One day I began working on squares and square roots of numbers and really got interested. I memorized the squares of numbers from 1 to 100. Then I began hunting for fast systems of squaring. For example, the squares of numbers between 10 and 20 have the same right-hand digits as those between 60 and 70, and the relationship follows through. So the square of 40 is 1600; the square of 41 is 1681, and the square of 42 is 1764 —and the square of 90 is 8100, the square of 91 is 8281, and the square of 92 is 8464.

If you are not interested in mathematics this sort of thing may drive you to pounding your head against the nearest wall; but believe me, it kept me from beating my head against one. I finally rationed myself to squaring five hundred numbers a day, no more. So I always had something to do the next day.

U Eun Chur was still in charge of me during the early part of the year and continued to waver in his attitude, worrying terribly when I was sick (perhaps more because of his responsibility than because of any sympathetic interest), but in virtually the next breath restricting my activities even further. The top in restrictions came one day when he caught me counting to myself. My hands were swollen from disuse and beri-beri, as were my feet, so I had worked out a cross-finger exercise, which consisted of pressing the thumb and the forefinger together five times, hard, then the thumb and second finger five times, and so on across both hands. By then I knew better than to let the guards see me doing anything unusual, so I did this exercise with my hand hidden by my side while I sat on the floor with my back against the wall. But as U Eun Chur passed me once he saw my lips moving. Immediately he said in Korean, "What are you doing?" and made me understand by mimicking my lip movements.

I said, "Counting–*il, ee, sahm, sah, oh.*"

He scowled, and there was no mistaking his negative. I must not, he indicated, count without permission.

I'm still of two minds about this man. He was a great nuisance, enforcing every restrictive rule to the letter and making up new ones of his own. He had been one of the guards during some of my worst interrogation sessions, in September 1950, and I'm sure he had taken his cue from the lovable Colonel Kim.

But U was also a fine soldier and scrupulously fair. As an officer I admired the way he drilled his squad, made them study their propaganda, and divided the work. However, my final experience with him was on the ludicrous side. In this Communist army, soldiers stealing from each other was the standard order of procedure. So when a guard acquired some small personal treasure he often would hide it in my suit-coat pocket, which hung from nails at the end of my small room. Sometimes two or three guards had things hidden there simultaneously, although for some odd reason no two of them ever happened to choose the same pocket. Of them all, U was the only one who never had done it.

On May 6 the guards had a party–the first I'd ever known them to have–complete with special food, sake, and a great deal of talk and laughter. In the middle of the festivities U slipped into my room, lifted the back corner of my sleeping mat, and under it dropped a package of almost a hundred cigarettes (he knew I didn't smoke), smoothing the mat carefully over them. The party continued without interruption.

When, on May 11, U came in with another guard for one of his special surprise searches, I didn't have a thing to find except one little handkerchief, which I had hemstitched for myself, with a borrowed needle and small skill, but this became an issue, although he let me keep it after long argument. Then he lifted the mat—and really did jump up and down and go into a lather. This obviously was going to be a super performance—until I began to laugh. I couldn't help myself. All I could do was to point at him and repeat, "*Tongsun*" (you).

He might have been able to pass it off if the other guard hadn't been watching his histrionics. Apparently U had been given those cigarettes for all the men at that May 6 party but had decided to keep them for himself, then had forgotten them when he sobered up. Now the only thing he could do was to make a somewhat shamefaced equal distribution. It was a trivial thing, but one of the high points of my year.

The next day U came to say good-by. He was wearing the shoulder boards of a second lieutenant. The May 6 party had been to celebrate U's upcoming commission.

This was a dismal period. For what they're worth, I think I should repeat the two clairvoyant obsessions that bothered me during my lowest moments. These were that both Lieutenant General Walton Walker, of the Eighth Army, and Colonel Henry (Hank) Hampton, my close personal friend, had been killed. I'm positive that no one had mentioned either name to me for months, but I was just as sure as if I had read the news somewhere. I even had dates—early November for

Colonel Hampton and early January for General Walker, and was sure General Walker's had come from artillery fire while he was visiting the front lines.

In midsummer I learned that I had been right about General Walker's death, although wrong about the time and circumstances; and after I was released I found that Colonel Hampton had indeed been killed at Suwon in the autumn. I have no explanation.

De Soon Yur took over as chief guard when U left, but my situation improved more slowly than I had hoped. I still could not stand or lie down during the day, and De apparently was afraid to modify those orders. I had another week-long sick spell—hepatitis, I think. Bombers increased their raids in the long spring days, and we spent a lot of time in that stinking air-raid trench.

I objected to the trench on various grounds, among them the fact that going to it interfered with my newest game—killing flies. I had done a little strictly amateur fly-killing the previous autumn; now I got serious about it. In April 1951 the first of the season's fly crop appeared, and I started batting at them with my palm and keeping track of strikes and hits. I had to keep my records mentally, but I ended May with an even three hundred flies killed and a batting average just over .300. In the first half of June my average was better but total hits were the same—an even three hundred. Then De presented me with a fly-swatter he had manufactured from a willow branch and the old half-sole of a shoe. My average immediately took a terrific jump to .760. I was studying flies and think I eventually might have batted .850. The trick is never to try to swat a fly when he's standing still. Wait until he starts walking, or lifts his front feet to wash. Then you bust him, because he can't take off without shifting position first.

The guards were interested but insisted that I couldn't count my score unless I produced the corpus delicti. So I carefully saved each deceased fly during the day, then crawled over to present them at night. This really was a dignified procedure. A guard would lend me a pencil to put down my total kill and batting average for the day. My June total (half the time with the swatter) was 2866. I had already figured this in my head; so when the time came for the official scoring I merely put down the blows struck and totals without adding the columns. This fascinated one guard, who immediately checked my columns and claimed to have found an error. I rapidly added it and got my original answer, but he still insisted I was wrong. We argued loudly, in two languages, and then I foolishly became provoked, tore up the paper score, and told them to keep their flies, damn them.

Both De and the other guard were angry, and I kicked myself for indiscretion—I was afraid they might take away my swatter. But nothing happened except that I no longer counted total strokes.

Just to keep this vitally important record straight, my top day in 1951 was 492 kills; but my all-time best, in 1953, was a 522-fly day. I killed 11,016 in 1951; 25,475 in 1952, but in 1953 lost interest and murdered only 4180—for a grand total of 40,671. Anyone who wants to challenge my three-year swatting record will have to show me the flies.

I was not the only one periodically miserable during the first part of this year. Kong, one of the new guards, was older than most of the others, and became ill soon after he was assigned to watch me. For days he lay on the floor, rolling in agony and coughing almost constantly. I was sure he had tuberculosis, plus some stomach disorder. Finally he was taken away, presumably to a hospital, and was gone for three weeks.

When he came back his side had been split by a large wound, from which a drain still protruded. I thought he must have been operated on for an appendix which already had burst. He went back to limited guard duty, still coughing and spitting regularly.

My own second sick spell left me even weaker than before and again put off any half-formed escape plans I had. Even when I went to the kitchen, which also was my personal latrine, my legs sometimes would collapse; and a couple of times I passed out completely, just trying to walk. I don't think I'm normally a hypochondriac, but I was convinced that I had cancer of the gall bladder.

A doctor was called to see me—and at least he knew exactly where to press my abdomen so that it hurt the most. Through an interpreter he asked me what I would like most to eat if I were at home. I think he expected me to say something about steak, but the thing which sounded best to me was milk toast. I said, "Hot milk toast with lots of butter on it"; I knew immediately that I'd made a mistake—they couldn't possibly provide that, and they didn't even try. If I'd asked for something reasonable, perhaps they would have. The doctor ruined my opinion of his diagnostic ability, however, with one more question. Had I, he wondered, ever had a venereal disease? I was happy to tell him I had not. When I showed him my feet, still swollen and as painful as if they had just been frost-bitten, he was not in the least interested. So I continued to go barefoot because I no longer could get my socks on.

In the spring the food routine was changed. All the guards but the man actually on duty went next door for meals, but the duty guard's food and mine was brought to us. For a while we ate together; but one of the new people obviously thought it was beneath his dignity to eat with a prisoner, so set my food on the floor by the door of my room. Shortly afterward this became a standard practice.

The guards now were getting some military training, which they had not received all winter; and in the spring De conducted extensive calisthenics every morning. But I still got mine, if at all, in my room, and each day faced the dilemma of whether to get my full exercise while the off-duty guards were outside running and jumping or to wash my face. Washing was always a problem, and if I didn't get it done at this hour I seldom had a chance later. This too had to be handled with extreme caution. The surest way to miss a day's wash was to ask some guard directly for permission to do it. The answer almost always was a negative, although if he thought of it himself, washing was a good idea.

As the summer progressed and my fly-killing became more of a full-time operation, washing acquired special importance. Every time I'd smack a fly—especially when I was doing it with my palm—I'd raise a cloud of dust, and by the end of a day my face and hands would be filthy. So missing one of my daily chances to wash represented an esthetic as well as a practical problem.

The mosquitoes also were getting worse. Some of them hatched in the water always in the bottom of that air-raid trench, which was convenient for them, and other hundreds came in from outside. I noted that a great many of them had the habit—typical of malaria-bearing mosquitoes—of standing on their heads when they took a hunk out of you. In the morning when I was dressing I'd use my fly-swatter on the ceiling, and the whole ceiling and wall would be bloody with the carcasses. But they still came in.

The guards occasionally got sufficiently interested in my fly campaign to swat a few themselves—usually choosing a time when I was just trying for a big score and borrowing my swatter. But their system of controlling mosquitoes was to build an evening fire in the onder, even on the hottest nights, which made the floor so hot that we slept in pools of perspiration. Sometimes they brought in a hibachi, the iron kettle containing not only charcoal but a few brambles, which almost suffocated us with charcoal fumes and smoke. Neither had any noticeable effect on the mosquitoes.

Or the flies. My campaign kept down the number in the area where I was allowed to hunt, and this helped my comfort some but had one effect on which I hadn't counted. As the flies got worse more and more of the guards would sleep, during their off hours, in my little room, in order to get away from the flies. If a man was sleeping I couldn't get even my fifteen minutes a day of walking.

Our deadly routine was broken once when De Soon Yur's wife walked sixty miles from Haeju to see him and he took a night off in celebration—the first time I'd known any of the men to get a pass for personal reasons. De's wife brought him some very fine hand-worked underwear, also a bag of peanuts, of which I was given a few. After a winter of almost unrelieved rice they tasted wonderful.

On July 5 I had another visitor—Major Kim, with an interpreter, Captain Oh Ki Man. Kim said he had just come to see how I was getting along—and did I think the war could be ended by negotiation? I said I doubted it. As I remember, I stated, "I don't think there would be a chance in the world. The United States never starts wars; but when we do fight them, we fight to win. And we do win."

Kim said, "I didn't come to argue, but I feel that the only way the war can be ended so there is a permanent peace is by negotiation."

In early summer some of the guards were away for days, helping nearby farmers put in their crops. And all during July virtually all of the off-duty men were gone during daylight. On July 17 De Soon Yur announced with obvious pride that we were going to move to a "trenchee"—he had picked up the word from my designation of the air-raid shelter. That night we packed all our things, and three guards and I struggled out in the dark and about two hundred yards up the steep hill directly behind the house.

Here we entered a covered trench dug across the side of the hill. It was six feet wide, about fourteen feet long, and barely high enough for a man to stand between the rafters supporting a dirt-and-log roof. It was entered through a right angle at one end, and the floor was three feet below the doorsill. Five-foot bunks for two guards were in the main tunnel, and at the far end a bay had been dug back into the hill. This five-by-six-foot haven was all for me. Three and a half feet of the width was occupied by a wooden bench, my sleeping couch by night, my sitting room by day.

The cave, De assured me, would protect us against pi-yang-gi (airplanes) and flies. Although the summer outside was boiling hot, the cave was dank, full of mosquitoes, chilly, and completely airless. I put on my heavy underwear and winter clothing to keep warm. De had assured me that I would get sunbaths and outdoor walks at the cave, but I got neither, partially because of the weather. Rain started as soon as we moved in, and continued for days—rain such as I've seen only in Korea. The sky just bucketed. On the chilliest days the guard would bring in a hibachi, which raised the temperature a couple of degrees but filled the cave with choking charcoal fumes. The roof leaked, and guards dug ditches in a fruitless effort to drain the water off the floor.

Robbed of my fly-killing pastime, I spent my time looking at the rock walls, which contained mica, quartz, and, I'm sure, a few flecks of gold, and massaging my sore feet.

Food was poor that summer. Besides the diluted rice, about all we had were garlic beads and tops, the latter chopped up and extremely hot. They burned all the way down, and my stomach never stopped burning until it was time to eat more of them. My dysentery was back, so I was a little more miserable than before.

On about July 24—a day I should remember more exactly—a guard came home from the town with a loaf of bread. I felt like putting my torn-off chunk of it up somewhere, just to look at, but wonder gave way to hunger. I told the guard to forget about any other food that day. I didn't want anything else to spoil the taste of that wonderful bread. I learned later that De, worried about my inability to eat as many red-hot garlic tops as the guards, had gone to headquarters and stirred up such a racket that my food allowance was increased to 800 *ton* a day, compared to the 500 allowed for each guard, and to the sergeant's basic pay of 1250 ton a month. That loaf of bread represented the first of the ration increase—and was also the first I had seen since early in September 1950.

▸▸▸▸◂◂◂◂

CHAPTER XI

My Friend Wilfred Burchett

The rains continued, the roof leaked steadily, and the floor drains clogged. Some time after midnight on July 31 a guard shook me awake. I put on my clothes but was told to leave everything else—and stepped down from my wooden bench into water already almost waist-deep. It had covered the guards' bunks, a little lower than my own, and still was rising. We splashed the length of the tunnel, getting soaked to the armpits when we had to stoop under the roof beams, and, in pouring rain, sloshed back down the hill to our village castle. Three sleeping guards were routed out of my four-by-eight special section, and an old woman and a child, who had moved into the main room, were ousted the next day.

The rain kept right on coming. The air-raid trench filled and overflowed into the kitchen, and the mosquitoes had a wonderful time.

The guards were doing the cooking themselves, for a change, and once—a glorious day—they secured some potatoes. Boiled potatoes and rice may not sound like much of a dinner, but then—well, I still remember it, although now I have trouble figuring out why I should have been so overjoyed.

This arrangement continued only a few days. Then a woman was hired as a cook, which made it bad for me because the guards were adamant that she must never see me. Although she was there only at mealtime, this meant that I spent even more time in my lightless closet, and could not even run up my fly-killing score during those hours, for fear she might hear the swatting. I don't know how they explained to her the extra man's ration and extra rice bowl used at each meal.

On August 4 I began to run a fever with a typical malarial four-day cycle, which left me sleepless and half out of my head. I was gradually going insane from the sound of a wall clock, which hung in the guards' room where I could not see it. I swear this Korean clock made a special dull sound, dih-dah, rather than a normal ticktock; and I beat my brains out trying to figure the time from the sound. I couldn't get enough water to drink and was becoming more and more delirious. Finally I scratched a note, "Quinine or atabrine," and De went off to see a *weesah* (doctor), who I hoped would get the note translated somehow.

To my delight De came back in only a few hours with five big yellow atabrine pills, which gave me almost immediate relief. In Tokyo much later, U. S. Army doctors told me this may have saved me, in my weakened condition. Atabrine is a treatment for dysentery as well as for malaria.

When I began to feel better I thought once more about escape. Summer was full, brush was leafed out, and the fields were full of corn and other vegetables. If I ever was going to get through, this was the time. Fortunately we were getting a little dried fish with our rice just then, and I began to save it. I'd eat just enough to leave a few bones in my rice bowl for the guards and the cook to see, wrapped the rest in scraps of papers, and hid it in the pockets of the trousers hanging on the wall. After U left there were no more sudden searches of my belongings, so it was fairly safe.

On August 15 Major Kim came again. This time I found

out, after much muddled translation, that he wanted information about Robert Lovett. He was quite disappointed when I could tell him only that I didn't know the Secretary of Defense. It was he who told me then that General Walker had been killed the previous winter.

By September 6 I felt almost normal physically, for the first time in months, and my escape plans began to take definite shape. Again I picked a date for a United Nations offensive—September 15 or October 1—and hoped to be ready for it. I was saving dried fish like mad. But the guards were talking about moving back to the trench, on which they had been working ever since the heavy rains stopped, and I knew I'd have to get away before we moved. From the inside room of a cave, escape is too difficult to think about.

Major Kim visited me once more, on September 15. The interpreter, Captain Oh, explained that the date was Korean Thanksgiving Day, by the lunar calendar, and that on this date gifts were exchanged and visits made to friends. Kim brought me two dozen apples as a gift; also some more questions, just to pass the time of day: How in the world did I think we could win the war by fighting when we were being defeated at every turn? What political party did I belong to? What were the political affiliations of Generals MacArthur, Marshall, and Bradley? Then suddenly he asked, "Did you know that General MacArthur has been dismissed?"

I said, "No."

He said, "Yes, he was dismissed last spring."

I said, "That news is a great shock to me." But I could get no further details.

Each of us ate an apple then, and I enjoyed mine thoroughly. After the visitors had gone I gave the guards the rest except for four; but the next day De came into my room to tell me sad news. Pack was ill. He said, "Poor Pack" a few times, until I got the idea that the only thing Pack needed as a cure was an apple—a *sagwah*. Pack had been good to me, so I gave De two apples for him. I'm not entirely sure that Pack got them both.

The next day I felt that I'd like to eat an apple myself. I waited until no one was around except De, broke an apple, and gave him half, eating the other half myself. The following day I repeated this procedure with another guard—and all the apples were gone. So out of my gift of two dozen, I actually got to eat two. But guards frequently shared their special treats with me, so it evened out.

It was now a race between an opportunity for escape and moving back to the trench, but it never came to a showdown. Instead, I got another fine attack of malaria, which laid me flat on my back. This time, I called for medicine on the second day of it, and De again secured five atabrine tablets. They worked, but not soon enough. The day I was able to wiggle we moved back up to the repaired and improved cave.

So I ate the hoarded fish, to keep it from spoiling. The United Nations attack had not been on schedule anyhow, so perhaps it was just as well. I thought, "Well, the United States has probably had general mobilization by this time. They weren't able to get a full-scale attack mounted by autumn, but it will come March 15 of next year. On March 15, Dean, you've got to be in shape to get away and meet them on the beaches."

The cave was much improved, larger and better ventilated. At the entrance a wall was built up on one side, and occasionally I was allowed to sit beside it for a sunbath. As added insurance that no one would see me, guards cut saplings and stuck them into the ground, forming an artificial greenery wall almost all around the cave entrance. I was also allowed to walk—in an area just six paces long. Once in a while I managed to get in half a mile of walking in this space before somebody made me stop. Food was improving, in fits and starts. Once I was given a whole pound of butter, which I put in my soup, a spoonful per bowl, in place of meat stock, and four cans of Soviet-supplied evaporated milk, which I shared with the guards. They didn't care for butter, so I got all of that. Life in the cave wasn't bad, and I thought that I wouldn't mind if we stayed there all winter.

But on October 29 I was told to get ready to move again. I asked if our troops were advancing, and got no answer. Nevertheless I was sure that was what had happened, and that we'd be taking another one of those long cold rides to the north again. I thought, "Manpo, here we come!" And this time I decided to be ready for the trip. I put on everything I had—woolen underwear, then a pair of shorts, then the Korean cotton underwear I had been given, about three pairs of socks, my summer trousers, and then my Chinese padded trousers. I had on a shirt, a U.S. fatigue jacket, a summer suit coat, and a padded coat.

I was so bundled up I could hardly waddle, but at least I would be warm. When we started to walk from the cave De also put his cap on my head, so I'd be further disguised. We got into a jeep—one officer with no rank insignia, a driver, De Soon Yur, and De Han Gool, I in my padded layers of clothing, and all our gear, including my blanket roll and a thin cotton pad. That jeep bulged but got under way.

We started south, not north, then cut to the east across a railroad, and finally back north up on a ridge, where we stopped. I thought, "Well, we're going to walk to Manpo, but it won't be too tough now. I'm in fairly good shape."

However, we went down a trail only about a half-mile and came to the rear end of a newly built little concrete house, stuck right into the side of a hill, with the roof camouflaged by dirt. The whole building was only about seven and a half by twelve feet. It was divided into two sleeping rooms, plus the usual kitchen and onder-firing space, and I was shown to a room five by seven and a half feet, which had in it a three-foot-wide bench, so that standing space was an aisle two feet wide. There were two small windows, not big enough to stick my head through, but with real glass in them.

The house had been built especially for me. We had driven about three miles but were less than a mile and a half from the village where we had stayed since January 1951. Our food still came from the same kitchen, and guards had to walk over for it every day.

I was delighted. This was the cleanest building I'd seen in North Korea—and I had no desire to go north, adding to the miles I'd have to come back when I did get around to escaping.

For the guards one of the most important factors was that this house was away from Chinese concentrations. They could relax about keeping people from sharing my quarters and finding out about me. But there were difficulties. The onder didn't work, and they had to tear up the floor (of poor quality cement, which seemed to be in ample supply) a couple of times to remake the flues. And their own quarters were impossibly cramped until they cut down the size of the kitchen and added a foot or two to their own sleeping space.

My treatment improved some. De allowed me a few forty-five-minute sunbaths outdoors, screened by another row of saplings cut and set up in the dirt between the house and the latrine, twelve yards away. But when a young Korean officer inspecting the place caught me seated on my bench doing calisthenics, he apparently objected. Thereafter De informed me they were prohibited unless I had special permission—although I still got my few minutes each morning.

Otherwise life proceeded almost exactly as it had before, with a couple of added diversions. The new house was clean, but that sod-covered roof proved a special attraction for North Korean rats, who knew as well as anybody that a hard winter was on the way. These characters proceeded with all speed to dig tunnels for themselves under the sod, then kept on burrowing, down toward the heat of the room. That was their mistake. Terrible engineers, those rats. They dug so deep that only a thin skin of paper and dirt was between them and the open room below, and their tunnels took in water from the upper ends. The result was that the roof leaked—water much of the time, rats now and then. I don't know why every rat who fell through the ceiling had to choose a spot directly over my head, but it seemed to me they did. At least five times wildly flailing rats landed on my face while I was asleep.

This was disconcerting to me, and unfortunate for the rats. Each time it happened the whole house went into pandemonium while the guards held a wild and woolly rat hunt. It might not have been so bad if they had used an American system, just swinging clubs around until they beat the rat to death; but their system was to get him with a sharp-pointed instrument, a pencil, dagger, or bayonet, stabbing him to death.

There was always a terrific battle, and the rat always lost. The carnage was terrible. Four or five men would be in my tiny room at once, all stabbing. By the time they finally got the rat the room looked as if it had been bombed.

Suddenly, on December 19, Dean's prison life changed. The

first indication was another visit from Major Kim and Captain Oh, who arrived about ten p.m. and for once posed no new questions about the course of the war. Instead Kim said, "Wouldn't you like to write a letter to your wife? You don't want your family to worry. Don't you want to write and tell them you're all right?"

I felt something strange in the conversation, but I said only that I'd written a letter a year before and had given it to Colonel Choi, who'd promised to mail it.

Both of them said, "Oh? We didn't know about that." They insisted that I write another anyhow—and do it that night. Kim provided a pen and paper and seated me on the floor at a wobbly little table in the larger room of the house. The house was wired for electricity, but our bombers had been busy on the transmission lines, so we had only an oil can with a wick in it for light.

I had been without any sort of writing implement in my hand for sixteen months, except to make a few figures, and I had trouble. I was horrified at my own script. My N's looked like M's, and my M's like nothing legible. I struggled through a letter to Mildred, then tried to read it, but I couldn't even make it out myself, so I rewrote it twice more. Then Captain Oh read it aloud, in Korean, but it wouldn't do, because I had started: "This is a red-letter day in my life. I have just been told that I can have a pencil, and that I can write to you—"

That part about a pencil wouldn't pass, Major Kim said. I did the whole letter over, foolishly without insisting that they read all of it first. So the next version also was turned down, this time because I had written, farther down: "I haven't seen a fellow American since July 1950."

Version number five finally was approved, well after midnight. Major Kim said, "Who else do you want to write to?"

I said, "I don't want to write to anyone else tonight. I'll write tomorrow."

He said, "Oh no. It must be tonight."

So finally I wrote another letter, to my daughter, and dated it the twentieth. I had to make only two copies to get one that was legible. When I simply was too tired to write any more the two officers left, carrying my letters and some photos taken at Pyongyang shortly after my capture. These they had brought to have me sign, to show that they were genuine.

In January 1952, when I got my first mail, I learned what all the rush had been that night. Those two letters of mine were turned over to United Nations representatives as the first letters in the original exchange of prisoner mail, on December 20 or 21. But before they were given to our people the texts were furnished to the Communist press.

I slept very little that night. I was excited about having a pencil. And in the morning I had another visitor—a major general, no less, named Lee. With him was my old chum, Lieutenant Colonel Choi. This gave me an opportunity for which I'd been waiting, and I let Choi have it. One of the first things I said to the general was, "This is the man who told me that I could wash twice a day, and I've never been permitted to do it. Why?" I was getting adept at their own type of phraseology. "This is the man who was going to take up with higher authority my request to go to a POW camp. All right, what does higher authority say about it? This is the man who gave orders that I wasn't to play chong-gun. Why?"

The general was making a big act out of being friendly, so I really poured it on old Choi. Choi squirmed. He said, "Oh, I didn't say you couldn't play chong-gun."

I said, "Then why was I stopped immediately after you

visited me on the third of November last year? As soon as you left the guards said they had orders against it. Why is that?"

Choi said, "That must have been Colonel Kim who gave those orders."

The general was friendly but answered few questions and said nothing to my other demands—for exercise, for sunbaths, for something to read. I never learned what, if anything, he did to Choi, nor do I care, but he himself was demoted later for having failed to visit me, for having permitted such orders, and for my general treatment. I learned this months afterward, and it looked to me as if they were making old General Lee a goat for what undoubtedly was a general prisoner-of-war policy they now wished to repudiate.

But this day everything was just dandy. The general didn't approve of the thin cotton pad on my bed, so it was replaced by one much thicker. He ordered a sheet for me, so an aide brought in a strip of cotton cloth about twenty inches wide and seven and a half feet long. I never figured out what to do with it. To replace my summer-weight suit, the aide produced a pin-stripe woolen made in Eastern Germany and a new shirt of some material like nylon. The shirt was so small in the neck that I couldn't fasten the collar, and the sleeves caught me at about the elbows. So it was taken away again, but they forgot to bring a replacement.

Finally Lee suggested that I have a drink with him. The aide brought in a half-pound of butter in a tin, sliced bread, dried devilfish, black fish eggs, and sake. We sat down, and the general began to ask questions: What did I think about the war? Did I think we had any chance at all? Then he launched into a long statement, the gist of which was that we couldn't possibly win. The United Nations Forces had missed their opportunity when the North Koreans were at their lowest point; and having failed then, we never would be able to win. They had solved their principal problem, transportation, and I must know how important that was to an army. Now they were getting stronger all the time; and no matter what we did, we never could make it as bad again as things already had been. There was only one ultimate victor: the Inmun Gun, the People's Army.

I didn't do much talking, because I was too busy eating. The butter was delicious, and this was the first *sliced* bread I had seen. The fish eggs and the devilfish also were wonderful. I don't care for sake, but I drank two small cups of that too. The general ate very little. When I had finished he indicated that I could keep what remained—butter and sake. But after he left I learned that I had misunderstood him. He meant that I could have the sake; the aide came back and got the rest of the butter.

Early the next morning, December 21, Captain Oh was back. Would I state that I had not been beaten? "It would be," he said, "a great favor to the general, who wants to be your friend and to treat you kindly; also a favor to me. The general may be punished unless you do this for him."

I suppose that I'm a sucker for people who ask favors, but I was grateful to De Soon Yur, if not to the general. I mentioned De's kindness and demanded again that I be taken to a POW camp so that I could see how other prisoners were being treated. I said: "As senior prisoner of war"—I knew from what the different interrogators had said that I was the senior—"it is my duty to know how other prisoners are being treated and to see that their interests are protected, that they are being accorded the treatment provided by the Geneva Convention." This was the same request I had made verbally many times, to which the answer had been that the question would have to be taken up with "higher authority." When "higher authority" got the request, if he ever did, he didn't bother to answer at all.

That evening I began to understand some of the reasons for all the hoorah of the previous few hours. As I was getting ready for bed I heard people outside the house. When I looked from my room into the guards' seven-by-seven quarters, a whole group was coming in, all but one either Chinese or Korean, many of them with cameras. At the head of the group was an Occidental, just removing his boots. He strolled across the room, which wasn't much of a stroll, grinned widely, and held out his hand.

He said, "Hello, General Dean. I'm Wilfred Burchett, the correspondent for *Le Soir*, a French Left-wing newspaper."

I shook hands with him. In fact, I was so glad to see another Caucasian that I felt like throwing my arms around him. I asked him his name a second time and added, "Are you American or British?"

He said, "I'm an Australian, and I've come to get your story of how you were captured. Won't you come in and sit down?" I was still standing in the door of my room, and he indicated a spot in the center of the floor in the guards' quarters.

By that time there was a solid circle in the little room. All the Chinese and Korean newspapermen were getting their notebooks ready. I could hardly take my eyes off Burchett, a fellow Caucasian. You have no idea how important that can be after a year and a half. Burchett, Captain Oh, who had come along to interpret the conversation between Burchett and me for the benefit of the Oriental correspondents, and I sat in the center, cross-legged like the rest, and directly above the onder, which was going full blast. The floor was so hot that we sat there only a moment before getting blankets to fold under us. Still we sweated profusely.

Burchett said, "Now, to get started, I'd like to ask you what you know about the war situation."

I said I knew very little about anything that had happened since July 1950.

"Then I'll bring you up to date," he said. "I'll brief you." And to my amazement (after months of savoring the tiniest tidbit of news) he did just that, relating in a few minutes the whole course of the war, telling me how far United Nations Forces had driven north in 1950, how far south we had withdrawn, and how far north we had pushed the second time. He said that since the last of May 1951 the line had been relatively stable along the 38th parallel. The United Nations Forces were north of it on the east coast, and North Korean and Chinese Forces (which he always referred to in the first person, that is, "our" side or "we") held an approximately equal amount of territory south of the parallel on the west.

The briefing was quite accurate, the only bias being in the method of telling, not in the facts, as I verified later.

Burchett said that a Russian spokesman had suggested an armistice, that Kim Il Sung had agreed to discuss it, and that after a great deal of delay United Nations Forces also had agreed, sending representatives to meet with those from North Korea. Then he went into detail about the various interruptions that ensued, but in each case intimated that the difficulties were due to the Americans. He also said that the first meeting place was to have been in Kaesong, but that American aircraft had violated the truce area, almost ending the negotiations.

He said that the two greatest stumbling blocks still remaining were the questions of construction of airfields—he thought that would be the toughest because the United States Air Force would not accede to construction of airfields in North Korea during the truce, but the People's Republic needed such fields for peaceful communications within its boundaries—and the prisoner-of-war question. On this he thought there would be an understanding; but there was trouble in getting proper lists of names. The Americans, he said, had submitted a list, but it was unsatisfactory because it did not give the prisoner's organization or other details about him. But another list had been promised by December 27, and he felt that a truce would be concluded at that time if no further incidents occurred. "If," he said, "your Air Force doesn't violate it and your people are able to prevent Syngman Rhee from taking some overt action. Syngman Rhee is dead set against any truce."

He also said, "I'm certain that the American people want a truce, and that your Army and your Navy want a cease-fire; but your Air Force and Syngman Rhee do not want any cease-fire."

He pulled a bottle of Gordon's gin from his pocket. "Well, that's that," he said. "Now, I'd like to have your story of how you were captured. It's pretty warm in here, but I don't think a little of this would hurt us."

We had no cups, so the bottle was passed to me. I tried to pass it on, but they insisted that I take the first drink. I took a small one and passed the bottle to Burchett. Captain Oh, and a Chinese photographer, Chun, also drank.

I started to tell him of my experiences from the time I had left Taejon on the evening of July 20 until I was captured. Burchett asked me to go slowly. He was taking most of it down in longhand, and everything I said had to be translated by Oh for the others. The whole business took nearly three hours, and by that time the four of us had finished the bottle of gin.

Then Burchett said, "I have roughly copied notes on the letter you sent to your wife yesterday."

I said, "Do you mean to say that letter was turned over to the newspapers?"

"Well," he said, "I've seen the text."

I said, "Please don't publish those in full. Those letters were personal, and they contained references to people other than my own family. I don't want to embarrass others." My letter had suggested financial aid to some families whom I believed to be orphaned.

Burchett said, "Well, these letters have been given to the press, but I won't mention the things that you don't want mentioned." He scratched out portions of his notes—although when the letters appeared, all over the world, they were carried in full. I believe Burchett was true to his word, but that Alan Winnington, a correspondent for the *London Daily Worker*, whom I did not know at this time, or others published the full texts. Our own press people picked them up, so Mildred and June read their letters before the originals were delivered.

We then went to my room, and Burchett asked what exercises I took. I showed him exercises I would like to have taken—not the fifteen minutes I had been getting. I thought, "Well, if any of this gets published, perhaps I actually will get to do some of these things." I could see that the exercises met with his approval, and the photographer, Chun, took several pictures of me demonstrating.

When Burchett said, "Do you do any walking?" I answered, "No. I've been trying to get regular walks and sunbaths, and I certainly would like permission for them. But I'm not even permitted to stand up. The only time I get to stand is when I go to the latrine."

He said, "I'm certain that is not the will of the Supreme Command. That's not the policy of the Korean People's Republic. There must be some mistake."

I said, "Up until yesterday I wasn't permitted to have a pencil, and I'm afraid they'll take away the one I have now not later than tomorrow."

He said, "How is your food?"

I said, "I have no complaint about my food. I've always eaten as well as my guards. And while I have an interpreter here, I'd like to explain something to them. On November 27 they bought ten eggs, and they gave them to me one at a time—but the guards had no eggs for themselves. I protested, but it didn't do any good. I'd like to have the interpreter explain that I don't want food better than they can get for themselves."

He made no comment on this, but handed me a book. "Here's a book I'm leaving for you to read," he said. The volume was Pastofsky's *Selected Short Stories*, fiction pieces mainly concerned with rehabilitation of swamp and desert areas in the vicinity of the Black and Caspian Seas.

I said, "Don't give me that, Mr. Burchett, because they won't permit me to have anything to read."

"You may have this book," he said, "because I've already secured permission from the commanding general for you to have it; and I'm certain they won't take your pencil away from you. I also want you to know that your name went in on the prisoner-of-war list which was submitted two days ago. I've seen news items telling of your wife's joy."

I said, "Were my son and daughter mentioned?"

"Yes," he said, "your daughter was mentioned, and I understand that she is with your wife."

I said I was very much concerned about my son Bill, because I still didn't know whether he'd succeeded in passing requirements for entering West Point.

Again Burchett nodded. "I'm sure he's in the Academy," he said. "I have a recollection of a press association item mentioning him as being a cadet."

He asked me what I thought about the Korean type of food, and I said I had reached a point at which I really enjoyed both rice and kimchee, although I never thought I'd be able to eat the latter.

Burchett said, "Well, the first thing I'll do when I get back [to Kaesong or Panmunjom] will be to write a personal letter to your wife and send it through the newspaper people on the other side. I'll tell her I've seen you, that you're well, and that she should learn to cook rice as the Orientals do, and to make kimchee, so that you'll have the food you desire when you return."

I told him I appreciated his offer of the letter and hoped that he would send it, but not to bother about the cooking instructions. He did send a letter, and it reached my wife on her birthday, only two days later.

The interview with Burchett went on until well after midnight, with none of the other reporters breaking in on his questioning. Then the photographers went to work, taking pictures of Burchett and me sitting together on the floor, of my exercises, and many other poses. They all left a little before dawn.

There is one thing I should make absolutely clear at this point. The final twenty months of my captivity in North Korea were in sharp contrast to the first sixteen; and I'm convinced that Burchett, deliberately or otherwise, was principally responsible for the change. He is widely known, and opinions about him vary, but this man made nearly two years of my life livable, by treating me as a human being when I was out of the habit of being so treated, and by causing my North Korean captors to reverse their whole policy toward me. Food became more plentiful and much better, I kept the all-important writing materials, mail began to come through, and the petty restrictions—not being able to stand, not being allowed to lie down in the daytime—vanished gradually. I cannot honestly complain about the major points of my personal treatment after that day. So I don't think it's surprising that I like Burchett and am grateful to him. I'm also very sorry that he is where he is and sees things as he apparently does. In a couple of subsequent meetings I came to know a little more about him, but never arrived at any real explanation either for his choice of the Communist side in this war or for his special kindness to me.

The basic details of his story are simple enough. Burchett worked for British newspapers prior to World War II, and as representative of a large London newspaper in the Pacific War Theater he became known to many American war correspondents, as well as to Army and Navy officers. He worked almost entirely with United States troops and naval units and shared correspondents' quarters and privileges at Honolulu, Guam, and many other spots during the westward progress of that war. His reputation for competence was high, and newspapermen who worked with him have told me that they knew of no special political leanings he had at that time.

But as that war ended the little Australian with the receding hairline somehow seemed to get out of gear with the free world. He was in Europe for some years between the wars, changed employers a time or two, was divorced from his British wife, then changed sides entirely.

He arrived in Korea during the early part of the North Korean movement to the south, but sent no dispatches that aroused world interest until he suddenly appeared with the Communist negotiators early in the truce talks. From then on he was used as an unofficial courier and news source on several special affairs—American newsmen's attempts to get in touch with Frank Noel, an Associated Press photographer captured while working with the X Corps, messages sent to me, and other similar matters.

His visit to me was so exciting that I did not think too much about why he was there. I noticed his use of Communist terminology—"stubbornness of the Americans," "failure of the United Nations," "Comrade Captain,"—and his references to Kim Il Sung as the Supreme Commander with built-in capitals—but these were only matters of phraseology. In later meetings he rarely referred to politics and talked about American safety razors—the blades, he thought, were not as good as they used to be—and about his family. He said his present wife was a Bohemian girl from one of the "Eastern People's Democracies"; and in 1953 he told me of the birth of a son in Peiping. He also spoke often of his former wife and a fourteen-year-old son, still living in England.

When Captain Oh came to see me the next day he was all friendliness. He explained that there had been a special reason for General Lee's visit to me on December 20—that was Stalin's birthday, and cause for a celebration. But there were to be others, specifically, one on my wife's birthday, December 23, a date I had mentioned in talking to the general. I had no way of knowing it, but this was the beginning of a series of celebrations on virtually every conceivable occasion, which continued during the rest of my captivity.

I went from the status of being ignored to the state of being feted—or celebrated with—in one big jump, and I never quite got used to the idea. Nor can I give any explanation of why my treatment improved so much, that of other prisoners very little or not at all. I believe now that I may actually have been, as my captors claimed, the only American in the exclusive custody of the Koreans, certainly the only one under that particular administration.

I hate the thought—and always will—that I was well treated while others suffered; and there is very little satisfaction in the fact that I didn't know about it, and could not have done anything if I had. I should have been able to represent other prisoners and do something about their treatment; but I was not able to, and did not. So while the welcome I received when I finally got home was wonderful and heartwarming, in some ways it also was a little hard to take. I wish those other soldiers, thousands of them, could have shared it much more than they did.

Captain Oh's prospectus of the first celebration on my new schedule turned out to be a little overenthusiastic. The general didn't show up. But Oh did, bringing more fish eggs, both black and red, and dried devilfish. He and the guards and I ate it all, and finished the half-pint of sake remaining from Stalin's celebration.

Incidentally I think I should make myself clear about food items, in order to avoid being taken for a gourmand. When I speak of having had fish eggs or meat or fish, I do not mean such quantities as we consider normal in the United States. When an American housewife says, "I'm going to have roast beef tonight," she thinks of a roast as four pounds or more, roughly a pound of meat for each adult. When a Korean says, "What shall we have for dinner?" the first answer is always pop (cooked rice); if they're especially hard up, pop and cho (maize), or pop and susu (millet). There may be a side dish, such as kimchee or garlic tops, either to put over the rice or to eat separately, and a small bowl of watery soup. But kogi (meat) or moor-kogi (fish—literally, water meat) is something special. That's an appetizer, nothing more. Fish is served in less quantity than you would expect in an ordinary shrimp salad; meat may be three or four pieces, each the size of a sugar cube. If beef, it's always gristle; if pork, fat.

Our diet during early 1952 included one fish normally used as a fertilizer, something like a very small herring; and in the spring the real delicacy was the root of the Chinese bellflower, *tow-raw-gee*. About this they even have a song: "Tow-raw-gee, why do you grow so far up the mountains?" Occasionally we got tree mushrooms, which I have not identified in the growing state.

At the December 23 dinner Captain Oh hoped that I had noticed the improving food. "From now on," he said, "you're going to have the same food that Korean generals have. You're to have an egg every day, and you'll get only polished rice."

I argued with him about this, saying that I preferred the unpolished variety because it had more food value—but he had a point to worry American dietitians. He said, "No, that's not true, because polished rice is more palatable. You therefore eat more of it, which more than compensates for the extra food value which might be lost in the polishing."

I asked him, "Do Korean generals eat better than enlisted men?"

"Yes," he said, "because they have greater responsibilities. So they must eat better in order to fulfill those responsibilities."

I said, "Well, that shouldn't apply to a prisoner of war, because my only responsibility is to keep alive and well and not to cooperate with my captors."

Nevertheless I got polished rice much of the time thereafter, and eggs from time to time. These were served raw, broken over a bowl of rice. My interest in them waned gradually and disappeared almost entirely on the day I broke one neatly—and out into my rice dropped a fully formed chicken.

On the evening of December 23 I had a visit from another journalist, a slightly put-out individual named Liu, who arrived in some temper over the fact that Burchett had already interviewed me. Like most of the Oriental press people who came to see me, he was accompanied by a retinue—photographers, note bearers, pencil bearers, and just plain ordinary helpers—who listened in to the conversation.

Liu said he represented the "press of the Chinese People's Republic," so I assumed he was some sort of press-association man. His attitude was definitely hostile, and I never bothered to find out much more about him. He was less interested in the details of my capture, but wanted to know why I was surprised that I had not been cruelly treated by the North Koreans.

To this loaded question I responded that my answer would have to depend on what he meant by "cruelly treated." I had not been tortured but had been threatened with it, in that first month, and my treatment hadn't been exactly gentle under Colonel Kim's ministrations.

He and Captain Oh, who again was interpreting, brushed right past that, changing the subject to the old familiar question: What hope did Americans think we had of winning?

To annoy him I changed my answer. I said it was just a matter of time until we'd sweep the Korean peninsula clean. I said I had not the slightest doubt of that—which brought on a long statement.

This was an easy interview because so much of the time all I had to do was listen to what the journalist thought, without bothering to tell him what I thought. This was especially easy because he had such an unpleasant manner that I resented what questions he did ask.

The interview closed with my question: Was he related to the man who had been Chinese (Nationalist) ambassador to Korea in the pre-war period? This wasn't so much to get information as to annoy him, which it did.

He said, "No. Unfortunately we have the same name, but that's like Smith in America. I know Mr. Liu and I'm glad we're not related, because I would kill him if I could. He's an enemy of the Chinese People's Republic."

There was one curious aftermath to this interview. I saw Liu once again, in June 1953, and he was a changed man, affable, pleasant, soft-spoken, and personable. I think he must have gone to a male charm school in the meantime.

Burchett's visit and the attention given me by officers of rank had impressed my guards, who treated me with new respect thereafter. Captain Oh told me on December 23 that hereafter I could exercise all I wished, and the guards complied, more or less. I took more calisthenics in the mornings, and, irregularly, was allowed to walk the twelve-yard path, screened on both sides, between the house and the latrine. This was quite steep, with a ten-foot drop in the twelve yards, and some steps; in this frigid weather it was also slippery. On the first day that I was allowed to walk I decided to cover a mile and a half and had it all divided mentally into the necessary number of round trips. But my legs weren't equal to it. On the seventy-fourth single trip they gave out suddenly and I fell, cutting my hand on the frozen ground. It was only a minor abrasion, but it bled profusely in the cold air. De Soon Yur was so concerned about it—insisting that I go inside the house immediately and wash an extra time that day—that I feared he wouldn't let me walk again. But things really had changed, and the walking went on, except when the guards, who hated the cold, refused to let me. Some days they would not let me go out at all. Most of them objected to the length of my walks and wanted to know repeatedly how many trips I had made. I cheated a little, counting round trips as singles, and thus kept down the total count—their measure of when it was time to go back inside. By this system I sometimes got in a hundred round trips. The guard shivered but never bothered to keep count himself.

On January 2, 1952, I had confirmation of the fact that my family really did know I was alive. Captain Oh brought copies of three telegrams, dispatched via United Nations newspaper correspondents, and handed by them to Communist functionaries at the truce talks, then passed north to me. My mother had wired, "It's a miracle"; my wife, "It seems like a dream"; and my daughter, "You have a husky grandson, born March 24, 1951."

▶▶▶▶◀◀◀◀

CHAPTER XII

Mail, Books, and Movies

Burchett's visit started a parade of news correspondents to my little castle on the hillside. The third—and to me the most important—was Li Heng Peng, a Chinese, who arrived on January 16 with twenty-four wonderful letters for me. One was from my wife, written on December 27; two from my mother; five from friends; two from relatives of former members of my division who now were listed as missing in action, asking if I had any word of these men; one from a cheerful teen-ager who sent me—although I did not know her—the latest news on the Davis Cup tennis matches, along with her good wishes; and the rest from press and radio representatives, all interested in getting my story. Several of the correspondents had accompanied the 24th Division in the early days of the Korean war or were acquaintances from Japan. This was about the average break-down for mail I received thereafter, although both the size of the deliveries and their frequency varied widely. Once afterward I was five months without mail, and my family went from February until October of 1952 without hearing directly from me.

Whenever I received mail from relatives of missing soldiers I forwarded the names to the commandant of POW camps. I never received any acknowledgment, so have no way of knowing whether the demands for information even were delivered.

All told, I received three hundred and eighteen letters and two magazines, mailed on the United Nations side of the lines. Both the magazines, received May 10, 1953, curiously enough, contained definitely anti-Communist articles. Of the letters I wrote to my family, only about fifteen per cent were delivered. Anyone watching the way Communist mails operate—or, rather, fail to operate—would score this as about par for the course. Letters simply didn't mean anything to the people around me; and sometimes they would let their own letters lie around for a week after writing them. I was told that an officer had to make a special trip from Pyongyang to Panmunjom every time I gave them letters to be mailed; and, northbound, the mail might stall anywhere. Once Captain Oh rode a bicycle all the way into Pyongyang, at least ten miles, to get mail for me; and another time De Soon Yur walked several miles, missing his dinner, so that I could have mail the same day it arrived in the nearest village. In spite of the casualness of handling, the Koreans were highly particular about the mail's appearance. I had to rewrite letters because my script crossed a red margin on some sheets of paper, and once my outgoing mail was sent all the way back from Pyongyang because my homemade envelopes—folded sheets of paper stuck together with rice paste—were too untidy for somebody's taste.

Strange things happen to generals. During World War II—I'm a little ashamed to admit this—I just ignored the press. My division had no public information officer, and when war correspondents visited us I usually tried to arrange a quick trip to a hot part of the front—so they'd go away just as quickly. The foreign press in Korea, when I was military governor, had been small, so I had little additional contact; and in the first days of this war I'd been too busy to pay much attention to the newspapermen.

Now, when my mail started coming through, I was very much aware of—not to say dependent on—the correspondents at Panmunjom, as well as the Communist press men I saw. These Panmunjom people were my most regular contact with the outside world, and not only wrote letters of their own and forwarded messages from my family, but also did their best to ease the last months of my captivity. One news service sent through a whole set of photographs of my home and my wife for me; another provided a very badly needed pen and pencil set. Robert Tuckman, Howard Handleman, Robert Vermillion, Dave Cicero, John Rich, and others—correspondents all—became dependable friends in those months.

Li Heng Peng brought a tape recorder with him, to which he was very anxious that I should tell my whole story, for an American radio chain. When I refused, fearing that this would open the door to all sorts of Communist interviews and might even be used on the Communist radio, he was very unhappy. Li may have been a Communist, but you never saw a capitalist salesman more unhappy at losing a sale. I often wondered what he had been offered by the radio people to get that interview, and how they had planned to make payment.

Incidentally Li was looking after my interests too. He said, "I'll help you prepare your story. You don't want to tell too much, or you won't be able to sell your story when you get back to the United States; but you want to say enough so that they will know it really is you, and that you're safe."

I told him that I wouldn't make the tape and that I was

astonished at the publicity already given to me. I said, "I'm no hero, and the publicity is embarrassing. The sooner it dies down, the happier I'll be. I'm concerned only that my family should know that I am alive. I'm ashamed of being a prisoner; and as far as other people are concerned, I'm sure a two-headed calf will be born pretty soon, and they'll forget about me. The sooner, the better."

Li spent a night and a day at the house—partly because there was an exceptionally heavy air attack, I think by B-29s, in the Pyongyang area. During that time he assured me that one of my fears was unjustified. He had just come, he said, from a POW camp (not identified definitely), and I need have no worry about the American soldiers there. He said he had seen Frank Noel, the Associated Press photographer who was a prisoner, and told me Noel had been awarded a Pulitzer Prize for photos made in the prison camp. Li said he himself had been at the camp for some time, living in a little house nearby, to which prisoners were permitted to come to use his record player. He also described a Christmas celebration in which prisoners had exchanged gifts and even had a Santa Claus to add some gaiety to the holiday.

I suppose it would have made no difference in any event, but for some reason I believed Li. He spoke excellent English, said that both his father and his uncle had been graduated from the Vanderbilt Medical School, and generally told a straight story.

As yet I haven't talked to anyone who was at that POW camp or saw him, so still don't know how much truth there was in his story, whether the prisoners allowed to go to his house were the so-called "progressives," or whether the whole thing was a fabrication. At the time he convinced me. I thought, "My goodness, those lucky devils. My fears were all groundless. They're having it soft."

I didn't have a chance to find out just how far from the truth this was until I was freed in 1953.

Li was a pleasant visitor, and he did his best to make himself liked. His first gift to me was four American chocolate bars—which the guards enjoyed as much as I did; and he also presented me with a first issue of an English-language magazine, *China Reconstructs*, printed January 1, 1952, in which he had written two of the unsigned articles—one called "Private Enterprise in New China," the other, "Women in Industry." The magazine was carefully put together, and the stories had a convincing tone. According to them, the Chinese People's Republic had already achieved a heaven-like existence, with everybody happy, everybody well educated, no beggars, no thieves, and no unemployment. It was just wonderful. But of course, the editors couldn't let it go at that. They also had to insert pages vilifying the United States—Americans had exploited the Chinese, were responsible for most of old China's troubles, had enslaved orphans, ad infinitum, ad nauseam. The propaganda value, if any, was dissipated. I can't say I was thoroughly bored—reading matter was at so much of a premium that nothing would have bored me—but neither was I convinced.

During the next year and a half I acquired quite a library. Titles in and out of it included this magazine; the short-story collection Burchett had given me; *The History of the Communist Party in the Soviet Union*, which I reread several times; *Anti-Duhring*, a text in which Engels restated and clarified much of Marxist doctrine; two issues of the magazine *Soviet Literature;* a book including all of Stalin's

Orders of the Day, issued on special occasions during World War II; another text, *Stalin as a Military Leader*, in which I discovered that Stalin had invented all the theories of warfare which in my abysmal ignorance I formerly had credited to Hannibal, Napoleon, or von Moltke, but which, to be honest, also included some very straight thinking about modern campaigning. If Stalin actually was the father of these ideas about directing campaigns through territory where the civil population was friendly, as this book claimed, my respect for him as a military leader was increased, in spite of the book's absurdities.

Other titles included Stalin's own *Lessons in Leninism; Gentlemen of Japan*, by Havens; *Dollar Diplomacy*, published in 1925; Jack London's *Love of Life;* copies of *Masses and Mainstream*, an American Communist periodical; a British Labour party paper so dull that I couldn't read it, starved as I was for reading; and various copies of the *London Daily Worker*–not so dull, but guaranteed to make you mad at least twice on every page, although from it I could glean a little world news under the propaganda. The non-propaganda reading matter came from Burchett and the rest from Captain Oh. Much of the Communist doctrine was heavy going, but I'm glad I read all of it. At least I know now what theories we're fighting, as well as what men.

Li also presented me with his own blank notebook, apparently issued by the Chinese Army for an expense account record, which I used frequently and still have. And as the crowning gift he produced a bottle of American bourbon. I don't know what small bit of information had led to the idea that I was an alcoholic, but from the time Burchett visited me every Communist who wished to be nice to me produced a bottle of something to drink. At various times

I had gin, U. S. bourbon, Canadian bourbon, and almost endless gifts of sake, ginseng, and vodka.

Li asked me whether my treatment in prison had always been kind, and I told him, "No. It's becoming more considerate all the time, and since Mr. Burchett's visit it has become exceedingly kind—but that's a one-hundred-and-eighty-degree turn from what it was before. During the interrogation in September of last year it was a little tough." I repeated to him a story told to me by a Hollander who had been captured in the Dutch East Indies. The man had told me he never had things really bad until Koreans became his guards. He had said, "They're sadistic."

Captain Oh was around during Li's stay—not to interpret, but perhaps just to listen in on what we said to each other. He overheard part of this and really jumped me for saying it.

For once, I argued with him. I said, "Well, it's true. Maybe you can defend yourselves by saying that you were so fearful of the Japanese that you overdid your job to prove your faithfulness to your masters. But regardless of the reason, I've heard from many former prisoners that their Korean guards were more cruel than the Japanese—as much as you hate the Japanese."

Oh finally admitted this was true but tried to make a point that the Koreans are not naturally cruel. He said, "The Koreans aren't naturally cruel. They're kind and humane at heart."

Well, that was his opinion.

Perhaps the talk did have some effect. Li had brought along a photographer, and on the second day of his visit wanted photos of me playing chong-gun and getting my outdoor exercise. The guards produced a chong-gun board, and

I thought this might mean the beginning of more play for me, but it was taken away immediately afterward.

When the outdoor pictures were being taken I stumbled and staggered as I walked up and down that steep path. Captain Oh said, "What's the matter with you? You're awfully weak. Aren't you getting your walking daily?"

I told him that it had been sporadic. "One day they'll let me walk the round-trip a hundred times, and then they'll miss for several days."

Immediately he jumped on the guards, spouting Korean at them in a stream—and thereafter I had no more trouble. I usually got in about three miles a day, up and down that path.

After Li's visit my social life settled down, except for special celebrations. Li had refused to drink any of the whisky he brought, so I saved it and told Oh—who apparently was in charge of me now—to come by, and we'd have a drink before dinner.

I had some education still coming—mainly about drinking. Oh appeared a night or so later, bringing a large Chinese cup—and his idea of a small drink before dinner was to see how rapidly we could drink the bottle. This was true of any state occasion, and obviously this evening was such a celebration—the occasion being that we had a bottle to drink. We celebrated the end of Old Bourbon, finishing him off in quick order.

The next occasion came in February. Tal, the civilian interpreter, showed up on the sixth, bringing twenty-four more wonderful letters, including word from my wife and my daughter and letters from Clarke and Bissett, each of whom assured me I could quit worrying—he was not dead.

Two days later Tal was back, this time to join me in celebrating Inmun Gun Day, the anniversary of the formation of the North Korean Army, with the help of a bottle of sake. This called for toasts. The guards, Tal, and I drank toasts like crazy. Mine was, "May the Inmun Gun never fight again and may it suffer no defeats other than at the hands of the United States." Even though this was translated (I have no way of telling how well), they drank to it cheerfully. At other parties I proposed toasts to the early victory of the United Nations, and my Communist guards drank them down. So, though I may have lifted my glass to some strange things in Korean, at least we were even.

Often sake or vodka just appeared, with special food but no other guests, and it became obvious that these parties were to be regular affairs. I began a campaign to try to get somebody drunk—preferably the guards. I thought if I ever succeeded, that would be a fine time to take off for the south—but I never did. De Soon Yur claimed that liquor made him ill and never drank, and the guard on duty always limited himself to a single small glass of sake.

The only success I had was with one small fellow, a new guard who had just replaced somebody who had gone off to officers' school or had been discharged. Almost all my guards were husky types, but this one was a thin, long-haired little character, slightly on the pasty-faced side. At this celebration he was the one delegated to drink with me, while the others stayed sober. The liquor was sake, and the supply far too plentiful for my liking. But by this time I had discovered that the proper thing was for me to do the pouring. Thus I could get two or three drinks into a guard while taking only one myself.

I poured this fellow a glass, and to my delight he drank it straight down. I thought, "Oh-oh, I've found one Korean with a hollow leg. We'll just see . . ."

I poured another, and he drank it just as fast. A third glass also went down at full speed.

In about fifteen minutes I was extremely sorry. When I had been in the Requirements Division of the Ground Forces, in Washington, D. C., one of our jobs had been the preparation of training manuals. We tried very hard to write a manual to fit almost every military situation. But there in Korea I realized how badly we had failed. To my knowledge, there is no U. S. Army manual that says what to do when having drinks with a Korean sergeant who gets drunk easily, then turns queer as a three-dollar bill and tries to hug and kiss you.

What I did do was to pour him two or three more drinks, just as fast as possible—while dodging. Then he passed out, fortunately, and I poured the rest of the sake through a crack in the floor.

On April 5 Alan Winnington, the only Caucasian besides Burchett to whom I talked in three years, appeared in the early morning. He was pleasant, but the interview was not a great success. He was suffering acutely from dysentery, which was still plaguing me too. Again photographs were taken; and again props were brought in—this time a rough wooden bench on which to sit. I enjoyed every minute of this sitting, not having seen anything resembling a chair for a year and a half; but as soon as the photos were finished the bench was taken away, and I saw no more Western-style furniture until the middle of 1953.

Winnington interested me less than Burchett, perhaps for the selfish reason that he did nothing about my situation except bring another bottle of whisky, which I really didn't want. But like Burchett, he did a straight reporting job and tried to sell me no propaganda. He didn't explain how a

British national came to be operating with Communist troops.

Earlier, International News Photos had sent through Panmunjom a set of twenty-seven photos of my wife and the house she had just bought in Berkeley. Since we had never owned a home before, I naturally was tremendously interested and spent hours trying to figure out a floor plan from the pictures, and to identify such objects as a square chest in the living room. This I had to assume was a television set, although I'd never seen one.

The guards also were vitally interested, especially in one of Mildred leaning against the TV set, with a figurine of a Japanese fisherman visible on a shelf behind her. They wanted to know her age—and obviously thought I was lying when I traitorously told them how old she was—but most of all they wanted to know, "Who is the fisherman?" Various suggestions were made—a household god, a national hero. The idea of having a statuette just for decoration was too much for our two languages without translation. I finally said, "*Harabachie!*"—literally, my grandfather—and everybody was satisfied. Incidentally, those pictures did more to impress my guards than anything else. When they saw how big my *jeep* (house) was, they thought I must, after all, be somebody of importance.

In May we moved across the valley to a more traditional Korean structure about the same size as the hillside house, but one which Captain Oh claimed would be less damp. For me, this move meant principally a larger spot in which to do my daily walking, and the added interest of Chinese troops manning positions nearby. They indulged in song sessions and competed with the Koreans in trying to get interrogation teams to downed United Nations fliers first. But for the guards the move meant more walking to get their food. After having to cross the valley all winter to an old mess hall, they had just acquired a new food facility a few yards from the hillside house. Now they had to cross the valley, the other way, to eat and bring back my food to me.

We spent a rather lazy summer. In mid-June, Oh insisted that I needed a record-player and subsequently produced an old American wind-up phonograph, even though I said I wasn't especially interested. It was a real relic, and the ten records that came with it were worn almost smooth—perhaps because the guards resharpened the needle by rubbing it on a rock. One record had "Camptown Races" on one side and "My Old Kentucky Home" on the other; two Hawaiian pieces were on another record; and the rest were mostly Korean songs.

I could have done without this entirely, but De Soon Yur liked it a lot. He was the one who always wound and operated it, playing "Old Kentucky Home" first, then the Korean numbers he really wished to hear and learn.

I decided once to play the machine myself, but the guard on duty complained violently, saying "De" several times. I think De Soon Yur probably had told them that no one else was to play it, in order to avoid having it going all the time.

I hadn't really cared before, but this annoyed me. When Captain Oh showed up again I demanded, "Who is this record-player for, De or me?"

He said, "You," and I explained that I wasn't allowed to play it. Oh thereupon made it loudly clear to everybody that this was my machine and I could play it when I liked.

But I can be ornery too. After I got permission I never played that thing again.

The only other real breaks in the summer were three movie

showings especially arranged for me in a newly built "cultural hall" near the old hillside house. These were *The Fall of Berlin*, a fictionalized account of Russian World War II heroism; *The International Youth Congress*, a documentary that spent much of its footage on certain American youths talking about the decline of capitalism and about world peace under the leadership of the Soviet; and a film celebrating the anniversary of the victory of the Chinese People's Army over the Nationalists. This featured a lot of battles which seemed to consist mostly of mass charges, and a Peiping parade which consisted entirely of American trucks, tanks, and howitzers, now in the possession of the Communists. I can't speak authoritatively about the endings of any of these movies because in no instance did the electric power hold out for the full showing. That was a busy summer for our bombers, and the North Korean power system just wasn't up to par.

At one of the showings Major Kim went along with Captain Oh and me, and afterward came to the house for another celebration. He himself had very little to celebrate. His family had been living near the east coast in an area overrun by South Korean troops. His six-year-old son, meeting the newcomers, happily told them that his father too was a soldier, then just as happily led them to his home when they expressed interest. Kim's wife, who had just joined him this summer, was now a bed-ridden cripple, and her parents were dead. But Kim remained friendly to me and only shrugged at his family's misfortune. He said, "That is war," and then no more about it.

In the winter of 1951-52 my ear had become infected and had started to drain. The guards had brought in a very young Army doctor, who put some gauze in my ear—and, I thought, took it all out again—at the same time he was shooting me in the hip with some penicillin that De had obtained. He left what was undoubtedly the dullest hypodermic needle in the world, and De continued to give me a shot every three hours until I neither could sit down nor move my arms without extreme pain. Nor was I made much happier by the rudimentary sterilization of the needle or the fact that the penicillin was mixed with ordinary drinking water from the household bucket. That penicillin, it seemed to me, lasted forever.

When the ear started to drain again I didn't let the guards know about it, for fear of getting more treatment. In Tokyo in the autumn of 1953, an Army ear specialist removed from my ear some of the gauze that had been put into it—and overlooked—in December 1951. He said I was lucky still to have an ear, and I believe him.

But in the summer of 1952 this same doctor was called again when I developed an infected eye. He was willing to step aside—and I was willing to have him do so—when Captain Oh brought a civilian eye specialist from Pyongyang. He cured the infection promptly, but had to be dissuaded from operating on me to remove a ptyergium. He assured me that he was the best eye specialist in the Orient and had removed many such growths, but I finally managed to convince him I could get along with it just dandy until I got back to the United States. This has been removed since my return, and I still have my eyesight. But for a while there in 1952 I wouldn't have given much for my chances of keeping it.

My personal company had changed frequently during the previous months, but I came to know some of the men well. De Han Gool had lived in Kaesong when American troops had an outpost there in the prewar days and delighted in telling me about his contacts with them. He eventually went on to school and received a commission.

Kong, the tubercular, was discharged for health reasons, as was Um, a guard I never had liked. Pack went on to a commission, as did nearly every other member of the guard who stayed in the Army. I felt like a prep school for officers' training. De Soon Yur was the exception, and I was told by Captain Oh that he had refused to go, preferring to stay with me.

The habits of a lifetime are hard to break, and that was a summer when I was both bored and unsanguine. I had no real faith that there would be either an early peace or an exchange of prisoners, and reading material was short. I was badly in need of something to do, so I tried to make an officer out of De Soon Yur. I gave him any number of sales talks, which may or may not have been effective, considering the few words we knew of each other's language. When he was due to make a trip to Pyongyang, I'd encourage him to shine the buttons on his uniform. This helped his appearance and pleased him mightily.

About the same time—I must be vague on details about this and a few other matters in order to avoid hurting people who helped me in North Korea and still are there—I began to get suggestions that perhaps I was in the wrong army anyhow. It was a long campaign, which started with happy little thoughts that I should write to congressmen, telling them to have the war stopped, then shifted to my own responsibilities. The gist of these veiled hints was: "A man of your talents shouldn't be wasting his time as a prisoner. You should do something for mankind and become a true internationalist. If you're interested, it wouldn't be at all difficult. You could have a division in the Inmun Gun, or perhaps even command a corps. Or, if you're weary of fighting, perhaps a political position. Song Ho (whom I had known as head of the South Korean constabulary) has already had his general's stars pinned on by Kim Il Sung himself. You could have the same—and your family could live comfortably in Peiping, where life is very good, and you could see them often." I can't be more specific than this, but I'm convinced that the repeated offer had some substantial basis—but of course, I had to go and spoil it. When somebody asked me what I intended to do for the sake of peace when I got home, I said, "I'll try to build up the military unit to which I am assigned in such a manner that it will impress any would-be aggressors." I don't think that's what my questioner had in mind; after that, not too much more was said to me about a corps in the Communist Army.

I had another attack of malaria early that summer, and it left me weak and debilitated. Shortly after the attack we walked one night to see one of the three movies I mentioned, and I found I had night blindness. I tripped in the smallest holes and fell down a couple of times. But I didn't fall far. Guards walking with me held my arms, to my considerable annoyance—although Captain Oh said they were just hanging on to support me. But I had a feeling they thought I might take off in the dark if I ever got a chance. Even more annoying was the fact that on another trip to the movies—this in a jeep—a guard held on to me all through the ride. Again the story relayed by Oh was that they were afraid I would fall out. I told him that, after all, I had ridden in a jeep a few times before and knew how to hang on, but the guard's clutch wasn't relaxed until we were safely in the cultural hall.

Except for bombing, the war was not bothering the people around me that summer. Food continued to improve, for me and for my guards, and everyone seemed relaxed. On May 1 my guards—except the duty man—went off to a big celebration in Pyongyang. De Han Gool was in some sort of a show, wearing a fake beard; Pak (the little one) played in a soccer match; and Big Pak, a newcomer who had been a guerrilla in South Korea before the war, got to wrestle. I was told there was also a huge political meeting in an underground auditorium, which would seat three thousand people, near Liberation Park.

The wives of two of the guards—one of them somehow having made her way from South Korea—moved into the little house near ours and immediately started making a garden and fixing up the shanty. The two husbands helped occasionally; and at least once took their wives for an evening walk—a rare treat for a Korean woman—but succeeded only in getting themselves picked up by a Chinese patrol because they were wearing only bits and pieces of uniforms. The two women were released by the Chinese, but Captain Oh had to make a major effort to get the two men freed. The Chinese were sure they were infiltrators or spies.

I asked De Soon Yur, "Why don't you bring your wife up here from Haeju, like the others?"

He said, "I have no wife." She had been killed months before in a direct hit on an air-raid shelter, but he had not bothered to mention the loss to me.

One thing about that summer I definitely didn't like. It looked to me as if United Nations planes had lost daylight control of the air over Pyongyang. I saw Communist jets overhead more than I saw our own, and there were quite a number of high-altitude dogfights. Once in August I saw one of our own planes knocked down, while the Koreans around me cheered. On another day United Nations aircraft made a major effort, aiming a terrific attack on Pyongyang. The bombers—four or five hundred of them, I think—came hour after hour, and explosions in Pyongyang were practically continuous. A regular umbrella of our jets stayed overhead, and there was no question about control of the air. I heard no cheering except what I was doing, quietly, myself.

The celebrations continued on every conceivable occasion. We celebrated my birthday, August 1, my wedding anniversary (and the anniversary of my capture), August 25; Korean Thanksgiving in October; then American Thanksgiving. It was getting so that I dreaded the sight of another bottle of Bulgarian vodka or sake.

In the autumn Captain Oh had an idea that attracted me more than the offers of Communist commands. It was going to be a cold winter, he said, and we should try to go to China. As a matter of fact, he was quite sure that if I made such a request it would be acted upon favorably—and Oh might get to go, as well as a guard of my choice.

This was a continuous pressure, which began in September and kept up. Oh said, "Wouldn't you like to see with your own eyes that what that magazine, *China Reconstructs*, told you was true? I know you haven't been to China yourself, but your friends have told you about the poverty, the beggars, and the great distress. Just from what you've heard from your own friends, not from us, and what you'll see with your own eyes, you'll find that all of this reconstruction story is true. You'll realize what the People's government has done."

I said, "Look, I'm a prisoner of war. I'd be a lame-brain, suggesting that I go there as a tourist."

But Oh continued to be positive that I would get a favorable reaction. He continued to tell me about how much he wanted to go to China himself. He had been there before and always had wanted to go back.

All that summer Oh visited me regularly, sometimes to test his English by reading passages from a book, *Gentlemen of Japan*, and having me correct his pronunciation, sometimes with a few guarded questions, but just as often with surprising information. From him I learned exactly how many men a B-29 carried, where each of them sat in the plane, and what his duties were. These people had some things about us down to a gnat's eyebrow—even some of our intramural arguments. Several times I was told that there was a disagreement within our Services about bombing—the Navy wanted nothing but strategical targets, the Air Force was willing to go along with ground troops by providing some close support, but the Army always was left out, in the end, on what it wanted the Air to do. The number of things referred to me was amazing, apparently after having been elicited from others or picked up from our own radio or press. Usually it was patent that all they wanted from me was some sort of confirmation, and I developed a fool-proof defense. I'd express surprise and ask for more details. I found out that if you acted surprised and dumb, they filled in your dumbness. Sometimes I learned quite a lot, without saying anything. The one thing I did not learn was that peace talks had begun on July 10.

Most of the time Captain Oh was trying to make things better for me, and I was grateful to him. So when this pressure about going to China kept up, I finally had a weak moment—another of those times when my sympathy worked against me, and I also thought I was being clever. I thought, "Well, he wants to go so much, and it can't hurt me. If I could really get to China, boy, I'll certainly be able to escape."

I remembered from military government days that Koreans

in whom I had confidence always said, "If you want to get something from a Japanese, you scold him; if you want something from a Korean, you praise him; and if you want something from a Chinese, you bribe him." I thought, "Well, if we get down there, at least the people around us will have been exposed to American dollars enough to know what I'm talking about when I promise them pay. Maybe I can bribe my way right out of this mess."

I told Oh, "All right, I'll ask to go to China."

So I made the request. I immediately regretted having made it, and did not feel bad when it was turned down.

By October, when no great United Nations offensive had developed, I figured there was no point in trying to escape just then. There's nothing to eat in the North Korean hills at that season, and I figured I would have to spend about another thirty-five days on any escape attempt. I thought, "Well, again I'll have to wait until spring. About March 15 the offensive will surely come."

In the meantime I began working on a biography of Kim Il Sung. Other captured people may have had occupations even more odd, but that one of mine should be up somewhere among the strangest.

Again Captain Oh was responsible. He explained that he wanted to translate the biography, a thin Korean volume, into English for his own amusement. He would translate a page or two and bring it to me. I'd correct the English—usually just substituting more suitable language for the literal translations—and he'd take it back and type it. It was slow work but did give me some idea about the North Korean leader, an almost mythological creature, whose age even has been disputed widely.

According to the biography, he now is only a little over

forty. His father had been a Korean revolutionary, jailed by the Japanese when the son was about twelve years old. When the father finally was released, his health broken by his prison treatment, the family went across the Chinese border, where the father died. As a high-school boy, Kim Il Sung joined the youth division of the Communist party and was put in jail himself. When he got out he organized a guerrilla movement against the Japanese, operating from beyond the Yalu and making sporadic raids to kill Japanese garrisons, then running back into the hills.

But, said the book, he always had Communist textbooks and political instructors with his guerrillas. When the Japanese surrendered, he took over the local area, where the Russians found him in charge and practically deified by the Koreans. Because he was a disciple of Marx, the Soviets gave him their blessing, and thus he was on his way to control of the country, taking along as national leaders many of the guerrillas who had joined him as youngsters.

Unfortunately I never finished this book. Oh told me one day that a friend of his had been officially commissioned to do a translation of the same volume and had it finished. Thereafter his interest lagged, and I saw no more pages. I think Oh had hoped to gain a promotion or notice by doing this job on his own, but the other fellow beat him to it.

We never got to China, but in February 1953 we went north again, to Kanggye. We had followed this same route twenty-eight months earlier, but now no fleeing army went with us. I was told the move was made to avoid expected heavy bombing, but I thought more likely it was to get me out of the way of that United Nations offensive which I still expected on March 15.

I now was definitely getting privileges of rank, and the

privileges consisted of one elderly American sedan, straight off a dead-line (out-of-repair area) in Pyongyang, and complete with the usual non-working starter and driver-with-peculiarities. This fellow's special belief was that he would lose face by shifting gears while going uphill—and the road to Kanggye goes over numerous mountains. Again and again and again, he let the engine lug until it died, then sat pleasantly behind the wheel while the huskiest of the guards wound the engine by hand. Sometimes it would start in half an hour, sometimes in two hours, and sometimes not at all—and the temperature was six below zero. We pushed the car into one village; were finally helped by drivers from a Chinese convoy in another two-hour emergency (our driver always managed to block the road when he killed the engine); and in a third crisis were pulled over a mountain pass by a truck.

When I wasn't wondering how soon we'd all freeze to death, I had my first real chance to see what the bombers had done while I was listening to them during the last two years.

For one thing, the railroads had been smashed but repaired. I think no important bridge between Pyongyang and Kanggye had been missed; and most of the towns were just rubble or snowy open spaces, where buildings had been. It gladdened my heart to see how much damage actually had been done—but I also noticed the countermeasures. For every bridge the Communists thought might be hit by our Air, another bridge was waiting, cached nearby against the day when they'd have to rebuild it quickly. I don't mean just piles of material. There were whole bridge sections all ready to be slipped into place. Sometimes duplicate highway bridges had already been thrown across the streams, so that a bomber would have to get both of them in order to stop traffic. The little towns, once full of people, were unoccupied shells. The villagers lived in entirely new temporary villages, hidden in canyons or in such positions that only a major bombing effort could reach them.

These people had been hurt by bombing and still were being hurt by it, but it looked to me as if their countermeasures were improving faster than our measures of destruction.

▶▶▶▶◀◀◀◀

CHAPTER XIII

The Long, Long Last Days

At Kunu-ri, which had been close to the highwater mark of our invasion of North Korea, but now consisted mostly of dugouts, we were fed in a state restaurant, one of the Communist innovations. As nearly as I could figure, the quite decent meal was free, except that if the traveler wanted meat in his soup he had to pay fifty ton, equivalent to a cent or two in our money but more than a North Korean sergeant's basic daily pay. But perhaps this is an unfair comparison, because pay scales and food costs have very little relationship. These same sergeants were drawing five hundred ton daily as food ration money, and more for me.

The entrenchments from the battle of Kunu-ri were still visible, and some old men told us they had been there and had seen American wounded in a hospital burned to death during that bitter fight.

Highway traffic was controlled by flagmen every two kilometers, and came to a dead stop whenever airplanes were over us. But when our stalled sedan held up a whole Chinese convoy of about fifty trucks, no planes happened to be near, in spite of my prayers for a quick air attack.

The town of Huichon amazed me. The city I'd seen before —two-storied buildings, a prominent main street—wasn't there any more. If it hadn't been for the river crossing I would not have believed this could be the same place. What few people remained lived in dugouts, and what had been a city was snow-covered fields.

We spent that night at a private house in a village some twenty miles to the north, sharing it with a woman and her half-grown daughter. In the morning the husband, who had been away on a trip, returned. He showed no surprise whatever at finding his home occupied by four members of the Inmun Gun, plus a strange-looking American. I suppose he must have been used to it.

This was February 8, another holiday, the Inmun Gun anniversary. We spent the morning watching schoolchildren in the village put on songs and dances, while our driver worked on the tired sedan. He got it fixed at long last—by soaking rags in gasoline, then throwing them on top of the car's engine to get it warm enough to start. Another of his habits was to fill the gasoline tank from an open bucket while smoking a cigarette. Why he didn't blow himself and the sedan up I'll never know.

Days later we reached Kanggye and were billeted in an excellent Korean house, on the side of a mountain about a thousand feet above the valley floor.

Here we lived as comfortably as anyone in North Korea does during winter and early spring. During my afternoon walks outdoors I noticed more and more U. S. planes, usually jets operating at high altitudes, without the obvious Communist aerial opposition that had disturbed me during the summer. I followed them with a good deal of satisfaction—and the guards watched them for bacteriological bombs. My worm's-eye view of this phase of the war may have no importance, but it was interesting. So far as I was concerned, the North Koreans had started their great defensive campaign against these nonexistent bacteriological attacks with a vigorous national inoculation campaign in February 1952. Everybody—soldiers, civilians, adults, and children—received four separate inoculations and revaccination. They were monster shots, and all of North Korea had fever and sore arms. Even I got one shot, which made my arm swell more and created a harder lump than any of the hundreds of shots I've received in our own Army. Captain Oh explained that this was a "combination shot," to combat various diseases. At the time there seemed to be no special reason for the campaign, but the mystery cleared up in May 1952, when I was shown alleged statements by American fliers confessing to the dropping of germ bombs.

Oh prefaced this evidence by saying, "I know you won't believe it when I tell you that your Army is engaging in bacteriological warfare." But, he said, he actually had talked to pilots who admitted dropping the bombs; and later he brought me a Korean newspaper with a photostatic copy of an alleged confession, hand-written by a U. S. pilot who described his training for the mission, the special low-level attack, and all the details.

I tossed it back to Oh. I said, "I'm not convinced. While this may be the handwriting of the officer whose signature appears there, the phraseology is not that of an American. He may have written it and signed it under duress. It sounds like a dictated statement. I have never heard a fellow American say that he was 'a slave of Wall Street.' And that expression of sorrow is the same phraseology I've read time and time again in alleged confessions of others. That's a pattern. The officer may have signed that statement, but I wonder how much he was tortured before he signed it—and I wonder who dictated it."

Oh said, "I knew you wouldn't believe it. You won't believe anything. But in your heart you must know it's true. What do you mean by torture? Are we torturing you?"

I said, "No, I've never been tortured, but I continue to worry about officers and men of lesser rank. That's why I still want to go to a POW camp."

He said, "Stop worrying about your men. They're better off than you are. They're all being taken care of by the Chinese. You're the only foreign prisoner of war still in custody of the Koreans."

He continued to talk about germ bombs, so I finally said, "What makes you think these are germ bombs, outside of some photos of flies crawling on the snow, which don't prove a thing? Has there been any more cholera, typhoid or malaria —any more than usual?"

He said, "No, but only because of our careful precautions. We had national inoculation of the population. Nobody could move on the roads without an inoculation card. We were ready for the germ bombs when they came."

The whole thing began to make some sense from a propaganda viewpoint: first, they inoculated the population (with what really didn't make much difference), then announced that germ bombs were being dropped by an inhuman enemy (the United Nations). They were able to whip up the national will to fight and a first-class hate campaign without the necessity of proving the bombing. A few carefully planted flies and some bomb fragments were enough to convince even people like Captain Oh that germ bombs actually had been dropped. I'm sure he still believes it. It was undoubtedly a big hoax, dictated from above. But man, it was sold to the people.

"We've got to get together. We're fighting inhuman so-and-sos, who know no limits. We must all fight harder"—

that's the line they were talking about and thinking about, selling to each other. And it worked. Korea has always been plagued by a strange and awesome variety of diseases—malaria, typhoid, encephalitis, cholera, dysentery. But this hate campaign succeeded in convincing the North Koreans that all these were the fault of the Americans.

The civil population became so inflamed that a downed airman had virtually no chance of getting away from his wrecked plane or parachute. Although Chinese and Korean intelligence officers always raced each other for downed airmen, most of the captures were made by farmers or villagers long before the military arrived.

Perhaps a digression is worth while at this point on the subject of propaganda. I was interested during these years to hear what the Communists said about us—how they argued their people into the idea that the American way was one of aggression, brutality, and exploitation of friendly peoples.

The one thing obvious from the first was that they were watching all the time for any sign of weakness, any scrap of information, true, half-true, or not-quite-false, which could be ballooned into "evidence" of American wrongdoing, the failure of capitalism, or the sad condition of little people living under U. S. rule.

Racial prejudice was their principal stock in trade. Every captured Negro soldier or officer was subjected to extra pressure. "Why should you fight for a country that treats your people so badly at home?" was the question they hammered at these men.

Every time they got hold of a bit of evidence (or alleged evidence) of racial discrimination, especially from Negro prisoners, it was brought to me—always with the query, "What is your conclusion?"

Usually I either had no conclusion or told them that I would not believe their particular story until I had reliable evidence of its truth.

Another weapon is their claim that capitalism is wasteful, an important point in a country like Korea, where everything is infinitely more precious than in the United States. Their pet phrase was "the anarchy of capitalist production," an accusation based on the argument that capitalism has no planning in its production, suffers from excesses, huge inventories, and overproduction, or from false scarcities. Such an incident as the burning of coffee in Brazil to hold the price level, or the destruction of government-owned potatoes in the United States, is hauled out as general evidence of a condition which naturally, in this light, looks horrible to a people near starvation.

Another point is that through their labor unions American workers complain about and fight against labor-saving devices, because they put men out of work. Under communism, runs the theme, everyone tries to devise labor-saving equipment because there will be work for all at all times. In the beginning everyone will have to work harder than he would like, and long hours, but it will all come out right in the end, with everyone's labor planned, no duplication, no human being working for an individual rather than for society as a whole. Then there won't be excessive hours of labor, and each will receive his requirements.

I repeat these highly colored claims because I believe we must understand how the Communist argues. My special point is for anyone who may come up against Communist argument, as a prisoner or otherwise. These are the things you will be told, so have your answers ready.

At Kanggye we began playing chong-gun regularly again.

There had been one false start in 1952, which had ended in an argument when I objected to kibitzing tactics. De, in anger, had burned up the chong-gun board. This put me in a position of not being able to suggest the game again, with dignity. I waited until De himself suggested that we resume playing. This he did in March 1953, and the game became our principal method of passing time.

I improved some and began working up through the chong-gun ranks—beating first the poorest player, then challenging the next, and so on. At first most of the guards gave me a handicap, and I'd be elated when each one would admit—by withdrawing the handicap—that I was getting into his class. I finally succeeded even in beating De Soon Yur a few times, and frequently made him resort to his special form of minor cheating. When he did this I figured I had arrived as a chong-gun player.

All cooks in North Korea apparently are known as Asimonie (literally, auntie). The one we acquired at Kanggye was a twenty-two-year-old widow, whose husband had been killed by South Korean police at Kaesong in 1949. She and her three-year-old daughter, a whiny child, moved in with us on the mountain. Myungja was such a spoiled youngster that I lost interest in trying to make friends with her during those first weeks when the cold was intense and the snow deep. Within a short time a softer wind—what we'd call a chinook in the western part of the United States—hit, and the sun came out. I began taking sunbaths outside, which also gave me a better light for hunting the cooties with which the house was infested. Occasionally I would read, while Myungja played around the kitchen door.

On one such sunny afternoon, while I was deep in some Communist tome, the child approached me and, saying nothing, extended a gift toward me. I took it without looking. From the circumstances and the texture of the goodie, I assumed it was dough, the ground-rice cake I have mentioned before, and which Asi-monie frequently steamed between meals. I put it into my mouth and had eaten about half of it before I realized that even Asi-monie could not have managed to get so much grit into a rice ball.

It was a mud pie, gift of the daughter (now watching me with fascinated eyes) rather than the mother. I prefer not to think of the condition of the soil from which it was manufactured—but my only suffering was mental.

Asi-monie also restored my faith that Koreans do have ordinary human emotions, even during a war. I had noticed as soon as we settled down that one of the guards, Sohn, a young widower, did many things for the cook, even carrying water for her, which was an unheard-of courtesy. And before we left the story was complete. A curtain was strung up to divide the guards' sleeping room, and Sohn thereafter slept behind the curtain with Asi-monie and Myungja. I suppose I was witnessing the start of a new Korean household.

I had a couple of other diet difficulties in Kanggye, which show, I suppose, that Americans remain squeamish to the bitter end. Once, on a walk, a guard discovered a rabbit, dead and frozen in the trail. The rabbit had a snare mark on its neck, so the guards were sure it was perfectly all right and cooked it promptly. They thought I was weak-stomached when I turned down my portion.

Also, there was a matter of a large dog, somewhat like a chow, that followed a half-grown girl around a nearby farmhouse during most of the winter. One day the dog was brought up to our place and walked past my doorway. Seconds later I heard a shot, and twenty minutes after that De brought me a nice piece of dog liver to eat. I was hungry enough to get that down, but the longer I thought about it, the less I wanted any more. The guards gorged themselves on dog meat for three or four days, but I passed. It was too much like eating an old friend.

During this time I was trading the guards English lessons, on a fairly formal basis, for help with my Korean, but the English classes proved harder than I had expected. They wanted to learn the whole language in a couple of lessons, including both capitals and script letters. Jealousy, too, began to raise its ugly head. De Soon Yur had known much more than any of the rest, but as the classes went on it was obvious that Sohn was the brightest. He even learned to sound letters well enough so that when he'd see a new English word he could pronounce it. And Kim Ki Mon, a very slow-minded man, made up for it by infinite patience, working at his English hour after hour, until I was completely exhausted. Both of them were doing well; and almost immediately De began to lose interest.

Just before going north I had acquired some cookies, two pounds of sugar, and some cocoa. At the conclusion of the English lessons I'd make hot chocolate (without milk, naturally, but with plenty of sugar) and pass this around with the cookies. Asi-monie didn't like cocoa but would hold out a rice cup of hot water and take two heaping tablespoons of sugar in that.

The classes continued until we used up all the sugar and De insisted that I let him take the rest of the cookies to trade for meat. After that the English course petered out, although Kim Ki Mon never stopped his individual efforts.

As spring advanced, more and more farmers came out to work their fields on the mountainside; schoolchildren were assigned to other fields, usually the rockiest and most difficult to reach; and each of my guards spent a day a week helping with the planting. Their activity cut down my exercise, because the rule that no one must see me still was in effect; but I got plenty of sunbaths.

We moved, finally, to a house farther down the mountain. The rest of those months were just boredom. Nobody bothered me, and absolutely nothing happened—not even mail arrived. I received no letters from December 27, 1952, until May 10, 1953, and then there was still no word about my second grandchild, whom I knew was due in late winter.

On June 16 we moved south once more, for once traveling in daylight, which gave me more chance to see the effects of bombing—the razed cities, villages built in canyons, and railroad and highway damage and repairs. I also saw elaborate truck hideouts in canyons and determined that supplies now reached the front from the operating railhead through a truck relay system that ran only at night.

Although the few houses remaining in old villages were empty of people they weren't unused. Almost every one bulged with sacks and boxes of military supplies or food. Other supplies were carefully dumped in wild disarray, so that they'd look like junk in aerial photographs or to the pilots of planes. I was amazed at the gangs of Chinese, usually wearing shorts and jerseys, working on the railroads; and others were tilling the fields. Apparently they had just moved in with the Korean country families, who worked side by side with them, in perfect harmony so far as I could see.

Captain Oh told me later that if a Chinese soldier misbehaves with a North Korean woman he is shot immediately. He said, "They have much stronger discipline in that respect than we have, and the conduct of our men toward women is much better than that of your troops. When we were retreating we lost many of our women soldiers because they were ashamed to take off their clothes to cross rivers, embarrassed to be nude; but the Chinese women soldiers think nothing of it, and the men behave. You may think they do bad things, but they don't."

The southbound trip was back on the truck-ride level (no sedan, this time), and we took all our goods—even a few crates of live chickens obtained from the Kanggye farmers—with us. On the second day our truck was stopped at a river crossing by a military policeman, who insisted that we let a couple of other soldiers and an officer ride. This brought on a terrific argument, with De, who was in charge of the truck, finally losing out. The truck driver, however, was like all North Korean chauffeurs, strictly independent, and perhaps somebody had hurt his feelings, for he flatly refused to go on, just sat there sulking, until a tank sergeant, one of those who had just got on, smoothed things over.

A mile farther on another soldier, armed, tried to flag down the truck. The driver wouldn't stop, and the soldier wouldn't get out of the road. Just as the truck hit him he jumped for the radiator cap and hung on.

This time the driver succeeded in making somebody mad. When he finally did stop and this soldier ran around from the radiator to yell at him, I thought there might be some shooting—but it ended with the soldier *and* his buddy getting on to ride. Through the whole affair De had very little to say, and the officer-passenger never opened his mouth.

We again passed much northbound traffic, but this was far different from 1950. An entire Chinese regiment passed, young troops, with their equipment in good shape, and I couldn't imagine why they were going north, as it obviously was no retreat. I'm now sure they were headed back to China, in view of the truce developments, and perhaps for Indo-China.

When we got back to the village near Sunan, Captain Oh was there. He explained the traffic movements. Only one question remained at issue in the armistice talks, he said, and they surely would be completed in two or three days. "General," he said, "you'll soon be going home. Within thirty days you'll be seeing your loved ones. It's only a matter of days now until there is an armistice."

I hadn't seen Oh for some weeks, and he was being so friendly that I too tried to be pleasant. I asked, "How is *your* family, Captain?"

And once again I received that shocking answer: "I have no family."

His mother, wife, and daughter had been killed in the bombing of a village a week before.

Before we had gone north to Kanggye in February I'd noticed the wives of the two guards working around their small house nearby; and once I thought that Pak's wife looked slightly pregnant. Now there was no doubt. On May 29 she gave birth to a husky son. The garden she had worked on in the autumn paid off too. She had corn, squash, soy beans, Chinese cabbage, and half a dozen other vegetables growing fine, where only waste land had been when she moved in.

The next time Captain Oh came to see me he said he had bad news for me. General Harrison, of the United Nations truce team, had just announced to the Communists that Syngman Rhee had liberated some twenty-five thousand non-Communist prisoners of war without consulting the United States.

I said, "That sounds to me as if there will be no armistice."

He said, "No, this has delayed it, but there will be one." He was still sure that my repatriation was only a matter of weeks at most, and he said, "You can't go home in those clothes. You must have a new suit."

I said, "Why bother? The whole peace is off."

"Oh no," he said, "it will be fixed up. You must have a white shirt and a new suit. What color do you want, brown or blue?"

I said, "Brown—I always wear brown."

Oh said, "I think blue is more becoming to you—you should have blue."

A day or so later a tailor came to make elaborate measurements, and finally the suit was delivered. It was blue.

Presently I moved once more, to a much nicer house on the edge of a village—complete with better food, a new cook, a chance to walk without worrying whether anyone would see me, and occasionally a swim in a river that ran at flood stage because a reservoir in the hills had been bombed.

I gathered that the move to this house was to provide a stage for an International Red Cross visit, but they never came. In the meantime I made no protest whatsoever. I was living better than I had in three years and had no intention of saying anything to spoil it.

The only visitors I had were photographers—a whole bevy of movie men, both Chinese and Korean, who wanted to make a story about one day of my life in prison. They were filming what would have been a wonderful day, because they included walking, swimming, sitting in a chair, eating bread (which I hadn't seen for over a year), reading, even a few feet of me fishing in the river with an old Korean all dressed up as if he were on a picnic.

The picture-shooting was interrupted by unaccommodating bombers who knocked out the power lines, and on July 16 I found out what a bride feels like when she's left at the church. The photographers got word that a peace might be signed at Panmunjom the next day—and left me flat. They took off like rockets, the Chinese for Peiping, the Koreans driving all night toward Panmunjom. I don't know what, if anything, ever happened to the film they already had shot.

By this time the general excitement over an impending peace was beginning to affect me. And its sudden coming on July 27—marked by a wild celebration in which hundreds of thousands of rounds of ammunition were wasted at Pyongyang—set a lot of things in motion. The very night of the cease-fire trains began running in and out of Pyongyang freely and at all hours. And with a speed remarkable when you consider the lack of communications, thousands of people suddenly surged out of the hills, leaving their caves and scattered shanties to pour back into the valleys, to their bomb-ruined homes.

I was informed of one more move—to Kaesong. The guards I had known for so long were left behind, and only one new fellow went along. I felt as if I were parting from long-time friends. We stopped in Pyongyang, and Captain Oh took me to lunch at a very nice Western-style restaurant, operating in the same building where I had waited briefly, in 1950, before being taken to see General Pak at the Security Police headquarters. He also let me see what obviously was a major headquarters, cut into the side of a hill near rice paddies, but he could not get me permission to see the 3000-seat underground auditorium about which my guards had spoken.

Finally he turned me over to a lieutenant colonel and rode in the jeep with us to a major intersection, then shook hands and left us. The last I saw of him, he was standing on a corner, waiting for one of the rickety buses which just had started to run again in that demolished capital.

For me there was yet one more typical Korean auto ride—this one in a brand-new Russian jeep. I was dressed in my new blue suit and new white shirt, by order, and had left behind all the familiar equipment of the last three years, my two blankets, my old clothes, and the dunnage bag that I had labored so hard to make.

I was anxious to get started south, in the belief that I would be repatriated that same day—August 5. On the road I noted with satisfaction the wrecked trains and shattered towns on which the bombers really had done a thorough job. But I also noticed that the jeep driver, every bit as independent as all the others, liked to chase trucks. On one stretch he galloped along for a full thirty miles, driving as hard as he could go and blowing the horn constantly in an effort to get around a convoy of six or eight trucks. But when Korean driver meets Korean driver, neither will give an inch of authority, and there's a real impasse. The trucks wouldn't get over, and our driver wouldn't give up the idea of passing. So we ate dust. My white shirt turned gray, the lieutenant colonel's uniform became indistinguishable, and still we chased. At the risk of our necks the jeep skinned past one, only to be stuck for more miles behind the next. We were well over an hour getting past the convoy. Then, the driver was in such a hurry to get to Kaesong (you'd have thought he was the one being repatriated) that he skidded on a mountain curve, let the rear wheel drop over the edge of a cliff, made a miraculous recovery, and turned the jeep clear around in the road before he could get it straightened out again. Still the officer didn't protest. And, remarkably, we got into Kaesong finally, without injury.

There I lived a luxurious life. My quarters were in a former museum, my food was prepared by an excellent Chinese chef,

I was able to walk twelve miles a day in a courtyard, and had a mattress and sheets again. Once my original disappointment at not being repatriated immediately had worn off, I was quite comfortable. I bathed when I liked (a wonderful privilege) in pools below a waterfall, built when American troops were occupying the town before the war. New underwear and socks were issued. When my blue suit, which fit very well, needed to be pressed, a woman did it by the typical Korean system, placing burning charcoal in what looked like a two-egg iron skillet, then pressing the suit on a blanket spread on the floor. It works fine, unless the presser gets nervous and spills charcoal on the cloth.

The guarding lieutenant (head of quite an impressive squad of guards who maintained a very military setup but no longer bothered to keep a man in my room) and I played chong-gun; and there was reading-matter. Also, there was far more to drink than I wanted.

There was one false start early in August when an officer told me one night, "*Naile, tan-sen pasio*" (tomorrow, you go). So I destroyed every paper which I imagined could delay my repatriation, saving only the letters that I had received. I especially wanted to save the sixty-four that had been written to me by my daughter. Someday I want her children to see them, so that they'll have an idea of what a wonderful person their mother really is. I packed my few belongings once more; and in the morning I dressed again in my best.

Nothing happened at the scheduled hour of ten a.m., or all morning. At one in the afternoon I shrugged off the premature hope and went back to my walking (twelve miles takes about three hours to do), figuring that I would have to wait at least until October 27, the ninetieth day from the cease-fire, before they would let me go.

On September 3 my guards worked all day to bring into the museum a big table and special chairs; and an extra cook arrived and began to prepare a feast in the cook-house in a corner of the courtyard. I asked questions, but all I could get from any of them was the one word, "*Planza, planza.*" It was midafternoon before I connected this—which means "French" or "France" or "Frenchman"—with Wilfred Burchett, who I had almost forgotten was French to them because he worked for a French newspaper. Shortly before dinnertime he arrived with a massive retinue of Chinese and Korean photographers and reporters. He said, "I have bad news. This is the last time I'll have an opportunity to eat with you. Bad news for me, but good for you. Tomorrow you're going home."

Presently we ate, drank, and had an orgy of picture-taking, centering on the presentation to me of two gift packages, one from the United Nations Red Cross and a somewhat larger one from the similar Communist organization. I was impatient to get the photographing over with, for the most wonderful item in the package was an American safety razor. I shaved that night and again the next morning, the two most satisfying shaves of my life. I thought then that maybe I really was going home.

But there was a little more delay. When I dressed in the morning my fine clothes didn't suit the local guarding officer. I must, he said, wear another outfit that day, a coarse suit of some material almost like denim, a pink shirt, and a little blue cap. So I changed, on his order, and bundled up my good suit and the white shirt, not doing a very good job for fear of delaying things.

About ten a.m. the lieutenant colonel who had escorted me from Pyongyang, but had not stayed at Kaesong, showed up and immediately jumped on the local officer for the way I was dressed. That outfit, he said, wouldn't do at all. There was great palaver, and I was told to put on the blue suit again. But it had been badly mussed by my quick wrapping, and they had trouble getting it pressed quickly with the little egg-skillet.

In all, by their directions I tried about three different combinations and ended up with a mixture—the new blue denim trousers, the pink shirt, tennis shoes, and the coat from the tailor-made suit. This satisfied nobody (except, perhaps, me, as I was interested mostly in getting away), but we obviously had passed some sort of deadline and had to go. The lieutenant colonel, a guard, and I took off in another new Russian jeep.

At the outskirts of Kaesong we came up alongside a column of trucks standing beside the road. Some of the gaunt Americans crowded into them recognized me and began to yell—those wonderful Yankee voices hollering, "Hey, General Dean! Hi, General! We didn't know we were waiting for you."

At the head of the column we stopped, and the Korean escort got out. An English-speaking Chinese officer and a Chinese guard with a sub-machine gun got in.

There were a few more minutes to wait—long enough to think briefly of three long years and the men I had known during them: Colonel Kim, whom I want very much to meet again, under different circumstances, when I might have a few questions to ask him; Choi, the man who disliked admitting his own orders but was terrified by the very thought of the Japanese; the various lesser Kims; Captain Oh, who believed simultaneously in the reality of germ warfare and the possibility of a permanent peace by negotiation. But mostly I thought about the guards, those sergeants who would hold a blanket for hours around the shoulders of a chilling man or laugh when they saw a dog being tortured to death; gorge themselves one week and share with you their last bowls of rice the next; steal from each other and give away their precious pens or buttons; enforce the most rigorous regulations or walk ten miles through the bitter cold for a letter because they knew you wanted it. I thought of U Eun Chur, the military man, and his hidden cigarettes; Kong, the tubercular who stood guard with an appendicitis drain in his side; Big Pak, the one-time guerrilla and skilled carpenter; another Pak who could make a watch crystal from a light bulb.

I thought of Lee and Tal, the scholarly interpreters; of Burchett, the kindly man who cut himself off from his own people for the sake of strange beliefs; of a couple of men who risked their lives for me and probably saved mine but must not be named because they still are in North Korea; of a South Korean mountain farmer to whom I'd like to take a carton of cigarettes and say, "Well, son, I *did* make it, in spite of what you thought."

Most of all I thought of De Soon Yur, the man with the short legs and stubby, wonderfully efficient fingers, the one who was kind all the way. I wish that he could visit me in the United States so that he could see with his own eyes just what we have. It is possible for men to be enemies and friends at the same time, and we were.

I won't pretend that I did more thinking at this one time; but in those last hours I tried to add up a little the results of three years in captivity, and to assess what, if anything, I had learned from them. Perhaps I'm naturally naïve, but the most important discovery to me was that the ordinary Communists who guarded me and lived with me really believed that they were following a route toward a better life for themselves and their children.

It's easy for us to say, "Oh, but they're so badly mistaken." It is not so easy to explain to these men of limited experience just how, just why, this ideology must fail. The one perfectly obvious thing is that we can't convince them with fine words. We cannot convince them at all unless we're willing and able to show them something better—which of course we can do if we will.

What I mean is illustrated by that election of 1948 in South Korea. It had faults, of course, but it was generally a free election, with a secret ballot. Nothing was attacked by the Communists with greater vigor. They tried to break it up at the time; and my interrogators were determined to prove that it had not been free, that it had been police-controlled, that Americans somehow had manipulated it to suit themselves. They desperately tried to discredit that election by any possible means.

I think the reason was simply that they in North Korea had never given the people anything to compare with it, therefore they had to tear it down, somehow, before word of this wonderful thing which Americans believed, and gave to the people they helped, filtered too far, made their own people ask too many questions. The better life means freedom, in anybody's language, and it was the one thing the Communists could not afford to allow north of the border.

I think the worst moment I had in North Korea was with one of my guards, the slow-brained Kim Ki Mon who was working so hard to learn English. Without warning one day he drew in the dirt a clear map of the Korean peninsula. He said, "Chosen (Korean) house, okay?"

I said, "Yes, Chosen house."

He said, "Not American house?"

I said, "No."

"But Americans," he said, "in Chosen house. Why?"

You and I know the complicated answer to that, but we have to make that man understand it too, if we would not have him hate us. For all of Asia we must have that answer, simply told.

I have mentioned before my own acute embarrassment when a North Korean interrogator said to me, "Did you explain to each of your men personally why they were fighting?" and I had to lie to him because I had failed to do that in the twenty days I was with troops on the Korean peninsula, although I always had made a point of it in World War II and in Japan. Of all the resolutions I made in three years, I believe that one—never to let such a question cause me to lie again—is the most durable. I think it needs to be expanded to a general principle. Each of us needs to know exactly why we're fighting, in Korea or anywhere else. If we fail to understand it—through ignorance, sloth, or insufficient explanation—we don't do a good job even though we win. An army can be a show-window for democracy only if every man in it is convinced that he is fighting for a free world, for the kind of government he wants for himself, and that he personally represents the ideals that can make a world free. And every individual in that army must realize that his whole country is judged by his behavior, at home and abroad, and not by the ideals to which he gives lip service.

I am a troop commander and in no sense a politician; and I speak for no one else and no organization when I make public these things I think. But I do believe them: that we must present a better world than the Communists. We must have an answer simple enough for the dullest to understand. We must, each of us, really know the things for which we fight. If I learned anything in captivity, those were the lessons.

Presently the column of trucks with our jeep at its head moved south toward Panmunjom, past increasing piles of American clothing—which would have been precious anywhere in North Korea—thrown away in the neutral zone by Communist repatriated prisoners as they rode north. We passed several northbound truckloads of these men, nearly naked, shouting and screaming and waving tiny little North Korean flags like so many truckloads of monkeys.

Beside me, the Chinese officer, in clipped English, said, "Now, when we get there, don't you get out until they call your name. A Chinese officer will come down the line and read off the names. But don't you get out of the jeep until your name is called."

We passed an American military policeman, standing at an intersection with his parked jeep, his boots, helmet, and equipment all shining and immaculate. Behind me the Americans in the trucks set up a concerted shouting; but for once no soldier taunted an MP. They were too glad to see him.

We pulled up to the exchange point, and immediately a big American colonel stepped to the side of the jeep and saluted me. He said, "Welcome back, General Dean. Will you step out, sir?"

Whereupon the Chinese officer spluttered, "No, no, not until his name is called."

The colonel swung toward the Chinese, and suddenly looked twice his size. I don't doubt that he had been tried beyond endurance by this same Chinese before and was technically correct when he said, "Your authority is finished, right here. We'll take over, right now." As he spoke he took a step toward the Chinese.

But I could see that this might develop into something

highly unpleasant—and there were truckloads of men waiting behind me.

I said, "Never mind, Colonel. Let them call off the names. A few more minutes won't matter now."

Nor did they.

CHRONOLOGY

INDEX

▶▶▶▶◀◀◀◀

Korean War Chronology

June 25, 1950	North Koreans cross the 38th parallel, invading South Korea.
June 30, 1950	President Truman orders U.S. ground forces to Korea.
July 31–Aug. 4, 1950	Americans retire to Naktong perimeter (high-water mark of Communist invasion).
Aug. 6, 1950	U.N. forces battle to hold beachhead in southeast corner of the Korean peninsula.
Sept. 15, 1950	U.N. troops make amphibious landing at Inchon, 170 miles behind Red lines, and begin offensive drive into North Korea.
Sept. 26, 1950	U.S. forces recapture Seoul.
Oct. 7, 1950	U.N. forces cross 38th parallel.
Oct. 19, 1950	U.N. forces capture Pyongyang.
Oct. 26, 1950	Marines land at Wonsan, on east coast; U.N. troops drive toward Manchurian border; Chinese forces in the war.
Nov. 26, 1950	Chinese Communists launch massive drive that eventually carries past the 38th parallel.
Dec. 24, 1950	Evacuation of Hamhung completed by U.S. forces.
Jan. 4, 1951	U.N. forces lose Seoul a second time.

Jan. 14, 1951	U.N. forces stop Chinese thrust 75 miles below 38th parallel.
March 18, 1951	U.N. forces recapture Seoul.
June 13, 1951	U.N. forces drive to 38th parallel.
June 23, 1951	Jacob Malik, Russia's representative to the United Nations, says: "Discussions should be started . . . for a cease fire."
July 10, 1951	Truce talks begin.
Dec. 18, 1951	U.N. and Communists exchange prisoner lists.
July 27, 1953	Cease fire!
Sept. 4, 1953	Repatriation of prisoners begins.

Index

MANCHURIA
YALU RIVER
Manpo
Chian
Choesin-dong
Kanggye
Huichon
Hamhung
HUNGNAM
Anju
Sukchon
Sunchon
Sunan
PYONGYANG
Wonsan
Korea Bay
IMJIN RIVER
Haeju
Paekchon
Panmunjom
Kaesong
SEOUL
INCHON
Suwon
Osan
HAN RIVER
Yellow Sea
Kongju
KUM RIVER
Taejon
Chonju
SANGJON-MYON
Chinan
TAEGU
PUSAN
CHEJU-DO
TSUSHIMA
Korea Strait
Sea of Japan
2. U.N. COUNTERATTACK, Sept. 15 - Nov. 5, 1950
4. U.N. COUNTERPUSH TO STALEMATE, Jan. 15, 1951
38TH PARALLEL
3. CHINESE PUSH, Nov. 26, 1950 - Jan. 4, 1951
1. U.N. BEACHHEAD Aug. 6 - Sept. 14, 1950
JAPAN
HONSHU
Yamaguchi
Moji
Kokura
Fukuoka
Beppu
Sasebo
Kumamoto
Nagasaki
KYUSHU

Limits of Attack and Counterattack
General's Route as Prisoner